D0044198

TERROR IN FRANCE

PRINCETON STUDIES IN MUSLIM POLITICS

Dale F. Eickelman and Augustus Richard Norton,
Series Editors

A list of titles in this series can be found at
the back of the book.

TERROR
IN
FRANCE

THE RISE OF JIHAD
IN THE WEST

GILLES KEPEL
with Antoine Jardin

PRINCETON UNIVERSITY PRESS

PRINCETON AND OXFORD

Copyright © 2015 by Editions GALLIMARD, Paris
English language copyright © 2017 by Princeton University Press

Published by Princeton University Press,
41 William Street, Princeton,
New Jersey 08540
In the United Kingdom: Princeton University Press,
6 Oxford Street, Woodstock, Oxfordshire OX20 1TR

First published under the title *Terreur dans l'Hexagone: Genèse du Djihad français*.

press.princeton.edu

ISBN 978-0-691-17484-6

Library of Congress Control Number: 2016959947

British Library Cataloging-in-Publication Data is available

This book has been composed in Sabon LT Std

Printed on acid-free paper. ∞

Printed in the United States of America

1 3 5 7 9 10 8 6 4 2

In memoriam Julien Jalaledin Weiss
and
Wladimir Glassmann,
who died together with the Syria we cherished

From Flash Infos, *"Communiqué sur l'attaque bénie de Paris contre la France croisée" (Communiqué on the blessed attack in Paris against Crusader France)*, 2 Safar 1437 (November 15, 2015; translated from Arabic and transcribed verbatim)

In the name of Allah, the All-Merciful, the Very Merciful.

Allah the Most High has said: and they that their fortresses would defend protect them from Allah. But Allah came upon them from where they had not expected, and He cast terror into their hearts. They were demolishing their houses with their own hands and the hands of the believers. So take warning, O people of vision. Surah 59, verse 2.

In a blessed attack whose causes Allah has facilitated, a group of believers, of soldiers of the Caliphate, to whom Allah gives power and victory, has taken as its target the capital of abominations and perversion, the one that carries the banner of the Cross in Europe, Paris.

Eight brothers wearing explosive vests and assault rifles took as targets places carefully chosen in advance in the heart of the French capital, the Stade de France during a soccer match between two Crusader countries France and Germany which the imbecile of France François Hollande was attending, the Bataclan where hundreds of idolaters had gathered in a celebration of perversity as well as other targets in the tenth, eleventh, and eighteenth arrondissements, and did so simultaneously. Paris trembled beneath their feet and its streets became narrow for them. The toll of these attacks was at least 200 Crusaders and even more wounded, the praise and the merit belong to Allah.

Allah helped our brothers and granted them what they hoped for (martyrdom)—they triggered their explosive belts in the middle of these infidels after having exhausted their ammunition. May Allah accept them among the martyrs and allow us to join them. And France and those who follow its path must know that they remain the principal targets of the Islamic State and they will continue to smell the odor of death for having taken the leadership of the Crusade, having dared to insult our Prophet, having boasted that they were fighting Islam in France and striking Muslims in the land of the Caliphate with their airplanes that have been of no benefit to them in the malodorous streets of Paris. This attack is only the beginning of the storm and a warning for those who want to meditate on it and learn from it.

Allah is the greatest.

Now it is to Allah that all power belongs, and to His Messenger, and to the believers, but the hypocrites do not know. Surah 63, verse 8.

CONTENTS

PREFACE TO THE ENGLISH EDITION

Between the attack on *Charlie Hebdo*'s offices in Paris on January 7, 2015, and the attack on an elderly French Catholic priest named Jacques Hamel, who was assassinated as he was celebrating mass in his church in Normandy on July 26, 2016, 239 persons of all nationalities and religious denominations were killed by jihadist terrorists in France. Included in this number are the 130 people murdered on November 13, 2015, in the attacks at the Stade de France, in the streets of Paris, and at the Bataclan music hall—the worst single massacre of French civilians since the one committed by the Nazis in the village of Oradour-sur-Glane during World War II. France was the first victim of this new Islamist terrorism during the second decade of the twenty-first century, but Belgium was also struck, notably in March 2016, with the suicide attacks on Brussels National Airport and the Maelbeek metro station—which serve the European Union's institutions. In addition, Denmark and Germany were attacked, as 2016 ended with Tunisian jihadist Anis Amri driving his black truck into the Berlin Kurfürstendam Christmas market on December 19, killing twelve, as a reminder of the attack in Nice that had killed eighty-six on Bastille Day. That first truck was white—black and white are the colors of the flag of ISIS, which claimed both attacks. Europe, seen by the jihadists as the West's soft underbelly, was the prime target of this "third-generation jihadism." Starting in 2005, this form of jihad spread after the al-Qaeda attacks of September 11, 2001, failed to mobilize the world's Muslim masses.

The United States has remained a tempting target of this new wave of jihadism, as was shown by the attacks committed in the name of radical Islamism in San Bernardino and, especially, in Orlando, at a gay nightclub called The Pulse, on June 12, 2016—just a day before the assassination of two French police officers by a jihadist in Magnanville, near Paris. The explicit objective of these multiple attacks in the West is to provoke reprisals targeting Muslims living in Europe and the United States. Such reprisals would, in the jihadists' imagination, cause Muslims to view themselves as victims of "Islamophobia" and would rally all Muslims together under the jihadists' banner, triggering religious war that would ultimately lead to the destruction of the West and the worldwide triumph of jihad. Such is the jihadists' dream, but they are far from realizing it, owing to the calm resolve of European societies, which have avoided conflating the Muslim population as a whole with jihadists trying to take that community hostage.

Nonetheless, the electorate's exasperation has been reflected in growing support for far-right and populist candidates campaigning on ethnic and cultural issues. The rise of Marine Le Pen and the National Front in France, of the Alternativ für Deutschland in Germany, and of Geert Wilders's party in Holland (which wants to ban the Quran), as well as the success of far-right groups in Austria and Denmark (which are at the center of governing coalitions pursuing policies hostile to immigrants and to Islam), have been in large part fueled by jihadist attacks on European soil—attacks committed mainly by young Muslims who were born and brought up in Europe and who are citizens of European countries. The election of Donald Trump, who promised during his campaign to prevent Muslims from entering the United States and to enact a government registry of Muslims, has galvanized these European right-wing, identitarian parties that are battling not only against immigration and Islam but also against the European Union and for the reaffirmation of a national identity that seems to them to be their sole protection against the anomie felt by a white lower middle class disoriented by a globalization that also threatens its jobs and its way of life. These groups feel that traditional European identities are being submerged both by migrations—which the far right calls "the Great Replacement"—from the southern and eastern Mediterranean region and by transfers of sovereignty to a European Union that is perceived as dysfunctional, bureaucratic, dominated by the business world, and favoring outsourcing and consequent unemployment.

In this context, and returning to the French scene in particular, the mobilization of French Muslim voters—which began with the 2007 presidential election but was decisively manifested by the contribution of this voting bloc to François Hollande's victory in the 2012 French presidential elections—has become a political factor. When numerous imams rejected the socialist government's proposal to authorize same-sex marriage, many Muslim voters abandoned the left, and various community-based lobbies subsequently sought to capture them for their own ends—notably during the struggle against "Islamopho-bia" led by activists connected with the Muslim Brotherhood, who wanted to use them to construct their political hegemony over their co-religionists.

The present book, which appeared in French in late 2015, just after the attacks of November 13, 2015, is intended to provide readers with information about jihadism in the West based on a precise knowledge of the facts. It is founded, first of all, on several decades of fieldwork in France's neglected neighborhoods, in particular its infamous *banlieues*[1] (one of the few contemporary French words to have passed into foreign languages and thus one that needs no translation here). It is also founded on a reading of the ideologically charged primary source material in the original Arabic that motivates this unprecedented form of jihad in the West. From these bases, this book places modern jihad into a historical and comparative perspective, from the first wave of jihad in Afghanistan and its fruitless sequels in Bosnia, Egypt, and Algeria (1979–1997), to al-Qaeda's second wave of jihad against America, whose high point was reached on September 11, 2001, and whose decline was signaled by the jihadist failure in an Iraq occupied by the American army (1998–2005). The book recounts the emergence of a third jihadist wave during the pivotal year 2005, with its focus on combat on European soil and its inclination to find recruits among the millions of second-generation immigrants from the Muslim world who have put down roots in Europe. Contrary to Osama Bin Laden's top-down organization of the attacks on New York and Washington, third-wave jihadism is network-based and organized from the bottom up. Third-wave jihadism also takes advantage of the spectacular growth of social media, which began in 2005 with the birth of YouTube.

What's more, 2005 was the year when France witnessed the greatest riots in its history in the disadvantaged banlieues where most of the second-generation immigrants from the Middle East and North Africa lived. Although these people had no connection with jihadism, their coming of age coincided with the appearance of an enclave-based ethnic-racial logic of violence on which the jihadists of the third-wave

---

[1] The term *banlieues* in our context refers to areas on the outskirts of Paris and other large cities that are now occupied chiefly by immigrants and descendants of immigrants.

jihadism have built their brand of terrorism. Third-wave jihadism was also facilitated by the matchless incubation chamber of the French prison system, where incarcerated jihadists became the mentors of petty delinquents to whom they offered an eschatological prospect of redemption through politicoreligious violence and even martyrdom. Mohamed Merah's massacre of Jewish children at their school in Toulouse in March 2012 marked the beginning of this kind of jihadism's operational phase, which was to continue in subsequent years, reaching peaks with the carnage at *Charlie Hebdo* on January 7, 2015, at the Bataclan on November 13, 2015, and in Nice on July 14, 2016.

France has been an especially tempting target because of the disastrously high unemployment rate among young people from immigrant backgrounds who live in the banlieues. The largely Arabic-speaking North African provenance of these children of immigrants—an echo of French colonial history—is a boon for Arab jihadist recruiters, who target this community in particular. (The appeal of jihadism among Turks in Germany and among Indo-Pakistanis in the United Kingdom is, by contrast, more limited, though the spectacular Christmas market attack in Berlin by a Tunisian ISIS jihadist showed that the old continent as a whole has become a target.) Hence the French situation is exemplary and premonitory, and a deeper knowledge of it can help us decipher situations in which we see jihadism spreading in the West, whether in the rest of Europe or in North America.

This English language edition was revised and updated by me.

G.K.
December 2016

PARIS, SAINT-DENIS, FRIDAY, NOVEMBER 13, 2015

On Friday, November 13, 2015, a group of killers connected with the Islamic State in Iraq spilled blood in Paris. This massacre came hardly ten months after the tragedies that took place on January 7–9 at the offices of *Charlie Hebdo* and at a kosher supermarket at the Porte de Vincennes. In response, the hashtag #jesuisParis (I am Paris) proliferated over social media, just as #jesuisCharlie (I am Charlie) had done at the beginning of the same year, and an immense movement of solidarity arose around the world. Monuments were illuminated with the colors of the French flag, and "The *Marseillaise*," remixed, was sung from America to Australia.

In Saint-Denis—a symbolic city that gave its name to a *département* known as the "93" (after its postal code) that was for centuries the burial place of the French kings, that became the showplace of the French Communist Party, and that is now the capital of French Islam—a failed attack targeted the Stade de France[1] and eighty thousand fans, including President François Hollande, who were watching a friendly soccer match between France and Germany. Three terrorists blew themselves up outside the stadium, killing, besides themselves, only one passerby. Five days later, in a squalid apartment building near the Basilica of Saint-Denis where drug dealers and illegal immigrants lived in squats, an armed group was flushed out and neutralized by the police using information provided by the authorities in Rabat, Morocco. The following day saw fingerprint identification of the bullet-riddled corpse belonging to the presumed brains of the

---

[1]The French National Stadium, located just north of Paris in the commune of Saint-Denis. (All footnotes are the translator's.)

attacks—the Belgian-Moroccan Abdelhamid Abaaoud, alias Abu Omar al-Belgiki ("The Belgian") or al-Soussi ("from Souss," a Berber area in southern Morocco). Abaaoud, a former hold-up man and ex-convict, the son of one of the prosperous grocers from this region who run *hanouts*, or retail shops, throughout Europe, had taken up residence in Molenbeek-Saint-Jean, a working-class district in Brussels that has been dubbed the seedbed of French jihad. After spending time in Syria in 2013, he became the gory hero of unbearable videos distributed by ISIS on social media.

Most other killers have been identified as people born and raised in France or in Belgium—the descendants of Algerian or Moroccan immigrants. Some of them had undergone a lightning-fast radicalization. Take, for instance, Bilal Hadfi, age twenty, a compulsive marijuana smoker whose Facebook wall shows him wearing a swimsuit and sipping a cocktail next to a pool as recently as 2014. He was one of those who triggered their explosive vests near the gates of the Stade de France when they were unable to get in. Or consider Hasna Aït Boulahcen, a twenty-six-year-old woman born in Clichy, one of Paris's immigrant suburbs, who had been placed in foster families after her parents separated when she was very young. Fond of vodka and a regular at discotheques, she was still using makeup and going out just a few months before posting on her Facebook account a photograph of herself wearing a niqab (face veil). She died in the apartment house in Saint-Denis that was raided by the police on November 18.

Samy Amimour was a Kabyle of Algerian origin. His family does not assiduously practice its religion, but its Berber cultural identity is strong, and it is well known in community life in Drancy, Seine-Saint-Denis, where it resides. For over a year, Amimour had been working as a bus driver for the Paris Transport Authority, which had begun recruiting its drivers in immigrant neighborhoods after its buses started being pelted with stones. In this milieu, the influence of "total Islam" (*Islam intégral*)[2] is now very visible and has become the object of polemics. Amimour began frequenting the Salafist mosque of Le Blanc-Mesnil in *Quatre-Vingt Treize*, then ceased to care about his work, and the police opened a file on him because he showed interest in going to Yemen. He ended up joining the ISIS forces in Syria and was one of the killers at

---

[2] "Total Islam," or *Islam intégral*, refers to an all-encompassing version of Islam that seeks to shape its followers' beliefs and actions at all times and in every sphere of life.

the Bataclan nightclub, playing cat and mouse with his victims before shooting them as impassively as people zap video game avatars.

Two brothers living in Brussels, Brahim and Salah Abdeslam, ran a café in Molenbeek that was closed by the authorities ten days before November 13 because drugs were being sold there. Brahim blew himself up in a restaurant on the boulevard Voltaire, but his brother, who fled to Belgium the day after the attacks, would be arrested in Brussels in March 2016, after a Belgian-French police onslaught on the network hideout, which would in its turn lead to the attacks on the Brussels-Zaventem airport and the Maelbeck subway station.

In addition to these killers, who are pure products of immigrant neighborhoods in France and Belgium and whose families believe in integration and social ascent, we find among the perpetrators of the attacks two individuals who came to France as part of the flow of refugees leaving Syria and Iraq for Europe. Thus we are at the heart of the link that ISIS has constructed between the jihad practiced in the Levant, where extreme violence and bestiality are communicated live over the Internet, and the world of the neglected immigrant banlieues that are seedbeds of the civil and religious wars that terrorist acts aim to provoke.

The "holy raid" (*ghazwa*), as the massacres of November 13 were called in Arabic versions of the communiqué reproduced earlier, struck Parisians indiscriminately, without respect to the diversity of their origins. The random machine-gunning of sidewalk cafés and restaurants in Paris neighborhoods with large numbers of immigrants or descendants of immigrants and the carnage at the Bataclan both attest to this, as does the systematic use of explosive vests in the manner of the suicide attacks carried out in the Near East. In contrast, the murders in January 2015 and those that Mohamed Merah committed in Toulouse and Montauban in March 2012 specifically targeted Jews, soldiers, and policemen of Muslim descent, who were called "apostates," as well as journalists stigmatized by the jihadis as "Islamophobes."

While these attacks are all part of a strategy that aims to foment in Europe, which ISIS's ideologists see as the West's soft underbelly, a war of all against all that seeks the implosion of the Old World and the establishment of a "caliphate" on its ruins, the indiscriminate slaughter in November 2015—dubbed "mass attack" in jihadi parlance—indicates a reorientation. This development is a key element in understanding the offensive that the "third-generation" jihad is conducting against the world in general and against Europe and France in particular, as well in understanding the motives of its members.

The effort made in the following pages to put these crimes in perspective leads us to ask whether the young men (and women) who commit them are capable of meeting such a broad challenge. Or, on the contrary, do the November 2015 mass attacks, and those of the same kind that would follow suit in Nice on Bastille Day, July 14, 2016, and in the Berlin Christmas market on December 19, 2016, paradoxically reveal the flaw in a reticular terrorism that delegates their execution to networks of activists, most of whom come from immigrant milieus and who are exceptionally violent but not very sophisticated? We will see how this model differs from the one typical of the preceding generation, which involved careful planning by a central organization and of which al-Qaeda is the incarnation and September 11 the culmination. Are the petty criminals Abaaoud and Abdeslam in Brussels and Paris; the banlieue gangster Coulibaly; the ex-cons Merah in Toulouse, Nemmouche in Marseille, Kouachi in Paris, and Anis Amri in Berlin, whose rudimentary intellectual level is reflected in their calamitous communiqués, really the generals of a "jihadi army" against which France and other European countries are "at war," to adopt the expression François Hollande used in speaking to a plenary meeting of the French National Assembly and Senate? Or should the stakes be defined more precisely to avoid risking an ill-considered response that falls into the trap that ISIS has laid for Europe? Apart from the anxiety that it elicits, this terrorism—which reached an apex in 2015 and 2016—is in fact intended to "savage" (*tawahhoush*) an "infidel" society fragmented into denominational ghettos until it collapses into a civil war between enclaves. This mad apocalyptic vision on the part of the jihadis feeds on the fantasy of a possible recruitment of their co-religionists, who are supposed to feel victimized by "Islamophobia," itself instigated by the massacres perpetrated by the jihadis, and thus be all the more prepared to assemble under their bloodstained banner. From this point of view, the massacres of November 13, 2015, in Paris, Nice in July, and Berlin in December 2016 differ from those of January 7–9, 2015, in Paris. The great parades that followed the latter on January 11, the largest in French history, marked the nation's refusal to allow itself to be drawn into the self-destructive spiral that ISIS is trying to set in motion. But the slogan #jesuisCharlie had a kind of ambiguity—analyzed in detail in the last chapter of this book—that estranged from the demonstrations certain groups, notably some Muslims, who saw them as expressing approval of the defamatory caricatures of the Prophet rather than solidarity with the victims of the Kouachi brothers and Amedy Coulibaly.

The situation was quite different in the wake of November 13. Despite the claim made by ISIS's communiqué, already reproduced verbatim, with its faulty, ill-educated French boasting that the "holy razzia" caused the death of a "minimum of 200 Crusaders," numerous targets had no relationship to "Crusades" or even to the Christianity that provided the pretext. If Paris is stigmatized for having "carried the banner of the Cross in Europe," the expression is ill chosen to describe Paris's tenth and eleventh arrondissements. As the contemporary Arabic scholar and historian Pierre-Jean Luizard put it:

> In the neighborhoods that were attacked, young people can be seen smoking and drinking as they socialize with others who are going to the mosque. That is what ISIS wants to destroy by pushing French society to turn in upon itself [. . .], so that each individual no longer sees others in relation to what they think or what they are, but in relation to their membership in a community.

Seeking further to justify the crime, ISIS's communiqué describes the audience at the Bataclan as an assembly of "idolaters" engaging in a "celebration of perversity." In doctrinal Islam, even if the Arabic text introduces other connotations, idolatry is punishable by death without reprieve. The "idolaters" are the *mushrikin*, those who associate other divinities with Allah the One and Only, and the concert was "an orgy of prostitution" (*haflat 'ahir fajira*). The disqualification in moral terms, which is excessive with regard to a simple rock concert and which only the most fanatical find convincing, reminds us of the scenes showing the killing of homosexuals by throwing them off tall buildings in Raqqa and Homs that ISIS put online in the form of educational videos, as if the morals that rule the "caliphate" had to be immediately transposed in Paris.

It is hard to see how such rhetoric could elicit support among the French Muslims whom ISIS wants to enlist in its crimes. Contrary to what happened in the days that followed the Merah and Kouachi-Coulibaly affairs, thousands of "likes" did not appear on Facebook walls or Twitter threads. If, unsurprisingly, the jihadosphere went wild, a large number of statements coming from Muslim milieus whose backing ISIS expected to gain described it as their worst enemy. Take, for example, the one made by Tarek, a thirty-three-year-old eyewitness to the failed attacks at the Stade de France, who told reporters: "France at war can count on its banlieues." And the same reactions were witnessed after the attack in Nice on July 14, 2016, where the truck that Mohamed Lahouaiej-Bouhlel drove into the crowd, an attack claimed by ISIS as a legitimate retaliation against the "crusader coalition bombings on the caliphate," killed 86 people—30 of them with Muslim names—including scores of children.

It is true that scenes that reminded us of the civil wars in Lebanon, Israel, Palestine, Syria, or Iraq, and that had previously been seen only on television screens, were suddenly transposed into the heart of continental France, and then Belgium and Germany. Does that mean that ISIS has succeeded in triggering the conflict it hopes for? Or could one say, as François Hollande did during his address to the legislators assembled in Versailles after the attacks, that "the acts committed Friday night in Paris and near the Stade de France are acts of war? They are the work of a jihadi army that is fighting us because France is a land of freedom, because France is the homeland of the rights of man"? By using in an unprecedented way the expression "jihadi army," which presupposes that the latter is the instrument of a genuine state, the president of the French Republic strangely provided ISIS with a confirmation of its claim. The struggle against ISIS in Syria and Iraq certainly requires military means—notably, the navy and the air force. But the fight against terrorism on French, Belgian, German, or any European and Western territory is first of all a matter for the police. It requires an ability to analyze the European terrain on which this phenomenon developed and to relate it to the mutations of international jihadism that have taken place since the latter's initial emergence in Afghanistan in the 1980s, passing by way of al-Qaeda and September 11. If we fail to understand the genesis of French jihad, for which we now have an in-depth case study that can be considered a paradigm for other Western countries, we doom ourselves to a political myopia that constitutes, alas, the mental horizon of a ruling class whose inanity jihadism has exposed—and that voters condemn in elections by increasingly casting their votes for far-right candidates.

The emotion aroused by the November 13 massacres had hardly begun to share the front pages of the media with other news before the posters for the French regional elections of December 2015 went up in front of schools that had been transformed into voting stations. In this election, the National Front achieved particularly high scores in Nord-Pas-de-Calais-Picardie and Provence-Alpes-Côte d'Azur, and it is in precisely these regions, as I repeatedly point out in my study *Passion française* (Gallimard, 2014), that we find the deepest ethnoreligious fissures in the social fabric.

In this respect, the massacres that occurred in November 2015, and prepared the way for what would happen in 2016 in France and its neighbouring countries, were revealing and can be explained only by situating them in their context. The communiqué that opens these pages, claiming responsibility for the "holy raid," makes sense only as an echo of a whole worldview that must be deciphered in all its dimensions. The following remarks, which are reproduced verbatim, can serve as an introduction. They were published online in 2015 and disseminated through the social networks of ISIS under the title "How to Survive in the West. A Mujahid's Guide 2015":

A real war is heating up in the heart of Europe. Many Muslims are putting a lot of effort into showing the world that we are peaceful citizens, we're spending thousands of Euros to do *Da'wah* (invitation to Islam) campaigns to show how good we are in society, but we're miserably failing. The leaders of disbelief repeatedly lie in the media and say that we Muslims are all terrorists, while we denied it and tried to be peaceful citizens. But they have cornered us and forced us into becoming radicalized, and that will be the cause of their defeat and the cause for the conquest of Rome. The people who own the media have had Europe and the Western world as their stronghold for over 1000 years, they do not want Islam to rise in their stronghold. They want to keep their authority, their adultery, wine and money and do not want to lose it. So they are doing a multibillion dollar media campaign to stop the Islamic State in the Middle East, and a multibillion dollar media campaign to stop the rise of real Islam in the West. All the major alcohol, gambling and *haraam* companies are funding this project because if Islam rises in the West, they will lose everything. It is a matter of life or death for both, only one will survive. Allah (God)'s last Messenger Muhammad (peace be on Him) promised us we will win and finally take over Europe's capital—Rome, but only after we have taken Persia (Iran) [. . .].

In the Ummah (Nation) of Prophet Muhammad (*saws*), we have been taught to physically fight to defend ourselves and our religion, no matter where we are in the world. If you disagree with Armed defense, and you are a pacifist, then remember that you will be imprisoned for your religion now or in the future, then ask yourself if you will be able to maintain your *Iman* (Faith) there. Those who go on the offensive earlier will learn how to react in different situations, and will more likely receive martyrdom (*shahadah*) instead of long-term imprisonment.

PROLOGUE

FROM THE MARCH OF THE BEURS TO *CHARLIE*

AND THE BATACLAN

Only two months separate the first anniversary of the massacres perpetrated in Paris by the jihadis Chérif and Saïd Kouachi as well as Amedy Coulibaly and the massacres at the Bataclan and in Saint-Denis on November 13, 2015. These killings occurred a decade after the riots that shook French banlieues in October and November 2005. The commemoration also took place five years after the Arab uprisings of the winter of 2010–2011 in Tunisia, Egypt, Libya, Yemen, Bahrain, and Syria.

The slaughter at the offices of *Charlie Hebdo* and at the Hyper Cacher [Kosher] supermarket at the Porte de Vincennes in January 2015 and the killing of police officers Ahmed Merabet and Clarissa Jean-Baptiste were part of the recent tectonic upheavals experienced by French society as it entered the "retrocolonial" era. This era was characterized by the return of the North African repressed in French postcolonial history, and the seismic revolutions in the Arab world from North Africa to the Middle East. The explosion of terrorism in France, which burst out with the double Paris attacks of January 7–9, 2015 (the European equivalent of the "double raid" of September 11), was part of a series of jihadi assassinations that began with Merah's killing spree in March 2012 and that lasted well into 2016, culminating in the Christmas market massacre of December 19 in Berlin. The reappearance of jihad on French territory, it having first emerged in

1995 and 1996 as a spillover from the Algerian jihad, caught the security forces off guard after sixteen years of successful security policy and was followed by a series of aftershocks that occurred throughout 2015 and 2016 and would spread in neighboring countries as well.

A series of incidents in 2015 and 2016 has made it abundantly clear that jihadism is firmly implanted in France. The fortuitous arrest of a jihadi suspected of having planned an attack on a church in April 2015, followed in June by the first decapitation in France (mimicking the abuses committed by ISIS in Syria and in Iraq) and then, in August, by a fortunately aborted shooting in a train, are all evidence of this. Such targeted attacks would follow suit in 2016 with the stabbing to death of a couple of policemen on June 13 in the outskirts of Paris and of an elderly priest performing his morning mass in a Normandy church on July 26. Moreover, several hundred French men and women have left to join the "caliphate" in the Levant, and in 2016, more than 1,500 of them were in the process of leaving or returning. Most of them were descendants of postcolonial Muslim immigrants, with the proportion of converts, whether young men or young women, being on the order of one out of every three or four.

Such figures force us to consider this terrorism unprecedented as an index of the French malaise and the inability of the political and economic elites to control social transformations. The irruption of jihadism, behind which looms the implantation of Salafism—a model for breaking with the values of the Republic and its secularism—is not an isolated phenomenon—and later jihadi developments in Belgium and Germany showed that it is not exclusively French. The far-right National Front's electoral successes and the invasion of the Web by sites appealing to ethnic identity and conspiracy theories, of which Alain Soral is the ideologist and Dieudonné the figurehead, constitute parallel "French fractures," from the housing projects to suburban homes. And in Germany, though the social environment is better than in France, with far less unemployment, we can observe a parallel rise of a strong extreme-right antimigrant and anti-Islam party—*Alternative für Deutschland*—which won a landslide in all elections following the 2015 arrival of more than a million Middle East refugees on German soil.

Nevertheless, the French case is stronger and deeper if we want to illustrate the paradigm of the rise of jihad in the West. During the decade between the three-week banlieue riots of autumn 2005 and the waves of jihadi attacks starting in January 2015, that country witnessed the deepening of new fault lines. The young people born in France to families that were part of the postcolonial immigration constituted the main symbolic stake. Among them, modes of violent confrontation with society and its institutions appeared, though the political expression of their aspirations or frustrations was not limited to these confrontations. However, the latter, which took various forms ranging from riots to jihad, constructed these youth as the media hostages of a kind of stigmatization. We shall see that this stigmatization fed, in turn, a siege-mentality fantasy of "Islamophobia." Paradoxically, this decade also corresponds to another, more widespread kind of behavior based on the opposite view: the entry of this new generation into French citizenship and into the electorate.

For the first time since the population group constituted by immigrants of Muslim extraction settled in France, it was participating in a significant way in elections, not only by voting in large numbers but also by proposing hundreds of candidates for various offices. In addition, in 2007 it involuntarily helped elect as president Nicolas Sarkozy—the former minister of the interior at the time of the disturbing riots in 2005. These riots were vigorously repressed, and Sarkozy benefited from the support of far-right voters, thus easily defeating his rival, the socialist Ségolène Royal, who won most of the first-time voters from the banlieues.

Conversely, the narrower victory won by Socialist François Hollande when he ran for president against incumbent Sarkozy in 2012 benefited from the support of more than 80 percent of voters who told pollsters that they were "Muslims" and who opposed his adversary and predecessor because of his controversial statements about immigration and Islam.

France has experienced intense social upheaval throughout the twentieth century—despite the strength of its national identity, which is built upon grand Jacobin and Napoleonic narratives that can be traced back to the era of the absolute monarchy. Such confrontations sustained a Communist Party that was one of the most powerful in Western Europe and that was the vector for a counterculture of class struggle that transformed working-class banlieues into Red bastions. At its apogee, the French Communist Party spoke for the members of the "proletariat," holding out the utopian promise of a radiant future while at the same time managing municipalities, labor unions, youth movements, and charitable organizations as well as seeing to it that its managers were upwardly mobile. But the French Communist Party did not survive the upheavals that occurred during the last quarter of the twentieth century—foremost among them the fall of the USSR.

The end of industrial society and strongly unionized shift work, along with the rise of a service sector that stressed individual initiative as opposed to solidary (by contrast with low-skill factory labor), have made the "worker's party" obsolete. Young people who are unemployed or who make a living in the informal economy and through various kinds of trafficking—of which there are a large number among children of immigrants and the "native" French poor alike—can no longer identify with the unionized "worker's party."

Instead, two kinds of protest movements have developed alongside one another: right-wing ethnic nationalism and Islamism as parallel conduits for expressing grievances. They both bear, as the French Communist Party used to do, a strong utopian element that restores a mythical dimension to a disastrous social reality by projecting onto it a utopia where those who are left behind today will triumph tomorrow. In this new version of the "radiant future," the red flag has been replaced by the brown flag of authoritarian right-wing parties or by the green banner of the Prophet Muhammad. The conflicts that used to be standardized by class struggle ideology no longer oppose the proletariat to the bourgeoisie; rather, according to some, they pit the "true French" against the "globalized Empire" (an updated reminder of the Judeo-Masonic conspiracy of the 1930s), and according to others, they divide the world between righteous "Muslims" and hell-bound *kuffar* ("infidels" in Quranic Arabic).

These two worldviews redefine group memberships, solidarities, and enmities along lines that are not defined in terms of social class, even though they are fed by an obsessive fear of losing social status. The new "imagined communities"—to borrow from Benedict Anderson's landmark book—to which those who adhere to these worldviews claim to belong, are transversal and heterogeneous. First of all, they revolve around moral certainties that are perceived as endangered and draw on a will to rebuild a code for the construction of a substitute ethics that the current political institutions, rife with corruption and compromises, lack.

The National Front has boasted that it is "France's leading party" since it received the largest number of votes in the 2014 European Parliament elections and the December 2015 regional elections. Yet this party's rhetoric does not entirely acknowledge that it is part of a more complex conglomeration. It includes organizations that urge a wider electorate to protest in the streets, as in the Manif pour tous (Demonstration for All) against the law authorizing same-sex marriage in 2014, and also a nebulous group that has emerged on the Internet and that is known as the *Fachosphere* (Fascist Web). Radical ethnic identity parties that call for all "native Frenchmen" to stand together against the "Muslim invasion" exist side by side with conspiracy theorists who seek to mobilize together true children of "our ancestors the Gauls" and "recent French people" (i.e., young French Muslims) against "Zionism" (i.e., Jews).

On the Islamic side we also find numerous generational, social, and political cleavages. Many groups are competing for influence over a population estimated to be 8 percent of France's inhabitants, trying to transform it into a closely bound "community" defined by religious and cultural barriers. This population is younger and poorer than average and is endowed with an exceptionally dynamic demography. From the 2005 riots onward, it has also been growing, partially because of a new development: a flood of conversions among "native Europeans" from the declining working class and the frightened lower middle class.

For the present and the foreseeable future, this population group represents a considerable stake in society and a major source of votes in elections. However, it is unlikely that it will be able to incarnate the united "community" that Islamic political and religious entrepreneurs are relentlessly working on by pressing for cultural frontier markers—which have ranged, since the end of the 1980s, from wearing the Islamic veil to respecting halal diet and demonizing same-sex marriage.

In the mid-1980s, the Union des organisations islamiques de France (UOIF), an offshoot of the Muslim Brotherhood, the main international organization for political Islam, gained a primacy that it retained until the 2005 riots. Controlled by Arabic-speaking *blédards* (those who were born and bred in North Africa or the Levant), it made its hobbyhorse the fight for Muslim female students' wearing of the veil in schools.

Having lost steam after the passage in 2004 of the law prohibiting the display of ostentatious religious signs in publicly funded schools and after the banlieues riots of 2005, the UOIF has since suffered strong competition from the Salafist movement in the battle for French Muslim minds. This "total" (in French, *intégrale*) view of the Muslim religion relies on a grand narrative promoting cultural separation from "infidel" French society. It recruits primarily among disenfranchised young people in the banlieues, where that blend of "total" Islam has become not only the norm in many places, multiplying ostensible markers in the urban fabric, but also a portentous *habitus* for their residents.

These two trends issue rules and prohibitions and construct representations of the world that challenge the established French identity.

Movements whose purposes are more explicitly electoral prey on them, the most effective of which is Union des associations musulmanes du 93 (UAM 93), which advocates a strategy of religious lobbying in Seine-Saint-Denis, the first *département* in France to have a Muslim majority, according to UAM's president. During the municipal elections in 2014, UAM 93 sought to take support away from the Socialist Party among voters in the disenfranchised housing projects by moving these voters to the right.

This shift has been aided by Islamic organizations' participation, alongside French Catholic traditionalists, in the 2013 Manif pour tous against same-sex marriages and also by certain imams' subsequent Friday sermons urging their followers to punish socialists for having become "corrupters on earth" by having authorized "homosexual marriage." Although most of the faithful themselves had still voted for the left in the presidential and parliamentary elections of 2012, largely owing to their social position, in 2014 their support for the socialists crumbled, partly as a result of the persistence of the economic crisis but also because voting socialist now conflicted with moral-religious values.

Nonetheless, these children of Muslim immigrants were not limited to a hard choice between a social position that pushed them toward the left and an ethnic-religious affiliation that pushed them toward the right. Since the collapse of the Communist Party, the French working class as a whole has ceased to vote for the left and has allowed itself to be drawn into an identitarian[1] vote for the far right. In 2015, polls indicated that the National Front had the highest number of blue-collar supporters. Moreover, in the 2012 parliamentary elections, some candidates who were children of colonial immigrants registered with the National Front or shared the conspiracy theory worldview advocated by far-rightists Alain Soral or Dieudonné M'Bala M'Bala—whereas others condoned Islamist rhetoric.

The entrance of this generation into politics has a history that goes back far beyond the vicissitudes it experienced from 2005 to 2015. Its chronology begins with the founding myth of the "March for Equality and against Racism," which the press dubbed the Marche des beurs (March of the *Beurs*—French banlieues backslang for Arabs) in autumn 1983. It was an initial attempt made by this new component

---

[1] *Identitaire*, a term referring to far-right politics that are based upon stressing native French identity and hostility to immigrants, particularly those of African descent.

of the French population to assert itself. The march came twenty-one years after Algerian independence—long enough for the generation of children born in France to Algerian parents to have reached adulthood.

Starting in the predominantly Algerian neighborhoods on the north side of Marseille, the march proceeded through the country, passing through Lyon and Roubaix and marking out a dispersed territory—the Algerian new France of the housing projects. The march sketched out an inverted mirror image of the lost French Algeria at the pivotal point between the former French Empire and what the retrocolonial era was to become. The March of the Beurs ended in Paris on December 3, 1983, with the presentation to President François Mitterrand, at the Élysée Palace, of demands for political participation. It issued from the heirs of the Algerian Front de libération nationale (FLN), regarding which he had declared, as minister of the interior, on November 5, 1954, just after the "Toussaint rouge,"[2] that "the only negotiation is war" with the FLN.

At the outset, the march appealed to the ideal universals that the participants felt had been taken away from them, particularly as a result of police blunders committed during "hot summers" and imputed to "racial profiling" (*délit de faciès*), which resulted in several deaths during checks of identity papers or security incidents. Beyond this declared intention, as evidenced by its being called the "March of the Beurs," it forcefully marked that ethnogeneration's appearance on the French political stage.

For Mitterrand, the "only negotiation" this time was to be trickery. These young people, whose hybridization—illustrated by their use of banlieues backslang in referring to themselves—was supposed to guarantee them better integration into French society and assimilation to it, were not urged by the President and his advisors to join political parties. Instead, they were limited to serving as an audience for a spectacular politics associated with antiracism.

Mitterrand's ruse was twofold: it consisted in broadly federating and publicizing the young people's movement in order to stir and then stigmatize as racist the far right, whose rise in power was to divide the right wing and allow Mitterrand's re-election as president in 1988. But it also consisted in diluting the marchers' specific demands (particularly those connected with the pro-Palestinian affinities that some

---

[2] "Red All-Saints' Day," a series of bloody attacks by FLN that took place in French Algeria on November 1, 1954. It is usually regarded as the beginning of the Algerian War for Independence.

of them expressed by wearing Yasser Arafat's checkered *keffiyeh*) in a broader antiracism in which French Jewish organizations played a driving role under the aegis of the organization SOS Racisme and its slogan "*Touche pas à mon pote*" ("Hands off my buddy"). We shall see how Mitterrand's Machiavellian malediction has endured down to the present and has been exacerbated to the point that the far right is now established at the heart of French political life, in a position to win its bet. Moreover, the ousting from established politics and marginalization of the children of Muslim immigration would pave the way for Salafism and jihadism as a compensation.

The following pages are devoted to the study of this epochal change and the birth of jihad within France. First, we shall see how, between the pivotal years 2005 and 2012, a specifically French jihad was incubated even as a deep transformation of society took place almost unnoticed. The riots that began in Clichy-sous-Bois in autumn 2005 gave birth to the third generation of French Islam at the same time when the third jihadi generation was emerging in the Middle East under the influence of Syrian ideologue Abu Musab al-Suri.

Born in reaction to the riots, Nicolas Sarkozy's presidency (2007–2012), which borrowed its political program from the far right, ended with the Merah affair—the test of the many jihadi attacks that would ensue. The intelligence services were unable to anticipate the latter's combination of a foreign Islamist ideology conveyed through social networks and the new political sociology of the radicalized French Salafism.

Second, we will see how François Hollande, who benefited from the "Muslim vote" in the elections of May 2012, rapidly lost it because of the law authorizing same-sex marriage (*Mariage pour tous*), which triggered a Manif pour tous in which Catholics and Islamists paraded together, partly to support conservative values. But the loss of the Muslim vote was also due to the worsening of the economic crisis that was causing serious distress in the impoverished banlieues.

That would be a terrain favorable to the eruption of the French jihad in a society squeezed between the resistible ascension of the National Front and the thrust of a Salafism whose most radical elements, their eyes set on Syria and ISIS, advocate the destruction of Europe by civil war. And in that, the French case is not only significant for France as such: as developments in 2016 showed, it is becoming a paradigm that can help us decipher the in-depth dimension of the rise of jihad in the West as a whole.

PART I

THE INCUBATION PERIOD:
FROM CLICHY TO SARKOZY

Between 2005 and 2012, a great change took place in French Islam. Only seven years separated the riots from the massacre perpetrated by Merah, but this very dangerous period was a time of missed opportunities. Paradoxically, the spectacular return of jihadi terrorism to France in March 2012 coincided with the beginning of a campaign that led to the election of François Hollande as president of the Republic. Hollande owed his victory in part to the fact that Muslims voted for him in large numbers. It was followed by National Assembly elections that included, for the first time, more than four hundred candidates from Muslim immigrant families. By seeking election, they declared themselves full-fledged members of the nation.

But alongside this ostensible political integration of a group previously excluded from most social institutions, an underground movement appeared. The third generation of French Islam emerged in 2004–2005, between the Stasi Commission[1] and the riots. This generation sought to free itself from the state supervision promulgated by former Interior minister Pierre Joxe's Council for Reflection on French Islam (Corif) and its successor, Nicolas Sarkozy's French Council of the Muslim Faith (CFCM); it claimed full citizenship, with the same rights enjoyed by Christians and Jews.

---

[1] A French commission headed by Bernard Stasi that was created in 2003 to reflect on the application of the principle of secularism in France. (Not to be confused with the former East German secret police, also known as the *Stasi*.)

The decoupling of this new political citizenship from its fragile social bases, added to a fractured Islamic religious field in France, created favorable conditions for the development of what its advocates call "total" Islam. The latter offers an imaginary alternative solution to the deadlocks in society that is all the more attractive because it manages to absorb, in part, the pre-existing radical utopian ideals of both the left and the right wings. It can also serve as a substitute for them, as is shown by the unprecedented increase in conversions to Islam.

This movement has been accelerated by the changes international jihadism has undergone. In January 2005, the Syrian-Spaniard Mustafa Setmariam Nasar, alias Abu Musab al-Suri, published online *The Global Islamic Resistance Call* (*Da'wat al-muqawamah al-islamiyyah al-'alamiyyah*). This 1,600-page manifesto conceived terrorism in Europe as the main vector of the battle against the West and identified the "poorly integrated" younger generation of Muslims as its preferred instrument. This text breaks with al-Qaeda's previous strategy, in which the leaders assigned agents from the Middle East to carry out attacks on the United States; instead, it gives priority to offensives in European countries, with the intention of fomenting civil wars in order to make them implode.

These ideas slowly matured as young jihadis left Europe to be trained on battlefields in Iraq and then Afghanistan, producing the milieu from which Mohamed Merah emerged. Conversely, the political integration of young French people from Muslim immigrant families was demonstrated by their willingness to vote and run for office in March 2012, at the very time when Merah committed the massacres in Montauban and Toulouse in the name of jihad—and as an enemy of society.

It is this political integration, the key to building a pluralist French society based upon shared values, that is deeply threatened by the emergence of jihadism at its very heart.

1

2005, THE PIVOTAL YEAR

The terrible riots that shook France in autumn 2005 and that forced the government to proclaim a state of emergency—the first since the end of the Algerian War and to be seconded as of the January 2015 jihadi attacks (still implemented until the summer of 2017)—took place in the context of deep national and international upheavals.

These riots occurred at a watershed moment when a new generation of young Muslims burst onto the scene, seizing control of the streets for three weeks in the areas where they resided. During the following decade, this irruption would take the form of both participation in elections and the assertion of Islamic identity. Many banlieues voters would register to elect thousands of officials in municipal, general, and regional councils. In the 2012 parliamentary elections, some 400 candidates out of 6,000 would be descendants of postcolonial immigrants; they were seeking, for the first time in history, to embody national sovereignty. Half a dozen of them would be elected members of Parliament, while the same number would become senators.

The riots were a rite of passage corresponding to the transition to a new age of French Islam, in which a generation born and brought up on French territory came to the foreground and shook up the Islamic institutions that had been controlled by earlier generations whose members had migrated to France from the southern or eastern Mediterranean shores and West Africa. This phenomenon occurred at the very time when the international radical Islamic movement began its own mutation. Whereas al-Qaeda had had a pyramidal structure with Osama bin Laden at the top and the United States as a target, as was shown on 9/11, the new approach was structured on a bottom-up, network-based model. It took Europe as its primary target and sought to recruit its "soldiers"among young Muslim Europeans.

During this period, bloody attacks committed in neighboring countries, such as in the United Kingdom in 2005 and when the caricatures of the Prophet were published in a Danish newspaper, had repercussions throughout the world. These events foreshadowed what would happen ten years later on a still greater scale, first in Paris and then in Copenhagen, while ISIS was expanding in Syria and in Iraq and when thousands of young Europeans had already joined the jihad.

The complex connection between the demographic and cultural changes in Europe and the transformations of jihadism are crucial for understanding what happened during the pivotal decade extending from the riots of 2005 to the attacks carried out in 2015 by ISIS.

THE DOUBLE TRIGGER FOR THE RIOTS

The most consequential outcome of the 2005 riots was that the children of postcolonial immigrants emerged as political actors. These young people took control of the streets in the banlieues to which they felt relegated. The three-week spectacle of vandalism, looting, burning of cars, and harassing of police officers sent an existential message to the rest of French society that left deep scars. However, the staging and the location of violence were carefully limited. The participants themselves restricted the violence to a register that was chiefly symbolic: between October 27 and November 18, only four deaths were associated with the events, including those of two teenagers electrocuted when taking refuge in an electrical transformer in Clichy-sous-Bois—the initial catalyst for the revolt. The riots' consequences were mainly self-destructive and included the burning of the public infrastructure—the housing projects, schools, gymnasiums, post offices, and means of public transportation—of which the rioters were, like other inhabitants of the banlieues, the main users. The incidents spread like wildfire all over France, creating a staggering mass effect for which the media provided both a vector and an echo chamber.

The sensationalist leitmotif *Paris is burning*, frequently repeated in American newspaper headlines, was false: Paris did not burn. Not only did the police take care to keep the riots outside the capital's beltway, but the rioters themselves proved incapable of leaving their own neighborhoods, to which the burning was limited. Contrary to what some people claimed, there was no national organization or coordination. This reactive and spontaneous movement was indefatigably fed solely by the vagaries of its own media and television image, its passionate upsurge giving way to an equally rapid subsidence. As was explained by young people from Clichy-Montfermeil, who had been directly involved in the riots or who had witnessed them, the riots were essentially limited to a few hours after dusk. The skirmishes occurred until their instigators got tired and went to bed in the same housing projects where the fighting had taken place—sometimes right below their own windows.

Continuous reporting in the media made it seem that the action was incessant and omnipresent when in fact it was spasmodic and circumscribed. The reality of the riots was largely dissociated from the way it was presented, but the scope of the phenomenon and its excesses led to an emotional interpretation that tended to exacerbate it.

The riots had two triggers. Noting this duality allows us to gauge the gap between the reality of the events and their representation. The first trigger was the death of two teenagers, one of Malian origin and the other Tunisian, who were electrocuted on October 27 when they tried to avoid arrest by hiding in a transformer. But this tragedy led to only a momentary reaction limited to the Clichy-Montfermeil area. The second trigger occurred at nightfall three days later, when stones were thrown at the police and the latter responded with a tear gas grenade that landed at the entrance of a crowded mosque. The sight of the worshipers choking and panicking gave new impetus to a weakening movement and extended it, over the course of a few days, to the majority of the housing projects in banlieues throughout France.

However, the account of the riots produced for general public consumption included only the dramatic episode of the electrocution, whereas it was the gassing of the Bilal mosque that provided the springboard for the events and caused their stupefying spread throughout the country. The tragic deaths of the two teenagers, Bouna Traoré and Zyed Benna, who had not committed the burglary of which they were suspected, supplied the occasion for an emotional response that is easy to understand and identify with and that gave the revolt a moral justification. This justification proved all the more necessary when the damage reached an unprecedented level, with more than nine thousand cars burned in the course of three weeks and tens of millions of dollars in damages incurred—and the majority of the population overcome by fear and indignation.

Less than two years later, in June 2007, the trauma would win the presidency for Nicolas Sarkozy, the hardline minister of the interior during the riots. And yet, as is shown by interviews with participants and witnesses in Clichy-Montfermeil that were published in *Banlieue de la République* (Gallimard, 2012), it was the "gassing of the mosque"—a normative Grand Narrative of the event that deprived it of its accidental character and turned it into a deliberate offensive launched by the police against Muslim worshipers—that remained the principal vector of the uprising.

In 2005, Islam was becoming an irrepressible marker of identity in the banlieues. The incident at the mosque dramatized the stakes involved at the very time when the younger generation, born in France, was competing with older generations, born and brought up in the Maghreb or the Levant, for the right to speak on behalf of Muslims. By revolting, they positioned themselves as the true defenders of the honor of their families—whose dignity, they claimed, had been deeply wounded by the profanation of their place of worship during their time of collective prayer.

As was explained by Hassan (a community activist who became a local elected official), after the spontaneous riots by the adolescent peers of Bouna and Zyed on Thursday, October 27, 2005, the situation could have been quickly calmed down by the intervention of the "elder brothers," who organized a silent march on the following Saturday. But then came Sunday, October 30:

> Things were turbulent near the Bilal mosque. Tear gas bombs were landing inside the mosque's enclosure, and there, in fact, it wasn't only the fifteen- to eighteen-year-olds, but all those who were peaceful! When you see your mother come out of the mosque and collapse, or your grandmother, because it was Ramadan, the sacred month, right in the middle of prayers. In these neighborhoods, the young people feel abandoned, completely neglected. It was that, not the death of Zyed and Bouna, that snowballed all over France!

Nasser, another community activist whom the media asked to speak for the young people in Clichy, and who was later a candidate in the parliamentary elections, described the tempo of the violence:

> It was Ramadan, so the young people were eating, I remember, at 6:30 p.m., and then they went to where the action was, for a short time, three or four hours. Then they went home. These young people have other things to do!

Ramadan thus supplied the temporal framework for the two events that triggered the uprising: Bouna and Zyed were hurrying back to their families' apartments so as to be on time for the breaking of the fast when they were forced to take refuge in the transformer, and the worshipers had assembled in large numbers in the mosque after the *ftour* (the meal eaten at sundown during Ramadan) in order to perform the sacred month's extra prayers. But although Ramadan ended on November 2, the riots continued for another two weeks. Thus the social and collective dimensions of the event went beyond the religious context. Nonetheless, the feeling that a sacrilege had been committed by the police not only served as an initial catalyst but also provided, according to Hassan, the rational justification for the violence:

> What set everything off was the attack on the mosque. What happened was not right, and what happened afterward still less: there were no apologies, nothing. People said to themselves that in France, a Muslim is worthless these days. A Muslim matters only during elections. Had it been a Jew or a synagogue, the reaction would not have been the same.

Bilal, a pious thirty-year-old computer engineer who was praying in the mosque when the tear gas bomb landed outside, constructed a vivid personal account of the event whose apologetic character seeks to rationalize the revolt's violence by putting the blame on the police:

> The women who were upstairs [in the mosque, in the area reserved for women] were poisoned by the grenades that were thrown outside. I was crying. People said: it's war. The guns they used to shoot their tear gas bombs looked like military rifles. It was scary to be facing them.

For Hamza, a Turk and an Islamic activist who was also present at the mosque and who stated that he "had tried hard to calm the young people who were throwing rocks," the atmosphere of war made his mediation impossible. He even situated the confrontations in the context of the conflict between Palestinian Muslims and Israel as it was seen on television:

> Bringing in helicopters over the housing blocks automatically made people think of Palestine. That was what one heard most often: "Look, this must be what our Palestinian brothers have to endure!"

FROM PROFANATION TO BLASPHEMY

The rationalization of the revolt as a reaction to the deliberate profanation of an Islamic place of worship by the state and its police force was facilitated by the international political context in which it occurred. However, the Israeli-Palestinian conflict was not the only international conflict that added fuel to the fire. In Denmark, on September 30, 2005, one month before the events in Clichy-Montfermeil, the newspaper *Jyllands-Posten* published a series of caricatures of the Prophet Muhammad in reaction to what its editors saw as a trend toward self-censorship within the media on issues related to Islam.

This initiative sought to respond to the trauma arising from the assassination of the film director Theo Van Gogh in Amsterdam a year earlier. He had made a short film entitled *Submission*, echoing the meaning of the Arabic term *islam*. (French novelist Michel Houellebecq would give the same title to his famed novel published on January 7, 2015, the day of the massacre at *Charlie Hebdo*.) In the film, Quranic verses are projected onto a nude female body—verses that Van Gogh and his scriptwriter, Dutch politician Ayaan Hirsi Ali, a Somalia-born atheist and erstwhile Muslim, considered hostile to the cause of women. Van Gogh was attacked and his throat cut on the street by a twenty-seven-year-old Netherlander of Moroccan ancestry. This event deeply upset the Netherlands, which had up to that point advocated unlimited multiculturalism. Moreover, French Jacobinism had been scorned there, especially after the Stasi Commission[1] recommended that conspicuous religious signs be prohibited in the schools, a recommendation that was made law on March 15, 2004.

The outraged reaction to the blasphemy against the Prophet's person in the *Jyllands-Posten*, publicized in the Muslim world by Danish Islamists, won the support of certain governments in the Middle East. The latter did not share the Islamists' ideology but nonetheless feared being accused of not having defended Islam with sufficient vigor. This kind of worldwide campaign, heightened by the media in the region,

---

[1] Named after Bernard Stasi, its president, this commission of "wise people" had been convened by president Jacques Chirac in 2003 to debate the threats against laïcite (secularism) that were posed mainly by Salafist attempts at making Islamic mores norms that would tamper French law. It recommended the banning of "ostentatious religious garments" in schools funded by taxpayers, in line with the French constitution's wall of separation between church and state. A law to that effect was passed in March 2014.

carried the concept of "Islamophobia" far beyond the Salafists' and the Muslim Brotherhood's usual networks. Let us note that it was the latter that publicized the term *Islamophobia* in the 1990s in an attempt to criminalize any criticism of the religious dogma they championed while at the same time constructing a specious symmetry with anti-Semitism so as to benefit from the moral dividends of victimization and turn them against Israel and Zionism.

The polemic surrounding the offense against Muhammad in contemporary Europe was not new. The 2006 campaign was in many respects a reprise of the one dramatized by Ayatollah Ruholla Khomeini's fatwa condemning Salman Rushdie to death, issued on February 14, 1989, for what the Ayatollah considered an insult to the Prophet in the British writer's novel *The Satanic Verses*. At the time, Khomeini was trying to make himself the champion of universal Islam, although he exercised authority over only the Shiite minority to which he belonged, which still amounts to only about 15 percent of the world's Muslim population. Since a fatwa's death sentence is applicable only in the "land of Islam" (*Dar al-Islam*), this call for murder symbolically extended that realm to include Europe. This fatwa was followed by many others, issued and sometimes executed by Sunni jihadis, as was tragically demonstrated by the slaughter at *Charlie Hebdo* on January 7, 2015.

Fifteen years after Ayatollah Khomeini's fatwa on Valentine's Day 1989, the Danish affair in 2005–2006, which also focused on the issue of blasphemy, rapidly became the subject of intra-Islamic competition. Initiated by Sunni Islamists, it was immediately picked up by that group's major media figures, notably Sheikh Yusuf al-Qaradawi of the Muslim Brotherhood, an Egyptian who was a naturalized Qatarian as well as the principal preacher on the Al-Jazeera television channel. He did all he could to make a worldwide cause of the caricatures that had appeared in *Jyllands-Posten*—a cause of which he proclaimed himself the knight in shining armor. Tehran went him one better by electing as president the radical Mahmud Ahmadinejad, who used provocation of the West as a mode of government and who made himself famous by proposing to wipe Israel off the map.

Cutting the ground out from under his Sunni rivals just as Ruhollah Khomeini had, Mahmoud Ahmadinejad announced that Iran would organize an international contest for the best caricatures of the Holocaust as a response to the Danish drawings. By so doing, he intended to deride the Holocaust in the same way the *Jyllands-Posten* cartoons had mocked the Prophet. Though the Holocaust is sacrosanct in the West, public opinion and media in the Muslim world—including some young Muslims in the West—see it as the foundational Zionist myth, which allowed the creation of the hated state of Israel. By means of this symmetrical outrage, the Iranian leader was seeking to regain ideological control over the Ummah, the international Islamic community, whose spiritual borders he extended from the Persian Gulf to Clichy-Montfermeil and Denmark. He found a henchman in Europe who echoed his sarcastic way of expressing hatred for Zionism in the person of the French humorist Dieudonné, who was to have a bright future that would involve the weaving of an improbable alliance between some of Islam's radical tendencies and extreme right-wing politics.

THE EPOCHAL CHANGE OF FRENCH ISLAM

The magnitude of the international Islamic campaign against Denmark led some European periodicals to reprint, out of solidarity and in order to defend freedom of expression, the cartoons that had appeared in *Jyllands-Posten*. Among these reprints was the February 8, 2006, issue of *Charlie Hebdo*, a weekly whose editorial team was to pay the price in blood nine years later, on January 7, 2015, during the massacre perpetrated at its offices by the Kouachi brothers, who cried "Allahu akbar!" and "The Prophet is avenged!" *Charlie Hebdo*, a satirical paper whose dated sense of humor and commercial model were losing it readership, nonetheless sold half a million copies of this special issue in 2006. (The circulation of the issue that followed the attacks in 2015 exceeded seven million.) After it republished the Muhammad cartoons, the periodical was immediately taken to court by the French Council of the Muslim Faith (CFCM), whose complaint was ultimately dismissed in the name of freedom of expression and because the secular republic did not recognize a juridical concept of blasphemy.

Similarly, the Union of Islamic Organizations of France (UOIF), which had issued a fatwa urging young Muslims to cease engaging in violence during the riots, had little effect. Although it denounced "an irresponsible act against the mosque of Clichy-sous-Bois at a time of prayer," it cited the Quran as authority for its fatwa: "Allah does not like those who sow disorder." The organization stated:

> It is strictly forbidden for any Muslim seeking divine satisfaction and glory to participate in any action that blindly attacks private or public goods or that might endanger others' lives. Contributing to these actions is an illicit act [*haram*].

Not only did the fatwa have no impact, but rather, on the following day, November 7, the number of vehicles burned (1,408), persons arrested (395), and policemen wounded (35) reached record highs for a single day. What's more, the riots continued for another dozen days. November 7 marked the definitive end to the preponderant influence the UOIF had gained since the first "veil affair" in a middle school in Creil, in autumn 1989, in which it had played an incendiary role. The baton was passed to young people born in France—the children of the immigrant workers, or *darons*, who had been the first Islamic generation in France.

During the difficult period before 1989, this first generation focused its activity on building mosques. The vast majority of Muslim immigrants then were neither French citizens nor voters and had no influence on the granting of construction permits by municipal authorities. After 1989, they were marginalized by the Brothers and the *blédards* who constituted the second generation, most of whom did not have French citizenship either. This second generation targeted very young people born and educated in France, seeking to inculcate in them rigorous Islamic principles and thereby counter the effects of the public school system's assimilationist education. The main theme of this shift in values was the demand that girls be allowed to wear the hijab in class. This was a recurrent irritant from 1989 on, and in the absence of legislation addressing the issue, multiple complaints brought before administrative tribunals and the Council of State complicated life in the schools.

The law of March 15, 2004, enacted as a follow-up to the Stasi Commission, put an end to the dispute and to Islamists' legal challenges. By depriving the UOIF of its main legal and political leverage, this effectively destroyed its ascendancy. Up to that point, the organization had maintained a sense of agitation and victimhood from which it benefited by presenting itself, in the eyes of its flock, as the advocate of its threatened Islamic identity and, in the eyes of the government, as the manager of a community defined within the nation by its particular religious values. This abrupt loss of influence occurred at the very time when a demographic and social mutation was taking place: the coming of age of the third generation, whose members, the descendants of postcolonial immigrants, had been born soon after the March of the Beurs in 1983.

The law prohibiting the wearing of the hijab at school preceded the riots of 2005 by only one year. This law also marked the shift of the center of gravity of French Islam from the UOIF to the banlieues and from the *blédards* to the "youth," as the discourse of the media described it from the outside. A number of these young people liked to use terms from *verlan* (a type of French slang that involves inverting the syllables of words) when they self-identified, calling themselves *rebeus* (Arabs), *renois* (noirs), or even *keblas* (blacks) and *keturs* (Turks), and thereby bringing the native language of the suburban projects into the public sphere, reversing its stigma. An increasing number of young *céfrans* (white French people) who had converted to Islam were involved in this development. Compared with their Muslim counterparts, who had been influenced by a conspicuous and strongly proselytizing re-Islamization movement, spearheaded by the Salafists, the *céfrans* were a minority in the housing projects. As we shall see, they would find it difficult to resist this socioreligious pressure.

But the young people who were front and center on the Muslim scene starting in the middle of the first decade of the twenty-first century were not limited to this neglected group. Elites emerged by pursuing educational paths that were far superior to those of their parents' generation and that led to high school and college degrees. Some members of these elites chose to become public servants, and some were initially associated with left-wing parties favoring a model of social redistribution that was part of the working-class tradition. However, the new development that put its stamp on the first decade of the twenty-first century was the arrival of a class of young entrepreneurs who had emerged from immigrant backgrounds and who were more open to the market and to right-wing values.

Of course, among them we find individuals who wanted to pursue careers that followed the conventional path of the republican meritocracy through which the preceding generations of immigrants had passed. In the course of this social ascension, these children of southern and eastern Europe had diluted their inherited identity, merging with the broader French identity and contributing to it. But what has been unprecedented has been the emergence of a new type of entrepreneur seeking to emphasize the identity of Islamic community with a view to gaining control over supposedly captive market shares. These businessmen, who can be figuratively described as "halal entrepreneurs," have played a major political role since 2005.

The great shift in French Islam in 2004–2005, during the period separating the law prohibiting the conspicuous display of religious symbols in the schools from the riots, had a series of notable consequences. In place of the institutions set up by the state since 1989 to provide for representation, which had failed to influence the young, a profusion of grassroots initiatives arose—some from associations, some from well-known individuals, some from mosques, and others from various interest groups. For the first time in the short history of Islam of France, the great majority of the social actors were French citizens who had been brought up, if not born, in France and whose native language was French. It was on the basis of their citizenship—whose ethical value and duties some contested even as they claimed the rights it conferred—that a series of demands were beginning to be formulated in the public sphere.

These demands range from strict respect for halal, whether in the domain of food or the choice of marriage partners, to the opening of private Muslim schools in which wearing the hijab is permitted and in which the teaching of "gender theory" is prohibited. These demands are pursued by lobbies that negotiate with candidates in elections, offering their support in exchange for a commitment to defend various Islamic causes. Whatever their specific orientation, most of these initiatives involve consumer pressure groups focusing on issues ranging from ritually slaughtered meat to education and voting. In this sense, the young citizens who participate in these groups are now taking a symbolic revenge, in the area of halal consumption in its broader meaning, for the situation in which France put many of their parents, who were excluded from the labor market after the crisis of the 1970s and who experienced widespread and extended unemployment.

This new generation, which consists of French citizens brought up in the world of the banlieues' housing projects, has found in the Internet a privileged way of expressing and propagating its values. These values combine the search for an all-encompassing conception of Islam inspired by the Salafism of the Arabian Peninsula and a fervent consultation of a digital "Islamosphere" full of norms and injunctions breaking with the "infidel" model of the West. This digital tool and the connections outside France to which it gives instantaneous access lead to the drawing of an increasingly sharp borderline between the spheres of the halal (licit, authorized) and the haram (illicit, forbidden). It favors the ambitions of associative or entrepreneurial networks, active in society as well as in cyberspace, that aspire to exercise religious, cultural, and political hegemony over young people.

The extension of these networks has been further increased by lightning-fast developments in the digital world. The Web 2.0 revolution, which occurred between 2005 and 2015, facilitated the construction of virtual communities through YouTube, Facebook, and Twitter.

It was by this means that the third generation of Islam of France—which became active, as we have seen, after the riots of 2005—came into direct contact with the third wave of jihadism. This jihad movement began to take form in the same year, after the online publication of the founding work of its main ideologue, Abu Musab al-Suri, entitled *The Global Islamic Resistance Call.*

This coincidence of social change in the banlieues' housing projects, the shift of generation in the leaders of French Islam, and the transformations of international jihadism's ideology looks like a perfect storm. Nonetheless, it was this coincidence that, through the social networks that were then emerging, produced the hybridization from which would emerge, ten years later, the cohorts of French jihadis enraptured by the battlefields in Syria and Iraq. By autumn 2015, more than a hundred and fifty of them had already died there, not counting those who followed the examples of Mohamed Merah, Chérif and Saïd Kouachi, Amedy Coulibaly, and Abdelhamid Abaaoud, perpetrating attacks on French territory or assassinations inspired by that ideology.

This latter phenomenon is obviously extremely limited in comparison with the number of people involved in the riots of 2005. Moreover, it represents only an extremist by-product of this third generation of Islam of France that has established itself in the meantime and that has taken various other forms of expression, as we shall see. But its spectacular character, its violence, and the forms of cultural hegemony that it has constructed in certain strata of the population, not to mention the perverse globalization that it illustrates, all give it an emblematic quality.

This requires us to identify precisely the context in which this phenomenon emerged, and neither to exaggerate nor to belittle its true significance. The paradoxical connection between these two spheres—the Islam of France in the banlieues on one side of the Mediterranean, and North Africa and the Middle East caught up in chaos on the other side—has produced the new dialectic of jihadism.

THE DIALECTIC OF JIHADISM

In January 2005, the 1,600 pages of *The Global Islamic Resistance Call* were made available online. This mixture of activists' encyclopedia and instruction manual for third-generation jihad was written by al-Suri, a naturalized Spanish engineer then in his forties, and it would put its stamp on the decade that followed.

Drawing up a balance sheet of international jihad successes and failures over the past quarter of a century, the text elaborates a dialectic of the movement that sounds almost Hegelian. According to al-Suri, everything begins with the "moment of affirmation" corresponding to the victorious Afghan jihad of the 1980s and then to its fruitless sequels in Algeria, Egypt, and Bosnia in the 1990s. It was followed by a second phase—that of al-Qaeda, symbolized by September 11, 2001.

This latter is the "moment of negation." Osama bin Laden and his organization turned away from armed jihad against the nearby enemy (*al 'adu al qarib*), which had led to the sterile guerrilla wars that had concluded the first phase. For it they substituted spectacular actions against the faraway American enemy (*al 'adu al baid*), which were intended to weaken it and expose it, in the eyes of the Muslim masses, as a colossus whose feet were of clay. But according to al-Suri, this second phase also led to a failure, because al-Qaeda's business model (based on terrorism alone, with satellite television, especially Al-Jazeera, as its vector) had no concrete expression among Muslim populations. The attacks that followed September 11, until the bombings in London of July 2005, merely exhausted its substance without triggering a popular mobilization.

The Global Islamic Resistance Call was situated at this historical juncture. It theorized a third wave to come, which in its quasi-Hegelian dialectic would correspond to the "negation of the negation"—that is, to its "transcendence" (*Aufhebung*). For al-Qaeda's pyramidal organization, which was not integrated into society, Al-Suri substituted a jihadism of proximity, based on a network-based system penetrating the enemy societies to be overthrown from the bottom up rather than from the top down. The spectacular attack on America was dismissed as the hubris of an Osama bin Laden intoxicated by his own image in the media. According to al-Suri, September 11 merely succeeded in giving George W. Bush an opportunity to destroy al-Qaeda's infrastructure.

Instead, the Syrian ideologue advocated civil war in Europe, drawing on poorly integrated, rebellious young Muslims of immigrant descent after they had been suitably indoctrinated and trained militarily on a nearby battlefield. This was supposed to be how the final dislocation of the West would begin, paving the way for the worldwide triumph of Islamism. Such a "rhizomatic" jihadism, which passes below the enemy's radar and turns its own adopted or natural children against it, is constructed in opposition to the centralized, almost Leninist model implemented by Bin Laden. Al-Suri summed up his program in a formula that flourished in the jihadosphere: *Nizam, la tanzim* ("a system, not an organization").

Having been posted on the Internet in January 2005, when al-Suri, hidden in Baluchistan, the vast tribal region on the western borders of Pakistan was fleeing the American army's offensive against al-Qaeda before his eventual capture. A decade later, in 2015, *The Global Islamic Resistance Call* appeared to be a visionary text. Even before it served as a literal instruction manual for terrorist activities, from Mohamed Merah to Abdelhamid Abaaoud, it was available, in PDF form and in both Arabic and English, on the Facebook pages of French, European, and Arab jihadis who had gone to Syria. Its importance was shown in 2008 by the Norwegian orientalist Brynjar Lia in a monograph entitled *Architect of Global Jihad*, as well as by my own book, *Beyond Terror and Martyrdom*. These works received little attention; the *Call*, which is long and difficult to read as a whole, was thought to be merely a jumble of wild theoretical imaginings whose reticular strategy would have no foreseeable practical effect.

However, it must be admitted that the "phase of transcendence" prophesied by al-Suri corresponds exactly to what gradually transpired during the decade following the publication of the *Call*. Two phenomena proved crucial to its realization. First was the concomitant appearance of social networking sites. (For example, the YouTube domain name was registered on February 14, 2005, a month after the *Call* was posted online.) These sites quickly became the vector par excellence for third-generation jihadi indoctrination, just as satellite television stations like Al-Jazeera had been for the second generation and faxes had been for the first generation. However, Western intelligence services failed to recognize in time this mode of radicalization, which relied on the sharing of images and other digital content in a virtual universe, and instead remained focused on the surveillance within mosques of activists linked to al-Qaeda.

In France in particular, this surveillance was successful—up to a point. It made possible the neutralization of the Franco–Algerian Khaled Kelkal and the terrorist network responsible for the Islamist attacks carried out in 1995—and then the preventive arrest of his compatriot Djamel Beghal in 2001, before he could blow up the U.S. embassy in Paris. And it was also this surveillance that led in 2005 to the dismantling of the "Buttes-Chaumont jihadi network," which was sending young Parisian recruits to al-Qaeda in U.S.-invaded Iraq. Thus the country remained under tight security until March 2012, when those who had considered al-Suri's *Call* to be of negligible importance

were caught off guard by the carnage perpetrated by another Franco–
Algerian, this time equipped with a GoPro camera: Mohamed Merah.

The second phenomenon that facilitated al-Suri's schema was the
occurrence of the Arab "Spring" and then, especially, its chaotic collapse
from 2012–2013 on, particularly in Syria and Libya. These upheavals
created an exceptional site for military training and propaganda only
a few hours' flight from Europe, and at a very low cost. Young Europeans who came from postcolonial immigration backgrounds or who
had recently been converted to radical Islam through social media networks could realize the fantasy of a "total Islam." Slaughtering "infidels" and other "apostates" in the same way that they killed player
avatars on their PlayStations, confounding the virtual world with the
real one in an Ummah without territorial borders, posting images
online in order to terrorize the enemy and galvanize sympathizers, they
connected the terrains of Middle Eastern jihad with the banlieues of
Europe. And some of them returned to the Old Continent to continue
their murderous mission there, thus giving concrete form to the vision
formulated in the *Call* in January 2005.

Al-Suri wrote his text on the basis of lessons drawn from his experience during more than three decades of activism. This red-haired
jihadi, born in 1958 to an old aristocratic family from Aleppo, learned
his trade from the Muslim Brotherhood in his country and during the
Afghan jihad of the 1980s. He knew Europe well, having lived there
for several years; he began by studying to be an engineer in France and
then became a naturalized Spanish citizen through marriage.

During the 1990s, al-Suri found refuge in the Islamist networks of
London (nicknamed "Londonistan"), clustered particularly around the
Finsbury Park mosque. At that time the United Kingdom was gener-
ously granting asylum to jihadis from the Arab world—who after the
establishment of the Taliban regime in 1996 would return to Afghanistan to join forces with Osama bin Laden. Al-Suri won a flattering
reputation by sending, from London, a magazine entitled *Al-Ansar* and
by providing support to the Groupe islamique armé (GIA; known in
English as the Armed Islamic Group) in Algeria. In the years before the
use of e-mail became widespread, this statement was faxed to the main
radical mosques throughout the world in order to spread the cause of
jihad in Algeria and to situate it in tradition of the triumph of jihad in
Afghanistan during the 1980s.

After his return to Kandahar around 1997, al-Suri served as a public relations officer for the head of al-Qaeda, for which he organized
meetings with foreign journalists. Thus he was associated with the

leadership of the second wave of jihadism after having participated in various stages of the first wave, from Afghanistan to Londonistan. He experienced the excitement of the Afghan battle, which forced the Red Army to withdraw from Kabul in February 1989, and saw its victors persuade themselves that they had played a decisive role in the fall of the USSR, of which the destruction of the Berlin Wall a few months later remains the symbol.

In the Islamist worldview, the only history of humanity is that of the Revelation and its accomplishment. If the world is not yet entirely Muslim, that is the fault of tepid believers who turned away from doctrinal rectitude. As the Egyptian Sayyid Qotb (the Islamists' principal mentor, who was hanged by Nasser in 1966) explained, it is up to believers to constitute a "new Quranic generation." After centuries of decadence when Muslims were lukewarm in their political and religious zeal, the new generation must take up the cause where the contemporaries and successors of the Prophet (the *salafs*) left it.

For Bin Laden and his doctrinal brothers, the fall of the USSR was the modern analogue of the collapse of the Sassanid Empire (the last pre-Islamic Persian empire) in the first decades of Islam's existence. That having been accomplished, Bin Laden urged Muslims to destroy the other impious superpower, America, just as they had captured Byzantium by multiplying raids on Constantinople until it was finally seized in 1453. Although it took centuries for the Greek Empire to fall, the apocalyptic acceleration of time, he claimed, would bring about the destruction of its current equivalent much more quickly.

The "twofold blessed raid" of September 11 was situated in a similar cosmology. According to al-Suri and his comrades in combat, the jihadis embodied the "spirit of the time," the Hegelian *Zeitgeist*. They were convinced that their Afghan apotheosis could be easily duplicated on other battlefields: in Egypt, in Algeria, and also in Chechnya, areas from which several hundred members of these international brigades hailed. In Bosnia, they thought they could transform the civil war that followed the collapse of Yugoslavia into a jihad that would allow them to gain a foothold in Europe.

These dreams were not realized. In the euphoria of the victory in Kabul, the jihadis forgot that they owed their military superiority over the Red Army to Stinger surface-to-air missiles provided by the CIA and that the Islamic *casus belli* constituted by the Soviet invasion of Afghanistan was an idea more productive for recruiting militants than for overthrowing governments that had Islamic legitimacy, like those in Egypt and Algeria.

The Dayton Accords of December 1995 marked the end of the war in Bosnia, forcing the jihadis to leave. In autumn 1997, the Egyptian and Algerian jihads, which caused about ten thousand and a hundred thousand deaths, respectively, turned into massacres of civilians. The very populations that militants were trying to mobilize to bring down the "apostate" regimes in Cairo and Algiers turned against them. However, al-Suri initially made himself the publicist par excellence for the GIA, justifying the rectitude of its actions by reference to its goal even as the group's image was being tarnished by suspicions that it had been infiltrated by the Algerian secret services—suspicions that led its members to tear each other to shreds and to massacre civilians. However, al-Suri himself finally became disillusioned with the group and left Londonistan for Kandahar. There, protected by the sympathetic Taliban regime, he worked alongside Osama bin Laden in the elaboration of the doctrine of the second wave, that of al-Qaeda, until he moved beyond it in his own writings of 2005.

JIHAD'S FIRST TERRAINS

During the first phase of jihadism, young Frenchmen had already left for the battlefields; sometimes they had humanitarian intentions, but subsequently they got involved in armed Islamism. In Alsace and the Lyon region, the war in Afghanistan was a catalyst for the Islamization of people who had become disillusioned with the antiracist beur movement of the 1980s. The conflict was also a factor in the conversion of the first young céfrans. When these converts returned to Europe, they became the contingent of radicals within a community of converts that had up to that point been dominated by older Sufi intellectuals. The gang of Islamist hold-up men in Roubaix, whose hideout was stormed by the police on March 28, 1996, was partially composed of jihadis who had fought in Bosnia. The ringleaders, two converts from northern France—one of whom would be killed by the Belgian police—tried in vain to relight the flame of jihad in France itself after returning from Bosnia.

For its part, the jihad in Algeria awakened considerable sympathy among young French people whose families had emigrated from that country. Even before terrorist activity shifted to France proper, there was ample evidence of support for the movement in France. The various bulletins issued by the Fraternité algérienne en France (FAF, or Algerian Brotherhood in France), which were regularly banned by the ministry of the interior; the meetings expressing support for the movement (notably, again, in Roubaix); and the collection of funds all testify to this sympathy. The hijacking of an Airbus plane flying from Paris to Algiers shortly before Christmas 1994, and then the attacks carried out in the following summer and autumn, which killed eight and wounded 175, are attributed by most observers to the GIA, led by Djamel Zitouni, alias Abu Abderahmane Amine. Its main operative on French soil was Khaled Kelkal, from Lyon, who was killed by the police on September 29, 1995.

Contrary to what was to be seen twenty years later, the cycle of violence in which Kelkal was the main figure—along with a small band of petty delinquents from the banlieues housing projects—found only scant support in groups descended from postcolonial Algerian immigration. The generation of the *darons* (fathers) still had a strong grip on the "Algerian colony in France," as it has been called by its great sociologist, Abdelmalek Sayad. These immigrant workers, who labored mightily to build a future for their children, invested in real estate, and endured xenophobia and unemployment, could not accept seeing decades of hard work and saving destroyed by the acts of a few young fanatics.

For their part, the Muslim Brotherhood's *blédards*, who dominated the Islamic institutions created by the state from 1989 on, did not approve of these terrorists, who threatened the Brotherhood's control over these institutions. These terrorists showed that the communal hegemony of which UOIF boasted to successive governments remained deficient. Finally, specialized police forces recruited numerous Arab-speaking officers who had been trained by French universities and who were well acquainted with the Islamist movement's networks, particularly through surveillance of radical preachers.

After the executions of Khaled Kelkal in the Lyon banlieues and, on March 29, 1996, of Christophe Caze from Roubaix, there were no more attacks connected with Islamist terrorism on French soil until those perpetrated by Mohamed Merah in March 2012. This sixteen-year period of domestic peace is rightly attributed to the reorganization of French intelligence services, but it was also the result of the supervision exercised by the generation of the *darons*.

For France, the second wave of the jihadi dialectic, that of al-Qaeda, was thus not directly manifested by violence within it. A few young French citizens of North African heritage were in fact arrested in Afghanistan or Pakistan after the Western offensive against the Taliban and al-Qaeda after September 11, 2001, and incarcerated at Guantanamo, but their influence remained limited, and their cause did not mobilize much support. The attacks carried out in Madrid in 2004 and in London in 2005 had no equivalents in France.

THE PRISON INCUBATOR

Al-Qaeda's only large-scale operation planned to be carried out on French soil in the wake of the second phase of jihadism came to light in 2001. The Franco-Algerian Djamel Beghal was intercepted as he was returning from the organization's Afghan camps to prepare an attack on the U.S. embassy. To realize his goal, he had to rely on a complex network, whose members were subsequently arrested in various European countries. These preventive arrests were made possible by surveillance techniques and by the lessons learned from the battle waged in France in the 1990s against the Algerian GIA, with which Djamel Beghal had been associated.

Djamel Beghal was incarcerated until 2009 and then put under house arrest in the Cantal region of France because he could not be expelled legally to Algeria; he was imprisoned once more in 2010 and remains so. Even though he was put out of circulation, he embodies the transition between the second and third phases of jihadism. A pure product of al-Qaeda—a rare case for a Frenchman—his planned action in Paris was conceived as a continuation of the September 11 attacks. It was in the Fleury-Mérogis prison that he met Chérif Kouachi and Amedy Coulibaly, the future killers in the January 2015 attacks, who were being held there as well.

Chérif Kouachi was part of a network established in Paris's nineteenth arrondissement. Its goal was to send young, radicalized Salafists to the Iraqi branch of al-Qaeda commanded by Abu Musab al-Zarqawi, which was fighting the coalition army led by the United States in Iraq. This network was dismantled by the police in January 2005, the same month that al-Suri's *Call* was posted online. It was nicknamed "the Buttes-Chaumont Islamist network" because apprentice jihadis jogged in the Buttes-Chaumont park in northern Paris to prepare themselves for future combat.

Their mentor, Farid Benyettou, was a Franco-Algerian preacher. Only twenty-four years old in 2005, he had been born in Paris on May 10, 1981, the day a Socialist president was elected. This improbable child of the "Mitterrand generation"[2] was also and especially a

---

[2]The generation that was young during François Mitterrand's presidency (1980–1995).

spiritual son of the Algerian jihad. After losing his father at age sixteen, he was educated in this form of Islamism by his brother-in-law Youssef Zemmouri, a former activist in the Groupe salafiste pour la prédication et le combat (GSPC; Salafist Group for Preaching and Combat) who had taken refuge in France in 1997 after the Islamist massacres in Algeria that hastened its defeat.

Arrested and imprisoned in France for having fomented an attack during the World Cup soccer competition in 1998 (which was won by the French team led by Zinédine Zidane, who is also of Algerian descent), Zemmouri was expelled from the country in 2004 after he was released from prison. The GSPC, one of the products of the disintegration of Algerian jihad, was to give birth in 2007 to al-Qaida au Maghreb Islamique (Aqmi, or al-Qaeda in Islamic North Africa), the North African and Sahelian franchise of Bin Laden's organization, some of whose members later pledged allegiance to ISIS.

Farid Benyettou recruited his followers by means of Salafist teachings he communicated to certain worshipers at the Adda'wa mosque in Paris, the best-attended in Europe at that time. Known as the "Stalingrad mosque," it was situated in a former textile depot near the Stalingrad metro station, but it was closed for renovation in 2006. Benyettou, who had a vast knowledge of Arab-Islamic culture, had great influence on young people who had only an elementary education. Making headlines, he led the street prayers that accompanied the demonstration of January 17, 2004, protesting the Stasi Commission's proposal to forbid the wearing of ostentatious religious symbols in public schools and in private schools under contract with the ministry of education. Organized by a nebulous "Muslim Party of France," the demonstration sought to radicalize the opposition to the "veil law" by going the UOIF one better.

The Buttes-Chaumont network was prosecuted in 2008 on the charge of being an "association of criminals associated with a terrorist undertaking." Benyettou was accused of having played a decisive role in the departure for Iraq of about a dozen young people, three of whom died there. The other important member of the network was Boubaker al-Hakim, alias Abu Mouqatel, who was in Iraq as early as 2003. From Damascus, where he was receiving Islamic training, he arranged for the entry of combatants into Iraq. Among them was his younger brother Redouane, alias Abu Abdallah, who died "as a martyr" in Fallujah during a suicide attack on the American army. Shortly before his death, Redouane made the following statement, dated March 18, 2003, to a French journalist he had met in Iraq:

I'm from the nineteenth arrondissement in Paris! We're going to kill everyone who wants to kill Islam! I tell all my friends from the nineteenth: come join the jihad, I'm here, it's me, Abu Abdallah, all my friends who are over there, come defend Islam! The Americans are all faggots and clowns, nothing at all. We know they're scared. They fight with their planes. They have to be told! Let them come at us on the ground, let them fight us, with guns. . . . If they come like that, in two hours we'll have destroyed them, all the Americans. I'm ready to fight in the front line, I'm even ready to blow myself up, strap on sticks of dynamite, and then [shouting] Boom! Boom! We'll kill all the Americans. [Chanting in a North African rhythm] We're the Mujahedeen! We want to die! We want to go to Paradise!

After being imprisoned in France from 2005 to 2011, Boubaker al-Hakim returned to Tunisia and then joined the international jihad, playing leading roles on both stages. In a video posted in December 2014, he took responsibility for the July 2013 assassination of Mohamed Brahmi, the secular Tunisian Member of Parliament from Sidi Bouzid, the cradle of Arab revolutions. In March 2015, in the eighth issue of ISIS's Anglophone online magazine *Dabiq*, he boasted that he had riddled Brahmi with bullets. He went on to outline his whole career, from his enrollment in the precursor of ISIS in Iraq, Abu Musab al-Zarqawi's movement, up to his imprisonment in France, and he gave his opinion about the present outlook for jihad in France.

In this article, one of the movement's most important activists explains with great clarity his journey, between 2005 and 2015, from Buttes-Chaumont to Iraq and Syria by way of Tunisia:

Prison was hard. We were humiliated by those infidels [*kuffar*], but at the same time it was a marvelous gateway for calling people to Allah and explaining His path to the young prisoners. Glory be to Allah! Today, I say to my Brothers in France: don't look for specific targets, kill anyone at all! All the infidels back there are targets. And I tell the *kuffar*, soon, Allah willing, you will see the flag of *La ilah illa Allah* ["There is no God but Allah," ISIS's banner] flying over the Élysée Palace. The Islamic State is now very close. Between us and you there's only the sea. And Allah willing, we will sell your women and your children in the markets of the Islamic State![3]

---

[3] Boubaker al-Hakim was killed by an American drone on Islamic State territory in November 2016.

Chérif Kouachi, the future killer at the offices of *Charlie Hebdo*, was arrested by the French police in January 2005, as he was about to board a plane for Damascus with the intention of going to Iraq. At that point he was simply a potential soldier for this jihad. Farid Benyettou, in the numerous statements he made to the press in early 2015 to testify to his own repentance, did not conceal Chérif Kouachi's low intellectual level and his simplistic violence. During Kouachi's incarceration in Fleury-Mérogis, he met Djamel Beghal, who enjoyed the prestige of having passed through the camps in Afghanistan. It was this meeting that was to transform an apprentice jihadi seeking martyrdom in Iraq into the perpetrator of attacks in Paris ten years later, on January 7, 2015.

In addition, Amedy Coulibaly, who in 2005 was also imprisoned in Fleury-Mérogis for robberies in the southern banlieues of Paris, was also in contact with Djamel Beghal.

Although between 1996 and 2012 France enjoyed genuine security, from 2005 on, the Fleury-Mérogis detention center served as an incubator for a new kind of attack that was implemented starting in 2012. The prison put in contact individuals from different backgrounds, such as Djamel Beghal, with his aura of an international jihadi and his knowledge of al-Qaeda; Chérif Kouachi, an apprentice jihadi whose tendencies were strengthened by Beghal's example; and Amedy Coulibaly, a petty criminal who, like many others, discovered in prison a redemptive radical Islamism into which he threw himself headlong.

The ground was being prepared for the sowing of the ideas of Abu Musab al-Suri, which targeted vulnerable young European Muslims like Kouachi and Coulibaly. Benyettou, arrested in January 2005, at the same time that al-Suri posted his *Call* on the Internet, was the last of the flesh-and-blood preachers whom traditional surveillance by the secret services was capable of detecting. The following years were to be those of the cyber-jihad that took form on YouTube, Facebook, and Twitter.

Just as the intelligence community missed the transformation of jihadism into its third generation after 2005, the French authorities failed to see what was going on behind bars—where the drifting away of the impoverished housing projects of the banlieues was being exacerbated and crystallized. In his *Islam in Prison*, published in 2015 after the Paris attacks, Mohamed Oueslati, a jurist and Muslim chaplain since 2001, notes that in French jails, "Islam has become the primary religion." He estimates that Muslims constitute between half and two-thirds of the inmates, depending on the prison. According to him, they have "the same characteristics as other prisoners: rather young, little educated, from poor, broken families."

Oueslati rapidly identified the causes of religious radicalization in prisons, which is facilitated by lack of privacy and the prisoners' psychological vulnerability. They often fall under the influence of "self-proclaimed imams" who preach "war and violence." In addition, there is the reinterpretation of television news through the prism of their situation: "The West mistreats Muslim countries, seeks to annihilate them. Then they [the prisoners] perceive an echo of what they have experienced [. . . and] say to themselves that others are experiencing it in a certain way [. . .]. They imagine that their religion is a battle, a war to be waged to defend its principles and establish it. That is how, for someone who wants to be a good Muslim, violence becomes the royal road."

Although the phenomenon was pointed out over a decade ago in pioneering works such as those of the sociologist Farhad Khosrokhavar, *L'Islam dans les prisons* (*Islam in Jails*) and *Quand al-Qaida parle: témoignages derrière les barreaux* (*When al-Qaeda Speaks: Testimonies behind Bars*), the state proved incapable of gauging its importance. Over the following years, a high price was to be paid for this blindness.

2

FROM MUSLIMS VOTING TO THE MUSLIM VOTE

We have seen that the suddenness, intensity, spatial dispersion, and temporal extent of the riots in autumn 2005 marked a turning point. At the same time, no party or organization succeeded in transforming the anger of the young people who took part in the confrontations with the police into a common cause or a concrete demand. The riots gave way to a silence that could be interpreted in many ways, and politicians tried to benefit from this silence by producing an intelligible interpretation of it.

More than twenty years after the March of the Beurs in 1983, the festering problem of the banlieues led to an unprecedented political crisis. Although the riots shocked French society into questioning itself, France failed to learn from them and to orient its politics accordingly. The left, which was then focused on the Socialist Party congress held in the Loire region of northern France from November 18 to November 20, 2005, right after the riots, gave the situation in the banlieues only minimal attention. Those attending the congress were preoccupied with the party primaries and with strategic positioning in the run-up to the 2007 presidential election. François Hollande, the compromise candidate, was re-elected party leader purely on the basis of internal party politics.

By contrast, the right was marked by the latent confrontation between Prime Minister Dominique de Villepin and Minister of the Interior Nicolas Sarkozy. Faced with the riots, it was unable to respond with a single voice. That did not prevent the latter from taking full advantage of the hard-nosed approach that he would make the springboard for his election as president of the Republic in 2007.

During the preceding years, the marginalized neighborhoods of the large French cities all underwent profound political changes. No matter how surprising they may seem, the events of 2005 were certainly not a bolt from the blue. Over time, the old alliances between migrants from countries that had been French colonies and organizations in the world of labor eroded—slowly but deeply. The ability of the labor unions and the Communist Party to subordinate differences in origin and religion to a feeling of class solidarity declined as the Communist Party adopted, under the impact of its electoral competition with the Socialist Party, a more nationalistic pose.

In the eastern Parisian banlieue Clichy-sous-Bois, the Communist mayor André Deschamps, denounced by his party for having made racist remarks during an electoral campaign, moved toward the National Front. (As early as 1983 in another former Communist bastion in Paris's eastern banlieues, Montfermeil, the far-rightist Pierre Bernard took advantage of the weak Socialist Party presence to put down political roots.) The descendants of migrants, who were excluded from stable employment and employees' collectives but who continued to adhere to the old logic of fraternity, no longer had the resources and connections to formulate and put forward common political demands. Moreover, the development of xenophobic discourses, marked by the electoral breakthrough of the National Front in 1984, shattered the solidarities that had emerged from the world of unionized workers, thus accelerating the ethnicization of the social fabric.

The topic of immigration, which had until then played a minor role in political debate, became a bone of contention. The failure of the left to grasp the pressing problem of the banlieues before the riots of 2005—the "*rendez-vous manqué*" (missed opportunity), as sociologist Olivier Masclet described it—became evident in the rioters' lack of leftist sloganeering. Powered by a shared indignation at the death of two adolescents hiding from police in a power station and the explosion of a tear gas grenade on the threshold of a mosque in Clichy-sous-Bois, the protesting public showed little awareness of any of the prior, deeper causes of the riots.

A community organization in Clichy, the Association collectif liberté égalité fraternité ensemble unis (ACLEFEU[1]), was formed to provide a

---

[1] Association and Collective for Liberty, Equality and Fraternity, Together United. When spoken, the group's acronym evokes a call to nonviolence, sounding like the French phrase "*Assez le feu!*" ("Enough fire!").

political response to the "social revolts" of autumn 2005. The group's very name was part of its attempt to draw attention away from the violent nature of the riots and toward the economic causes and the conditions of everyday life that led to them. In the immediate wake of the disturbances, group leaders maintained a presence every evening in the neighborhoods in hopes of maintaining a relative calm while at the same time negotiating with public authorities new measures to help these marginalized areas.

The list of grievances[2] compiled by ACLEFEU during a tour through France's "sensitive" housing projects and written up just after the riots concludes with the following words:

> This collection of testimonies reveals an accumulation of instances of neglect. Nonetheless, those with grievances [les "doléants"] still want to believe in the Republic and its values. The French support one another and want to participate "together and united" in a positive transformation of society.

ACLEFEU sought to reinforce a feeling of belonging-as-citizens by leading the rioters to abandon demonstrations of strength in favor of becoming politically engaged as a pressure group using the model of American "community organizing." The cahiers text goes on to emphasize the organization's objective of converting violent protest into political mobilization and, ultimately, voting. The appeal then addresses the political class:

> [French citizens] now intend to use their right to vote, to examine how your programs address their expectations, and to assess the effectiveness of your action. Determined to become actors in this change, they expect that you will take the necessary actions to improve their everyday lives, that you will listen to them, that you will involve them.

For ACLEFEU, the low level of voter turnout and the rise of social tensions were the consequence of the lack of interest and effectiveness on the part of politicians incapable of responding to the demands of residents of the banlieues. The association's activists themselves could not fall back on the support of a social consensus in France as a whole.

---

[2] "List of grievances," an expression borrowed from the period of the French Revolution.

Their demands, associated with a left-wing tradition long established in the marginalized neighborhoods of large cities, were now out of step with the attitudes of the majority of the population. The violence and destruction of property that took place during the riots alienated the country from the young people of the banlieues, preventing the growth of shared solidarity and sapping any political will to take action to help them.

The "toleration index," published each year by the National Commission on Human Rights to measure the extent of the French public's attitudes toward minority groups, fell abruptly in 2005 under the combined impact of the fear of the "Polish plumber"—cheap labor coming from new Eastern European EU member states threatening French jobs—and the crisis in the banlieues. At the same time, the riots marked the return of state activism in urban areas through an ambitious "Program of Urban Redevelopment" (PRU), which continued the plan adopted two years earlier under the auspices of the charismatic Minister for Urban Affairs Jean-Louis Borloo. Immediately afterward, the Agence nationale pour la rénovation urbaine (ANRU, or National Agency for Urban Renewal) was established, with the mission of demolishing more than two hundred thousand housing units and constructing the same number of new units, as well as remodeling an equivalent additional number. These political measures were limited to improving the conditions of housing and the organization of local life. They did not include provisions for expanding urban transportation or for improving access to employment.

Numerous elected officials applauded the PRU, which was accompanied by a temporary increase in economic activity and which provided new resources for the municipalities concerned. Others condemned the lack of democracy in the planning and implementation of this program.

Although the mechanisms for consulting the affected residents put in place and widely promoted by state officials could have served as a complement to political participation, they could not make up for the lack of political representation. In short, even before the world economic crisis of 2008, public policies deployed in the French banlieues neglected the economic issues that caused marginalization and that reinforced social and ethnoracial segregation. The measures put in place in urban areas proved insufficient and could not prevent an increase in unemployment and economic insecurity. Moreover, the demands for political participation were given little attention, thus undermining the legitimacy of urban activists and reformers.

In this context, the process launched by ACLEFEU, later complemented by other (sometimes rival) associations such as Au-delà des mots (ADM, or Beyond Words) and Mouvement de l'immigration et des banlieues (MIB, or Movement of Immigrants and Banlieues), adopted the twofold objective of channeling violent protest toward institutional participation and opening up political avenues for young people from immigrant families. These demands for equality were situated in the tradition of French immigrant movements and revolutionary history through the references to the aforementioned *cahiers de doléance*. (These grievances, submitted to the National Assembly at the end of a march on November 25, 2006, one year after the riots, assembled more than twenty thousand contributions from a hundred cities.)

At that time, the national mood was still shaped by the events of the 2002 French presidential elections four years earlier. These elections were marked by the elimination of former Socialist prime minister Lionel Jospin in the first-round voting, while the second round featured a contest between right-wing incumbent president Jacques Chirac and the far-right Front National leader Jean-Marie Le Pen. The 2002 campaign had focused on the lack of security in the impoverished banlieues, and the community organizations working in these areas, including ACLEFEU, were led by people attempting to lead the participants in the riots away from violence and into a new form of partnership with the left.

These attempts failed—at least in part. Voter registration of banlieue residents increased, but the incentives offered as a way of turning the protests expressed during the riots into a political force failed to yield a workable and effective electoral option. Neither was public policy changed. In light of these failures, the politics of compromise that was being sold to the young people in the projects came with a significant social and symbolic cost. Disappointed, they turned away from the compromise inherent in electoral politics and took a different path—that of confrontation without a clear political agenda. Later on, this focus on confrontation was to be co-opted and instrumentalized by certain groups, first and foremost Islamist movements, whose discourse already advocated a break with French society. Thus did the processes of religious radicalization in the decade between 2005 and 2015 take root on ground made fertile by the failure of the efforts at political reform.

In the wake of the riots, an ideological change took place within the electoral base of the right wing in the National Assembly. Nicolas Sarkozy, who was then minister of the interior, opted for a divisive strategy after having tried to make an alliance with Muslim organizations such as the Union des organisations islamiques de France (UOIF), which had a conservative agenda on issues concerning morals and ethics. He had attended the UOIF congress with some fanfare in April 2003, but during the 2005 riots, the organization failed to exercise the social control it claimed to have over the residents of the projects. The UOIF's demonstrated ineffectiveness would pave the way for a new generation of Islamist leaders with a far more radical social agenda.

At the same time, public opinion was clearly becoming more hostile to immigration. Polls in late 2006 showed that almost 45 percent of the French blamed the riots on the failures of the young rioters' parents, and 25 percent blamed immigration in general. This provided the minister of the interior, eying the upcoming presidential election in 2007, with the incentive to pivot toward an unparalleled tough political message. This step of Sarkozy's put distance between him and the legacy of outgoing president Jacques Chirac. In Sarkozy's eyes, Chirac had become too soft from June 1997 onward due to his "cohabitation" with Lionel Jospin's government after the latter's Socialist Party won the parliamentary elections and remained in power for a five-year tenure until May 2002, when Chirac was re-elected president after an electoral battle with Jean-Marie le Pen.

By contrast, Ségolène Royal, the new Socialist candidate for president chosen to face Sarkozy in 2007, opted to develop ties with the banlieues. On February 27, 2007, and with great fanfare, she made a public appearance in Clichy-sous-Bois to sign ACLEFEU's manifesto. Adopting an opposing stance to her competitor, she stated: "The disenfranchised neighborhoods are not a problem, they are part of the solution to France's problems." The mobilizing effect was to prove real in the banlieues, but it was not enough to change the outcome of the election on the national level. Her position also served to alienate Royal from that part of the left's middle-class base that was attracted to the law-and-order discourse of the right in response to the riots. Sarkozy's victory in 2007 owed a great deal to the consolidation of a wide-ranging socially conservative electorate from the center-left to the extreme right.

On the left, five years after the trauma of Lionel Jospin's elimination from the contest for the presidency after the first round of voting in April 2002, Ségolène Royal became the Socialist Party's presidential candidate by winning the party's internal primary against the wishes of the party's top officials. Throughout her campaign, she chose to oppose Sarkozy at every turn so as to minimize dissent in Socialist ranks, and she used strong leftist language to that end. While on the campaign trail, for example, she went to the island of Martinique in the French Caribbean in January 2007 and met Aimé Césaire, the famed poet of negritude and a former Member of the National Assembly who had long fought for the recognition of slavery as a crime against humanity. During this public meeting, Royal criticized a law passed by the right-wing French Parliament in February 2005 that introduced into school curricula a statement about "the positive role of the French presence abroad, notably in North Africa." According to Royal, "[t]his revisionist interpretation of history is unacceptable. Colonialism is a system of domination, spoliation, and humiliation." Césaire gave her his support. She then promoted the notion of a "racially mixed France" (*France métissée*), a slogan that elicited a chauvinist reaction and ultimately favored her right-wing opponent. Moreover, the universalist conception of humanity that she repeatedly evoked sidestepped the contentious issue of the relation between Islam and secularism, a notoriously difficult issue for the French left and about which the left's different traditions have yet to come to a consensus.

In the wake of the riots of autumn 2005, France's very self-image was destabilized. Sarkozy was able to take advantage of this crisis by positioning himself as a stabilizing force on the right. He succeeded both in siphoning votes from Jean-Marie Le Pen's National Front and in undercutting the left. The ebbing of the far right plunged the National Front into political and financial difficulties from which it would emerge only after several years of disorganization and ideological retooling that included Marine Le Pen's ascendancy to the party leadership.

Serge Laroze, a National Front politician who in 2012 would become a party candidate in the legislative elections of that year in a district near Toulouse in southwest France, recalls this difficult patch for the far right in an interview with the authors:

> In 2007, Nicolas Sarkozy siphoned off the National Front's votes, taking over our themes, and to some extent our solutions. But he didn't go that far: he created a sort of "soft" version of the National Front. Many Front supporters said to themselves: "He's like Jean-Marie Le Pen, but more credible!" We lost a lot of votes, and we found ourselves in financial difficulty: our subsidy collapsed, and wherever we didn't reach 5 percent of the popular vote,[3] we had to pay back the campaign costs.

---

[3] Campaign costs are reimbursed only to candidates of slates that received at least 5 percent of the votes.

THE "MUSLIM VOTE"

In the banlieues, 2006 and 2007 were marked by a significant rise in registered voters—from 637,000 to 708,000 in the northeastern Parisian *département* of Seine-Saint-Denis, an increase of 11 percent. This surge was twice the national average, which was estimated at 6 percent. In some communes with large disenfranchised neighborhoods, it was even greater: 29 percent in Clichy-sous-Bois, representing 1,500 additional voters; more than 14 percent in the north-central division of La Courneuve; more than 12 percent in Vaulx-en-Velin, a large outlying district of Lyon; and 11.5 percent in Argenteuil in northwestern Paris.

These local dynamics did not concern all the areas where riots occurred in 2005. But the increase in these areas was greater than in the rest of the country, with spikes in the especially sensitive zones that had been a locus of confrontation with Sarkozy a few months before the riots. As minister of the interior, Sarkozy visited the *Quatre-vingt treize* city of La Courneuve in June 2005 shortly after a child, Sid-Ahmed Hammache, had been shot dead by a stray bullet during a conflict between two rival gangs. In front of the television cameras, Sarkozy made his difference with Jacques Chirac clear: "Starting tomorrow, we're going to clean out this place with a Kärcher.[4] We'll bring in the necessary personnel and stay as long as it takes, but it will be cleaned up." Such parlance made a stir even with some of his colleagues in Prime Minister Dominique de Villepin's government.

On October 26, 2005, Sarkozy visited police headquarters in Argenteuil, in Val-d'Oise. His motorcade was booed by a large group of young people. Sarkozy addressed residents observing the situation from their balconies: "Have you had enough of this? Have you had enough of this bunch of riffraff? Well, we're going to get rid of them for you." Thus did Sarkozy use the fresh collective memory of the riots to reinforce an existing polarization rather than producing a new one. Such gestures succeeded in tilting the French right-wing vote away from Chirac and Villepin's moderation and toward a tougher stance on security matters linked to banlieues' unrest.

Among the inhabitants of the marginalized neighborhoods, people from immigrant families were overrepresented among the new voters of 2007, and they voted mainly for the left. Thus Nicolas Sarkozy's victory and the right's tougher language coincided with the entry into politics of these second-generation immigrants who had been marked

---

[4] A Kärcher is a German-made high-pressure washer widely known in France.

by the riots. The electoral triumph of their nemesis, Sarkozy, despite their unprecedented level of political mobilization left a bitter taste in the mouths of these new voters and had long-lasting effects.

Henceforth the "postcolonial" immigrant vote would play a significant role in French electoral politics. Second-generation immigrants have registered to vote in increasing numbers since 2007. Because of their French nationality, they enjoy voting rights that their foreign-born elders do not share.[5] And as a consequence of the spread of mixed marriages, other forms of naturalization, and changes in the structure of immigrant families, it has become exceedingly difficult to speak of a clear-cut divide between scions of immigrants and the "majority" population. Social mixture has become a fact of French life that is not readily acknowledged in popular depictions of French society. Many French citizens have at least one person in their family of postcolonial immigration origin. Data provided by the Institut national de la statistique et des études économiques (INSEE, or National Institute for Statistics and Economic Studies) in 2008 show that the French population included 3.2 million immigrants from Africa and Asia as well as 1.4 million of their direct descendants. France has entered what populations studies scholar François Héran has called *Le Temps des immigrés*—"The Time of Immigrants."[6]

Theoretically, the increasing proportion of second-generation immigrants in the population should translate into greater political power for this community. However, their political clout remains undersized relative to their increasing demographic weight. Banlieue youths did not begin registering to vote in significant numbers until 2006—even though voter registration had been made easier under the Jospin Socialist government in 1997. Moreover, their increased but uneven political mobilization was counterbalanced by an increase in the right-wing vote made possible by the aftershocks of the 2005 riots and the incendiary, polarizing language of candidate Sarkozy.

By the time of the 2012 presidential election, the political conditions were quite different. The young people from the banlieues who hadn't bothered to vote the first time Nicolas Sarkozy ran for office regretted their inaction and were eager to see him defeated in 2012.

---

[5] Foreign-born legal residents in France are not allowed to vote in local elections in France—unless they are citizens of an EU member state.

[6] *Le temps des Immigrés: Essai sur le destin de la population française* (*The Time of Immigrants: An Essay on the Fate of the French Population*), Editions du Seuil, Paris, 2007.

Their views were shaped not only by the situation in France but also by international events—particularly the turmoil in the Middle East. The war in Iraq, like the conflict between Israel and Palestine, served to mobilize them and reinforced their mistrust of Sarkozy. This is one reason why the 2012 Socialist Party presidential candidate François Hollande succeeded where Ségolène Royal had failed five years earlier.

ECONOMIC CRASH AND IDENTITARIAN REACTIONS

In its intensity, the economic crash that exploded during the summer of 2008 echoed the Great Depression of 1929. The resulting loss of jobs hit the banlieues hard as unemployment increased rapidly and enormously. People holding informal jobs, whether temporary or "under the table," were hard hit by the general deterioration of economic activity. Between 2008 and 2012, unemployment rates for men rose by 49 percent and those for women by 55 percent. The gaps between "sensitive urban zones" and the rest of society grew larger.

This crisis also damaged the quality of the positions held by people whose financial situation and social status had up to that point been relatively stable. Young college graduates found it harder to secure an internship or find a first job, and in most cases, new hires were offered limited-term contracts, thus decreasing job security. These cumulative effects spread in already segregated areas where lack of public transportation made the difficulty of finding work insurmountable.

In addition to these structural developments, the growing scarcity of jobs intensified discrimination in employment and housing. The manufacturing sector, which is essential to the general economic activity of sensitive industrial zones, was seriously impaired. The planned closure of the Peugeot-Citroën car factory in the northeastern Paris district of Aulnay-sous-Bois threatened almost a hundred thousand people in Seine-Saint-Denis, which has a million and a half residents.

With the economic crisis of 2008, questions of unemployment and social security became of great concern, particularly among second-generation immigrants because of their vulnerable position in the labor market. This was how Farouk Khanfar put it one year after he ran as an independent candidate in the 2012 legislative elections in the Lille banlieues of northern France:

> It's the politicians who are creating the crisis! And then they talk about unemployment, about reducing family allowances, taxing them, reducing unemployment benefits. . . . That amounts to taking

food out of people's mouths! They say: "It's your fault, you don't want to work!" But in reality, there isn't any work!

Starting in the autumn of 2008, France was shaken by a process of political polarization based on heightened opposition and conflict. This process mostly went unnoticed, because it was not channeled by social movements or other institutions. Even before the global financial crash of September 2008, however, Sarkozy gave people a language with which to express their anger when he placed the subject of French identity on the national agenda.

Sarkozy's presidential term was characterized by a paradox: the economic question, although it obsessed everyone in the wake of the 2008 crash, was rapidly relegated to the background. Instead, a set of disparate issues relating to identity and involving immigration, French history, secularism, and Islam was substituted for it, while the problem of social and economic discrimination was not directly addressed.

In the absence of a clear strategy for responding to the economic crisis, the quest for an essence of French national identity reopened wounds caused by the crisis in the banlieues. It became the crucible for a confrontation between "us" and "them" and legitimized the propagation of particularist identities.

Criticized for having played the identity card, Nicolas Sarkozy defended himself by quoting Claude Lévi-Strauss: "Identity is not a pathology." During a November 2009 speech in La Chapelle-en-Vercors, a site associated in the collective memory with the French resistance against the Nazis, the president observed that

> we may be living through one of those times when landmarks fade away, when identity becomes unclear, when we begin to feel that something that is essential for us to live is being lost. [. . .] I want to say this because I think it so: by trying to do away with nations out of fear of nationalism we have revived identitarian tensions. It is in the crisis of national identity that a narrow nationalism is reborn, replacing love of country with hatred of others.

In this period, the decline of the National Front seemed irremediable, and no pundit foresaw that in the forthcoming years, the extreme right would be reborn as a dominant political force. Sarkozy, convinced he had dealt a lethal blow to the National Front in 2007 when he siphoned away so much of its constituency, gave himself license to play the identity card for all it was worth—hence, in his 2009 Vercors speech,[7] his decision to place the Republic in the long tradition of the French monarchs:

> Let us examine how the Republic realized the old Capetian dream of a France one and indivisible, as a state that did away with feudalism. The kings dreamed, the Republic realized. [. . .] Over the centuries, France has never ceased to mix, to interbreed—I'm not afraid to use that expression—and, through this mixture, through this interbreeding, through this assimilation, to transform and enrich itself.

Answering Ségolène Royal and the left more generally, which vaunted the benefits of social and racial mixing (*métissage*) while disparaging assimilation (associating it with restrictive standardization and oppression), Sarkozy attempted a synthesis, praising both. The rest of the speech seemed to prefigure the 2010 law forbidding the wearing of any veil that covers the face in the public sphere: "France is a country where there is no place for the burqa, where there is no place for the enslavement of women, on any pretext, under any condition or in any circumstance." He concluded by contrasting "those who know France's national identity" with those who do not: "Some do not want to engage in this debate because they are afraid of it. If they are afraid of the French national identity, that is because they do not know it. That is an additional reason for opening a debate that will basically teach them what the French national identity is."

This question thenceforth became a major subject in quarrels among media personalities, politicians, and public intellectuals. A few days after this speech, riots broke out in Marseille (a city with a large population of Algerian descent) after a qualifying soccer match for the World Cup between Algeria and Egypt. Maurad Goual, who stood as an independent right-wing candidate from Marseille in a later round of parliamentary elections, testifies to these events:

> It's true that every match played against teams from Algeria, Morocco, or Tunisia leads to havoc in Marseille. But that was a scandal, it was shameful!

---

[7] It was written by his advisor Henri Guaino, who also wrote the speech Sarkozy gave in Dakar addressing the youth of Africa on July 26, 2007.

On January 16, 2010, Jean-Claude Gaudin, the mayor of Marseille—and a member of Sarkozy's right-wing party[8]—declared during a meeting organized by the Minister for Immigration, Integration, and National Identity, Éric Besson, that

> we're glad that Muslims are happy about the match, except that afterward, when fifteen to twenty thousand of them surged down La Canebière [the main avenue in Marseille], there was only the Algerian flag, not the French flag. That does not please us.

These remarks triggered a national controversy and led to a schism between second-generation immigrants and Sarkozy's right-wing party.

Meanwhile, a parliamentary commission on the aforementioned proposed legislation restricting the public wearing of veils that cover the face (targeting the niqab as well as the burqa)[9] submitted its report in early January 2010. The proposed law was based on an older initiative of the Communist Member of Parliament André Gérin, the president since June 23, 2009, of an investigative committee on the public wearing of veils that obscure the face. The 2010 parliamentary commission's report, recommending a ban on the niqab and the burqa in public spaces, was submitted to Minister of Justice Michèle Alliot-Marie and became law on September 14, 2010. The majority of the legislators in both the National Assembly and the Senate voted in favor of the law, although most legislators representing the parties of the left abstained.

The National Front managed an unforeseen return to the center of the political stage in the run-up to the 2012 presidential election when it reaped the benefits of the identitarian fire imprudently lit by Sarkozy. Although its new leader, Marine Le Pen, the daughter of the party's founder, subtly muted the party's older racially based nationalist rhetoric on immigration, she ensured that Islam and Muslims would become one of her party's targets. Her strategy was to beat Sarkozy on his own ground and win back the voters lost in the 2007 contest.

Serge Laroze, the National Front politician of Haute-Garonne we already mentioned, illustrated this rhetorical change:

---

[8] The Union pour un mouvement populaire (UMP). Created in 2002, this party changed its name to Les Républicains in 2015.

[9] The niqab is a garment that covers a woman's upper body and face, except for her eyes, whereas the burqa covers the entire body, including the face, and features a piece of netting that obscures the eyes but allows the wearer to see out.

There are twenty million [*sic*] people of Muslim immigrant extraction [. . .]. I'm not talking about politics, but about arithmetic! [. . .] France has always been a country of immigrants, that's clear.

But he added:

The problem with Islam is that it isn't just a religion, but a civil code, a political constitution, a moral law. [. . .] It's not up to us to adapt to Islam, we have our laws, our Constitution, our temperament, our way of eating and slaughtering animals, etc. We're not going to eat halal meat, we're not going to prepare special meals, establish special hours in swimming pools.

He concluded by evoking the prospect of a confrontation:

I think the major problem of France and Europe, and here I'm sure I'm not wrong, is the collision course with Islam.

Stéphane Ravier, a National Front candidate in Marseille's northern neighborhoods and, since 2014, mayor of that city's thirteenth and fourteenth arrondissements, developed the same theme using a culinary analogy:

The problem is diversity. By being diverse, a large part of the population no longer knows who it really is: "Am I French? Am I Algerian? Am I Moroccan? Am I secular? Am I a Muslim, since I live in a country that is traditionally Catholic?" All this mixing produces something indigestible. We're trying to combine couscous with sauerkraut and *daube à la provençale*. It's inedible.

Behind the rejection of cultural mixing, symbolized by an inedible dish, he is at pains to praise each gastronomic tradition separately:

If you take each of the dishes, they're all excellent! I love couscous, on the condition that it's made like couscous. The mixture of kinds is a collective suicide. And that's what we're preparing for ourselves.

This argument makes it possible to reject Muslims not as such but rather as a group that French society cannot assimilate ("digest") and whose own essence must be preserved. The principle of purity no longer follows the path of race but that of culture.

The National Front's turn toward culture was also adopted by other elements of the French far right. In late December 2010, the Riposte laïque movement, led by former Trotskyite and Union activist Pierre Cassen, joined forces with the Bloc identitaire and other like-minded European groups of the far right to conduct what they called an Assises de l'islamisation (Symposium on Islamization).

The new anti-Islam discourse denies that it is racist. Anti-Semitism, which played a pivotal role in the history of the traditional far right for decades, has been set aside and replaced by denunciations of the "Islamic threat." The battle against the "Islamization of France" had already begun in 2002 with the program of National Front dissident Bruno Mégret's Mouvement National Républicain (MNR—National Republican Movement). Marine Le Pen and her team reformulated the concept and combined it with a selective understanding of French secularism (*la laïcité*) to justify the rejection of Islam and to denounce the ritual practices of many Muslims.

During this phase of her rise to national prominence, Marine Le Pen took issue with the fast-food chain Quick, which had opened exclusively halal restaurants in certain banlieues. According to her, the government had the right to intervene because it was one of the chain's investors via the state-run *Caisse des dépôts et consignations*:[10]

> It is the state that is breaking with the principle of secularism (laïcité) and is imposing not multiculturalism but "monoculturalism," since in this case what is offered is not multiple but single. It will be halal and nothing else. This is a genuine scandal that breaks with one of the values of our French Republic, which is laïcité. [. . .] I'm sorry, but if I have to be the last hold-out, the last person who refuses to allow the law of the market to take precedence over our traditions, our ways of life, and our values, well then, I'll be that person.

In early summer 2010, riots broke out in the Villeneuve housing project neighborhood in Grenoble following the death of a hold-up man of Algerian origin who had been shot dead by the police. On July 17 and 18 of that year, the confrontations turned into a riot in which firearms were used, something that had been extremely rare in the riots of 2005. After these events, Nicolas Sarkozy gave what came to be known as "the Grenoble speech," in which he laid out a new doctrine:

---

[10] "Deposits and Consignments Fund," a public investment arm of the French state.

What has happened isn't a social problem, it's a problem of criminals, it's values that are disappearing [. . .]. We must have the right to strip French nationality from any person of foreign origin who has voluntarily endangered the life of a police officer, a gendarme, or any other person who holds a public office. French nationality is something you earn, you have to show that you're worthy of it. When you shoot at an officer assigned to maintain order, you're no longer worthy of being French. I also believe that a juvenile delinquent should no longer be able to obtain French nationality automatically as soon as he reaches the age of majority.

The events in Grenoble in 2010 marked an intensification of the violence in a context of increased social tension. The National Front's return to center stage put strong pressure on the executive branch, and Marine Le Pen's party used the Grenoble riots to portray the office of the president as weak. Le Pen bolstered her public image and name recognition by ramping up her attack on Islam. In a speech in Lyon in December 2010, she drew a parallel between the Muslim presence in France and the Nazi occupation. According to her, the public prayer performed every Friday in the street on the rue Myrha in the traditionally Algerian neighborhood of Barbès in Paris was a form of occupation:

Now, there are ten or fifteen places where, in a regular way, a certain number of people are coming to seize territory. It's an occupation of bits of territory, of neighborhoods in which religious law is applied: it's an occupation. It's true that there are no tanks, no soldiers, but it's an occupation all the same.

The sheikh of the mosque on the rue Myrha, in reply, pointed out that the neighborhood had a shortage of mosques: "We were running out of space. We're using the street, we're not occupying it."

SORAL AND ISLAM AGAINST "AMERICAN-ZIONISM"

It was in this context that far-right journalist, essayist, and activist Alain Soral spoke out on behalf of his movement *Égalité et réconciliation* (Equality and Reconciliation). The trajectory of this complex and controversial public figure has been erratic and unpredictable. Although he presents himself as a former Communist activist, the French Communist Party denies any connection with him. Nonetheless, he worked for a while for the periodical *L'Idiot international*, founded by writer and activist Jean-Edern Hallier, in which capacity he met Jean-Paul Cruze, the author of a pamphlet entitled "Vers un Front National" ("Toward a National Front") that made the case for an alliance between Communists and the far right. Soral joined the National Front after the 2005 riots and worked on Jean-Marie Le Pen's final campaign for the presidency in 2007.

At the same time, Soral created *Égalité et réconciliation*, which was simultaneously an Internet forum and a network that organized meetings in Paris and in the provinces. It has enjoyed great success by encouraging the sort of inflammatory "antisystem" rhetoric that the Web facilitates, adopting the same formulas that have proven successful for the latest generation of jihadists. *Égalité et réconciliation* claims to represent both the "labor left" and the values of the right, echoing an old National Front slogan: "Socially left-wing, economically right-wing, nationally French." Soral, the driving force behind this group, has a greater affinity for the older National Front of Jean-Marie Le Pen than for the newer version led by Le Pen's daughter. Thus the rhetoric of his own group reconnects with the racist, anti-Semitic French nationalism of a previous generation. In fact *Égalité et réconciliation* produces little if any online material hostile to Islam and to Muslims, emphasizing instead the far right's traditional Judeophobia.

Égalité et réconciliation seeks to reconcile young Muslims and the far right through the propagation of a worldview they call *Kontre-Kulture* (Counter-Culture). Endeavoring to establish his organization in the banlieues, Soral gives speeches in poor neighborhoods with titles like "*La France, l'islam et les banlieues face à l'empire mondialiste*" ("France, Islam, and the Banlieues against the Globalist Empire") that position Muslims as a key resource for French nationalists' battle against "Zionists." Soral also seeks to build a bridge between the traditional European far right and residents of the banlieues by challenging the French position on the conflict between Israel and Palestine, deemed too close to "Zionism."

Alain Soral has collaborated closely with the popular and controversial comedian and activist Dieudonné M'bala M'bala. His relationship with the French-Cameroonian comedian began when they both publicly supported the "anti-Zionist" slate for the European Parliament elections of 2009, which ultimately received more than forty thousand votes. This movement was a continuation of the

EuroPalestine collective, which had presented a list of candidates in the 2004 European elections. The famous *Charlie Hebdo* cartoonist known as Siné was a member of this collective's support committee, as was the Olympic judo champion Djamel Bouras. Alain Soral, who was also a member of the collective, met Jean-Marie Le Pen shortly afterward, and the two men quickly became very close. Thus the former claimed he had partly written the speech that Jean-Marie Le Pen gave in Valmy (a town symbolic of the victory of French revolutionary armies in September 1792 against the invading Prussian army) to launch his presidential campaign in 2007, in which he reminded those in attendance that

> Sarkozy is my exact opposite: the champion of a "yes" vote approving the Euro-Globalist constitution, whereas I was the champion of the national and republican "no";[11] he is communalist-oriented and clientelist, willing to divide in order to rule, going so far as to help the most extreme Islam take root on our terrain the better to stigmatize French North Africans, whereas I am a stubborn and assimilationist patriot. . . . In short, Sarkozy is a servant of Atlanticism and Empire, whereas I am the defender of small, sovereign, unaligned nations.

In 2007, Jean-Marie Le Pen was the guest of honor at *Égalité et Réconciliation*'s first "Summer University."

Over the years, Alain Soral gradually adopted the slogans and arguments of influential old-guard, anti-immigrant, anti-Zionist populists of the far right such as François Duprat or Jean-Gilles Malliarakis, both founding members and former leaders of the National Front. This older far-right discourse, not well known to other political groups, produced a shock wave by its reintroduction in a very different Zeitgeist. Alain Soral declared that he had never had a problem with Islam or with Muslims and that he was mostly concerned with waging a battle against "Americano-Zionists." This position led him to strengthen his ties with activists coming out of the antiracist movement, who had more of a leftist background.

---

[11] Jean-Marie Le Pen alludes to the referendum on the Maastricht Treaty in 1992, which pitted "Europhiles" and "sovereignists" against each other, crossing party lines within both the right and the left.

During this period, far-right populists in Soral's mold tried, with limited success, to put pressure on new National Front party leader Marine Le Pen. At the same time, *Égalité et réconciliation* mobilized to defend Ba'athist parties, such as Syria's Assad regime, because Arab nationalism had long been seen by the right-wing populists as an opponent of Communism and Anglo-Saxon capitalism. Here, international politics resonated with certain expectations of voters in the French banlieues, according to whom the Israeli-Palestinian conflict has wrongly been excluded from French political debate.

This domestic political dynamic was soon influenced by events elsewhere. On July 22, 2011, the Norwegian Anders Breivik carried out a series of attacks in Oslo and on the island of Utøya against young social-democrats. The toll of 77 dead and 151 wounded traumatized a society that saw itself as open and consensual, that had until then imagined that it would be spared the social violence and radicalization that were afflicting other European countries.

Following in the conspiracy theory tradition, Alain Soral made a video in which he denounced Anders Breivik as a Freemason, claiming that the attacks were merely a plot that sought to cast opprobrium on the European far right. *A contrario*, Jean-Marie Le Pen indulgently suggested that the real culprit was a feckless government that allowed too many immigrants into Norway. On his blog, which was at that time hosted on the National Front website, Le Pen declared:

> The situation seems to me serious, not because of this incident involving an individual who, in the grip of a fit of insanity, even if it was temporary, started massacring his fellow citizens. [. . .]. What seems to me more serious, and what this case shows, is the naïveté and inaction of the Norwegian government.

The Breivik case was emblematic insofar as it justified violence by the white nationalist far right while at the same time fulfilling one of the wishes of jihadist Abu Musab al-Suri, who called for the rise of "indigenous" (*de souche*) violence in Europe that would spur a new generation of armed jihadists to retaliate on European soil in a manner reminiscent of the violent breakdown taking place in the Middle East with the post–Arab Spring upheavals. The hostility to the left, immigrants, and Muslims that animated Breivik, and the location of his attacks in a European country devoid of a colonial past where confrontations among ethnic and religious communities were rare, constituted a major shift in contemporary European history—a shift that also started in France on the occasion of the cantonal elections of 2011.

THE BEGINNINGS OF THE MUSLIM VOTE

The cantonal elections[12] of 2011 look in retrospect like a rehearsal for the 2012 presidential election. The comeback of the National Front, spurred by its new president, Marine Le Pen, provoked a change in political orientation at the head of Sarkozy's right-wing party, the Union pour un mouvement populaire (UMP). To cope with the competition from a far right that presented itself as the protector of laïcité against the "Islamization of France," the UMP, for the first time in its history, decided not to issue voting instructions to its electorate in the event that the second round pitted a left-wing candidate against a National Front opponent. This decision, which was debated at length within the party, became a leitmotif in the following years.

The UMP positioned itself at equal distances from both of its main adversaries, adopting a populist strategy known as the "Buisson line"— named after Sarkozy's advisor Patrick Buisson, whose personal résumé included editing the far-right weekly *Minute*. The strategy, piloted by UMP militant and former head of the National Front's youth wing Guillaume Peltier, targeted the right-leaning lower middle class.

For its part, the left also hoped to use these cantonal elections as a tryout for the 2012 presidential election. To that end, it conducted experiments that involved mobilizing support in banlieues inspired by American-style door-to-door campaigning, hoping to find more stable support in strata of society that had become wary of its progressive social agenda.

But it was the strategy adopted by the National Front in these cantonal elections that sent a shock wave throughout the entire field of French politics. From the outset, the Rassemblement Bleu Marine (literally, in a play on Marine Le Pen's first name, the Navy Blue Union) was intended to attract voters who did not identify with the old far right of her father, Jean-Marie. Co-directed by Marine Le Pen herself and prominent lawyer and media personality Gilbert Collard, the campaign was aimed at "de-demonizing" the party in the eyes of the voters. Making a serious bid for power required the party to work on its image and distance itself from the most repulsive episodes in its history, which were punctuated by the outrageous statements and

---

[12] A French canton is an administrative subdivision akin to a township that groups together even smaller subdivisions known as "communes" and that provides the communes with police and other municipal services. It is a significant echelon between local and national politics; accordingly, cantonal elections are considered by pollsters as an important indicator of national political trends.

legal battles of its founder, Jean-Marie Le Pen. In its founding charter, the organization claimed that it was capable of uniting "patriots on both the left and the right." Its discourse was strictly "republican," and while it accorded a special status to Christianity, it said nothing about other religions or spiritual trends:

> The Republic is secular and accepts no religion or state ideology in the public sphere. [. . .] It recognizes the role of Christianity in general and of Catholicism in particular in the history of France and in its contribution to French civilization.

Marine Le Pen's Rassemblement Bleu Marine took up some of the National Front's central themes, such as its rejection of the legitimacy of the international organizations to which nations transferred their sovereignty—for example, the European Union. Her campaign also embraced another key tenet that had been at the heart of the National Front's discourse for more than thirty years:

> The long-term viability of our national solidarity requires that we give preference to French nationals and restrict foreigners' access to certain benefits and jobs.

In these elections, the National Front's message was honed and recalibrated in accord with Marine Le Pen's view that "being French is an honor that is either inherited or merited."

TOWARD AN ISLAMIC ELECTORAL LOBBY

During this period, new political entrepreneurs in the banlieues, sensing voters' deep distrust of elected officials on the national level and of the leaders of the established political parties, saw an opening and began setting up new political lobby groups based on ethnic or religious affiliations. Paramount among these was UAM 93, the Union of Muslim Associations of the Seine-Saint-Denis *département* to the northeast of Paris,[13] the first ever lobby group in France based on Islam. The influ-

---

[13] The administrative and electoral district (*département*) of Seine-Saint-Denis, which as we saw is assigned the postal code 93, has a population of approximately 1.5 million and is the most culturally and demographically diverse of all French *départements*. Recent census data suggest that almost a third of the district is foreign-born—generally of North African origin. UAM 93 leaders claim that it is the first French *département* with a majority Muslim population.

ence of UAM 93 in the French Muslim population was initially quite limited, but it eventually became a significant political player.

Ahmed Khelifi was a candidate in the parliamentary elections held in June 2012 in Seine-Saint-Denis. During the campaign, UAM 93 published a video interview with him in which he explained why he was running for office:

> I stood for election on behalf of a new party called "Nouvelle Union Française" [New French Union], whose ambition is to federate all the segments of the population that are not represented in the major parties, that is, the disabled, the elderly, students, the unemployed, blacks, Arabs, Muslims, and non-Muslims.

UAM 93 and other lobby groups were inclined to support candidates from all kinds of political backgrounds, the only criterion being the candidate's promises and the advantages they hoped to receive in return for helping these candidates win public office. Freeing themselves from older working-class loyalty to the parties of the left, the heads of these lobby groups instructed their militants at the grassroots to give great weight to questions concerning racism, discrimination, immigration, and the status of Islam both in France and around the globe. Compared to this broad concern about representation (how Islam or immigrants are perceived, etc.), less attention was accorded to public policy.

Maurad Goual, a candidate for parliament in 2012, makes clear how difficult it is for young people in the housing projects on the outskirts of Marseille to sort out a political identity:

> Today, a boy from the northern neighborhoods, whether his name is Mohamed, Mamadou, or Ismaël, knows only one thing for sure about his identity: it's religious. He knows he's a Muslim, that's not negotiable. Beyond that, he doesn't know what he is.

At the same time, acute forms of segregation and marginalization were being felt—and resented—by residents in neighborhoods such as those in the western Parisian *département* of Hauts-de-Seine. Mohamed Bentebra, a candidate in the 2012 legislative elections in that district, here describes the stigma of life in *"les cités"* ("the projects"):

> What makes me laugh is that in the projects, everyone wants to leave. What people who live in the projects have in common is neither their origin nor their religion, but the fact that they all want

to leave. Today, whether your name is Laurent or Mamadou, if you live in Sevran or Clichy-sous-Bois [impoverished banlieues in the département of Seine-Saint-Denis], you're dead!

Whereas voting in "the projects" prior to 2011 was primarily reactive and defensive—as when immigrant voters cast their presidential vote in 2007 for the socialist candidate Ségolène Royal in order to oppose their nemesis, Nicolas Sarkozy—in the cantonal elections of 2011, young voters from these same areas were more inclined to support local candidates who understood residents' difficulties and who expressed sympathy for their religious practices. The mainstream parties seemed less than interested in—and at times positively hostile toward—such concerns. This perception was conveyed by Hamid Boujnane, a candidate based in Lille in the 2012 legislative elections:

[The mainstream parties] don't want new people to come in [into politics]. I can tell you that when you're new and you're not blond with blue eyes, it's even more difficult.

Candidates from established parties who were unresponsive to demands increased people's impatience.

Prior to 2011, UAM 93's political activity had been relatively small-scale. On February 26, 2009, it published a joint statement with the French Communist Party of Seine-Saint-Denis demanding the cessation of bombing when the Israeli army was conducting its Operation Cast Lead in the Gaza Strip. A few days before voter registration was closed on December 18, 2009, it exhorted people to register, stressing the importance of the 2010 regional elections. But only during the 2011 cantonal elections did it begin to intervene forcefully on the public stage. In March of that year, it released a public appeal from the Collective of Muslims of Montreuil, a banlieue east of Paris in the *département* of Seine-Saint-Denis that had been a longtime stronghold of the Communist Party and that was now home to the largest concentration of Malians outside of Mali.

This appeal began with a get-out-and-vote message addressed to Muslim voters, whose minimal political influence it deplored:

In a city like Montreuil, where the Muslim population is considerable, it is regrettable that Muslims do not make their voices heard in the various elections [. . .]. This cannot go on. If the right wing insults us, that is because we don't vote. If the left wing ignores us, that is also because we don't vote. Let's stop punishing ourselves. Our voices have to be heard! Political leaders have to know that we matter.

It is significant that the UAM 93 strongly opposed the right wing but also rejected the left. It sought to distance itself first and foremost from all elected officials, whom it accused of being deaf to the demands made by the association and by Muslims in general. It also seemed uninterested in matters of public policy or in ideological combat. UAM 93, for example, never mentioned the National Front, whose influence had been declining in the banlieues since 2002. Its grassroots efforts were focused on mobilizing voters solely on a religious basis:

> Muslims have to vote en masse and in an organized manner in order to obtain commitments from the candidates, so that freedom of religion and its practice are properly respected. [. . .] We think that Belaïde Bedreddine [a Communist member of the Montreuil municipal council] must be elected, we have to vote for him in order to punish Ms. Voynet [a former Green party cabinet minister in Lionel Jospin's socialist government, who was then mayor of Montreuil].

This is a classic call to a target community to cast a protest vote.

In emphasizing the importance of mobilizing Muslim votes, UAM 93 was inclined to persuade local officials that a coherent Muslim voting bloc in fact existed and that they were the ones to mobilize it rapidly. Later analysis of the data revealed that this was not the case at that time, but local candidates found the argument convincing.

On March 25, 2011, the branch of UAM in Aubervilliers, a poor city north of Paris, published a statement repeating the same argument point by point:

> It is regrettable that Muslims do not make their voices heard in the various elections. There is nothing surprising about the fact that politicians do not take into account the legitimate demands of Muslim citizens. [. . .] Muslims have to vote en masse and in an organized manner in order to obtain commitments from the candidates, so that freedom of religion and religious practice are properly respected.

The text explains UAM 93's strategy, making the connection between the legitimacy of Muslim bloc voting and the critical share of

Muslim voters in its constituency. The appeal to religious feeling justifies the demands relating to its expression (such as the need for more Muslim places of worship) but does not encourage voters to think of any other spheres of social life, such as education or transportation, as a potential voting issue.

The cantonal elections of March 20 and 27, 2011, provided the UAM with an opportunity to prove itself as an effective political advocacy and lobby group. In a communiqué published the week before the first round of cantonal voting, the association proposed to handle voting by proxy and to help voters who had trouble getting to the polls. These practices, rarely adopted by religious organizations, are common among political parties trying to mobilize their base. Presented as nonpartisan services, they were connected with positions taken by the association regarding the candidates to be supported or defeated.

Community initiatives such as those of the UAM have a real impact but do not decide the outcome of elections on their own. Despite the appeals to eligible voters in the impoverished banlieues issued by UAM and other religious organizations, voter turnout was low both in the cantonal elections of 2011 and in the regional elections of the previous year. Social problems and the very young age of many of the would-be voters in the banlieues kept more than a few away from the polls. The appeals to identity politics could not counteract the politically demobilizing effects of an economic crisis that had hit this cohort harder than any other social group.

Analysis of the 2011 election results reveals that there was no monolithic, homogeneous Muslim vote based on a surge of religious and communal feeling. There were, however, forces that pushed this constituency in that direction. The rise of the far right and polarizing rhetoric about national identity provoked frustration and even anger among residents of these neighborhoods. They felt targeted and denigrated, and all the more so after having manifested their willingness to participate in the country's political life. The will to make themselves heard and to count produced a new surge in 2012 that made a significant contribution to François Hollande's victory.

FRANÇOIS HOLLANDE'S DECEPTIVE VICTORY

The presidential election of 2012 ended a parenthesis in French politics that had been opened by the 2005 riots. As already noted, Nicolas Sarkozy had revamped the parliamentary right wing with a hard-line discourse on security and immigration. In the 2007 presidential elections, it siphoned many votes from the National Front and reduced its influence. It took over a space that allowed it to triumph over a left wing weakened by the calamitous memory of April 21, 2002, when Lionel Jospin had been eliminated in the first round of presidential voting, leaving Jean-Marie Le Pen to oppose Jacques Chirac. But once in power, Nicolas Sarkozy had succeeded in countering neither the effects of the economic crisis nor the rise of violence, as had been shown by the riots in Grenoble. On the contrary, the ideological schism over national identity orchestrated by the president's office had backfired.

Marine Le Pen's takeover of the National Front was a shot in the arm for the far right. The slogan she chose for her inaugural campaign as party head—"Rassemblement Bleu Marine"—put voters on a first-name basis with its new leader. The cantonal elections of 2011 illustrated this renewed competition and foreshadowed the rise of the National Front, which went on to earn more than 17 percent of the vote in the presidential election of 2012. A decade after Jospin's elimination, the National Front recovered its ability to exercise influence, positioning itself as an alternative solution to the failures of Nicolas Sarkozy. However, the leftist force that Le Pen's party faced in 2012 was no longer the demoralized Socialist Party of 2002.

François Hollande's victory on May 6, 2012, signaled a profound change in French society. For the first time since 1988, a left-wing candidate had won the presidential race. The mayorships of the main cities, the majority of the *départements*, and most of the regions also fell into the hands of the Socialist Party and its allies. These results were the consequence of three distinct trends. First, widespread hostility to Sarkozy stemming from the time of the 2005 riots lasted throughout his term of office, particularly among Muslim voters. These banlieue voters felt singled out by Sarkozy during his time as minister of the interior and then as president.

Second, the comeback of the far right fragmented the electorate that had given Nicolas Sarkozy his 2007 victory and subtracted a key voting bloc that his UMP party needed for victory in 2012. Marine Le Pen exploited the return of urban riots and the exacerbation of tensions caused by the increased visibility of Islam in French society to recover the National Front's traditional voters and to attract others disappointed by Sarkozyism.

Some commentators after the 2012 election expressed the view that Sarkozy lost because he positioned himself too far to the right, thus alienating centrist voters to the benefit of Hollande, particularly on social questions such as same-sex marriage and immigration. However, it seems more likely that his chosen strategy allowed him to limit his electoral decline relative to the far right. Attacked on his left and right flanks, he was the target of a political crossfire that led to defeat. Still, the results were close: Hollande won the race with 51.6 percent of the vote, only slightly more than a million votes ahead of his adversary.

Third and finally, the lingering aftereffects of the 2008 economic crisis provoked a strong rejection of the man who was perceived as the "president of the rich"—notably, but not exclusively, in the most disadvantaged milieus. This change took place among lower-middle-class voters on the right who had not seen their living conditions improve despite Sarkozy's promise that they could "work more to earn more." The crisis hit the country's industrial base particularly hard, and affected workers punished the sitting president at the polls.

François Hollande had been nominated as the Socialist Party's candidate after a bizarre primary marked by the disqualification of his rival Dominique Strauss-Kahn in May 2011, he having been arrested in New York on charges of sexually assaulting a hotel maid. In this tumultuous context, Hollande, who had served as first secretary of the Socialist Party for more than ten years, emerged as a figure without rough edges or any disqualifying negative characteristics.

Campaigning to be a "normal president," the candidate promised to end the polarization that had been associated with the Sarkozy era. In his inaugural speech in Le Bourget, in the heart of Seine-Saint-Denis, Hollande pledged to go after the "world of finance," thereby avoiding the fraught issue of the banlieues. Essentially, he coasted to power by letting hostility to Sarkozy play its mobilizing role.

The left's victory in 2012 was an amplification and an extension of Ségolène Royal's electoral gains in 2007. The personal relationship between Royal and Hollande, a former couple with four children, boosted the fame of a candidate who was little known in banlieues. And whereas part of the left and of the Socialist Party had expressed a certain distrust of Royal because of her heterodox deviations from standard leftist ideology, Hollande avoided obvious faux pas and managed to balance expectations that were sometimes contradictory.

From 2007 to 2012, a million and a half new voters were registered. The two elections brought out approximately the same number of individuals—slightly less than thirty-seven million voters for each of the first rounds. Sarkozy had got almost 11.5 million votes in the first round of voting in 2007, but five years later, his first-round total was only 9.7 million. Hollande modestly improved the Socialists' first round score, from 9.5 million to 10.2 million votes. The balance of power seemed to be shifting in favor of the left. But the most important surge in the first round of presidential voting was that of Marine Le Pen's revitalized National Front, which received 2.6 million more first-round votes than it had under her father in 2007.

Thus the left's advance was accompanied by a strong surge of the National Front, which attracted mainly right-wing voters who were disappointed by the previous five years and who demanded a more radical identity-based politics that Marine Le Pen ably provided.

The largely immigrant banlieue of Seine-Saint-Denis presented a very different face, in opposition to national trends. There Hollande got more than 38 percent of the votes in the first round, while Sarkozy and Marine Le Pen were limited to 19.5 percent and 13.5 percent, respectively. The vote in banlieues favored the left even more in 2012 than it had in 2007. The economic crisis, the debate on national identity, and the polarization regarding Islam led to an unprecedented mobilization of Muslims and of second-generation immigrants to the benefit of the Socialists.

Indeed, studies have emphasized that the vast majority of self-identified Muslims casting ballots in 2012 voted for Hollande. Polls conducted by the OpinionWay Institute revealed that 93 percent of them chose the Socialist candidate. The French Institute of Public Opinion (IFOP) came up with a similarly elevated figure—86 percent. An inquiry conducted by the Institut Montaigne in April 2012 revealed that 60 percent of young Muslims in banlieues intended to vote for Hollande compared to only 28 percent for Sarkozy. These estimates were, however, flawed because of the poor quality of the sampling of religious voters.

Because French law forbids census takers to ask questions about religious affiliation, there is a lack of hard data on the social profile of these groups. The standard tools used by pollsters to correct for bias are incapable of sorting out the statements made by religious groups. However, most expert commentators are agreed that Muslims disproportionately voted for the parties of the left. But it would be hasty to conclude that this was a "Muslim vote" motivated by religious demands and identity politics.

Immigrants, no matter their religion, have long been situated farther to the left on the political spectrum than the rest of the population. The vote of a large part of the Muslim electorate in 2012 was in line with this tendency. However, their voting behavior in this election can be seen as essentially defensive, in opposition to the re-election of

Sarkozy—who was seen as a threat—rather than as a positive endorsement of the Socialist candidate's platform. In this particular election, the party that benefited most from "communalist" identity politics was the National Front; Muslim voters did not coalesce into a monolithic "Muslim vote" based on a specifically religious group feeling.

The vote for President Hollande fostered for a time the illusion of a collective unity. But behind this temporary political realignment, which was attainable because of the rejection of the outgoing Sarkozy presidency, it is possible to discern fault lines that would steadily expand in subsequent years. From the riots of 2005 onward, the marginalized banlieues in particular experienced an erosion—initially almost imperceptible but real even so—of the social and political bond with the rest of the country. This breakdown was accompanied by an increase in the role played by religion in defining identities and in framing political demands, coupled with the rise of a certain moral conservatism that was sometimes tinged with radicalism. This overall movement went essentially unnoticed, because it did not follow the predictable trend of national politics.

Support for the left, which played a very important role in defeating Nicolas Sarkozy in the second round of the presidential election, soon disintegrated—and the disintegration was rapid. The Socialist and Communist parties, traditionally well established in the banlieues, were challenged by a myriad of independent nonpartisan candidates. There again the vote for Hollande masked the reality of local conflicts and the divisions within an electorate that lost its unity as soon as Sarkozy had been eliminated.

The new fault lines became clear in a series of legislative elections held after the 2012 presidential race. In a June 2012 legislative election in Beziers, a poor city in the southwest of France, the right-wing UMP candidate, Élie Aboud, was defeated by the Socialist Dolorès Roque by a dozen votes in a tight three-way race that included a National Front candidate who won almost 20 percent of the vote. This election was annulled by the Constitutional Court and took place again in December of that year. In the second election, Aboud won by a landslide, garnering more than 61 percent of the vote. Between the June and December votes, many imams in the district had expressed their outrage at the "homosexual marriage" law project advocated by the Socialist government, and a number of Muslim voters immediately manifested their discomfort with gay marriage at the ballot box.

The National Front's electoral surge in 2011 and 2012 proved to be sustainable, because it reflected a deep social and ideological trend.

Although the left had benefited from a conjunctural victory, the economic and moral disappointments that led to Sarkozy's defeat continued to undermine French society. Whereas the right's victory in 2007 had produced the illusion that the National Front had entered a permanent decline, the left's victory in 2012 gave the false impression that a resolution of the country's structural problems was possible.

In the following months, eleven more June elections that had been annulled by the Constitutional Court took place anew. All were won by right-wing candidates. The paradoxical situation of 2012 already contained within it the ingredients for the rise of radicalism and violence that was manifested in the crimes Mohamed Merah committed on March 15 and 19, 2012. Coming at the beginning of a hard-fought electoral campaign, these actions were dramatically continued in the course of Hollande's term as president.

THE MERAH AFFAIR IN CONTEXT

The Merah affair put a dramatic end to the sixteen-year illusion that France was immune to jihadist terrorism on its own soil—in contrast to Spain or Great Britain, which had been the target of major attacks in 2004 and 2005. On March 19, 2012, a young Franco-Algerian man by the name of Mohamed Merah murdered three Jewish children and a teacher in cold blood at a Hebrew school in Toulouse. This occurred exactly fifty years after the Évian ACCORDS—the ceasefire that ended the Algerian War—went into effect and also at the beginning of the presidential campaign that François Hollande won with the help of massive support from the Muslim electorate. In the course of the preceding week, this same killer had attacked four French soldiers, murdering three of them and seriously wounding the fourth. Three of the soldiers were of North African origin, while the other was from the French Caribbean island of Guadeloupe.

These acts not only were atrocious (Merah took pleasure in the massacre of little children, which he filmed using his GoPro) but also took on an exceptional symbolic dimension by injecting jihadist violence into the country's most important political event—the presidential election. Committed by someone who had grown up in the banlieues, these murders also called into question the French ideology of integration as the national secular and republican grand narrative, and they rewrote in blood a somber story of a country that had yet to overcome its colonial past.

THE RETROCOLONIAL BACKLASH

With this affair, France entered straight into the third wave of jihadism advocated by the aforementioned Syrian jihadist thinker Abu Musab al-Suri in his *Global Islamic Resistance Call*. The murders followed to the letter the instructions recommended by this book, which could be downloaded from the Internet: the killer chose his targets in his nearby environment and selected them because they were Jewish or "apostates"—the targeted soldier from Guadeloupe may have been the victim of a "racial profiling" that saw him as a lapsed African Muslim whose blood was therefore permissible to shed. A petty thief and juvenile delinquent of Algerian descent, Merah was radicalized by his time in prison, his trips to the lands of jihad, and propaganda videos posted on YouTube or shared on social media, as well as the regional Salafist milieu that he dealt with and of which his brother Abdelkader and his sister So'ad were prominent members.

But the terrifying carnage in Montauban and Toulouse did not testify solely to the efficacy of the jihad model that al-Suri had conceived. It also shed light in a sudden and brutal way on the existence and identity of French jihadists capable not only of appropriating ideas originally expressed by a Syrian-Spanish ideologue and then made commonplace via Islamist social media but also of translating such ideas into action. These jihadists were members of the generation born in the last three decades of the twentieth century and dubbed Generation Y by sociologists—referring, perhaps, to the wire of the headsets dangling from their ears to their navels, making a kind of Y and closely connecting them to the digital world like a postmodern umbilical cord that could no longer be cut. Bottle-fed on video games, this generation has blurred the line between the virtual and the real worlds, passing from one to the other with an ease that disarms its parents, members of a post–World War II Generation X who were educated and socialized before the digital era. In the French banlieues, this Generation Y came into the world in the wake of the political failure of the 1983 March of the Beurs. It reached adulthood, disillusioned, around 2005, the year of the riots and of the online publication of al-Suri's *Call*.

Merah's killing spree was the first of a series that was raised to new heights by the massacres committed in January 2015 at the offices of *Charlie Hebdo*, in November 2015 at the Bataclan nightclub, and on Bastille Day 2016 in Nice. That first incident thrust France into a global web of jihadism in which social dereliction, the colonial past, political disillusionment, and Islamist provocation were interwoven. Suddenly, the taboo on murder for a political/religious cause was swept away by a new, radical Salafist doctrine that redefined the boundary lines between good and evil by making it permissible to kill "infidels" on French soil. Jihadist violence, which people had become accustomed to seeing happen only on their television screens, had now penetrated the very heart of everyday French life and depended on modalities that remained incomprehensible for most people.

In the history of Islam in France as it has unfolded since the 1970s, the young people who personify the third stage of worldwide jihadism also belong to the third generation of France Muslims, who (with the exception of converts) are the children of postcolonial immigrants. Clearly, the radicalized activists in this cohort who have committed criminal acts represent only a tiny minority, but they constitute the avant-garde of a larger Salafist trend whose rapid expansion on French territory characterized the decade between 2005 and 2015. The all-encompassing, uncompromising Islam of this new generation scarcely existed prior to 2005, when community leadership was in the hands of the Muslim Brotherhood Filial l'Union des organisations islamiques de France (UOIF).

The irruption of Salafism corresponded to a complete disavowal of the values and mores of French society. In principle, this rejectionism should lead this third generation of believers to practice *hegira*, or emigration, to majority Muslim countries in order to live a "completely Islamic" life. In the absence of the ability, or perhaps desire, to take this logical step, the rejectionist orientation leads these young people to construct enclosed enclaves on French territory that mimic, as much as possible, the experience of living as a Muslim in a majority Muslim country.

The movement expanded after the 2005 riots, at a time when a majority of young French people who were Muslims by heritage or culture assumed the responsibilities of their recently acquired citizenship by getting involved in the democratic electoral process. Their involvement was, however, abhorred by the followers of "total Islam," who considered the republican notion of the sovereignty of the people an idol to be overthrown. Sovereignty, they maintained, was Allah's alone, and the only legitimate law was sharia, drawn from the commandments contained in the holy scriptures of the Quran and the hadiths (the sayings of the Prophet). But paradoxically, it was as French—they were the first generation primarily composed of French citizens—that these Salafists disavowed French republican values and practices in order to espouse a "total," all-encompassing version of Islam, which they viewed as their sole identity.

This paradox was exacerbated by the singular coincidence of the massacres in Toulouse and Montauban, perpetrated by Mohamed Merah in the name of this total Islam, with the 2012 political campaigns—first for the presidency and then for the French parliament. For the first time, a "Muslim" vote was forcefully expressed; an overwhelming majority of French citizens defining themselves as such voted for the Socialist presidential candidate François Hollande and then for the parties of the left in the parliamentary elections, as we have seen in the preceding chapter. Even if, due to the constraints of French law, it is impossible to quantify the extent of Muslim support for the left in these elections, it is clear that in a close electoral race— Hollande ultimately won by only 1.13 million votes—the left owed a good part of its success in these elections to the massive mobilization of these voters.

Thus even as the first jihadist massacre of the twenty-first century in France took place, a significant and effective Muslim voting bloc came into being for the first time in the course of two major French elections. Moreover, this vote seems to have been determined for the most part by standard social and economic concerns such as are typically part of any election cycle. These two concomitant phenomena—Muslims' first large-scale participation in elections and the irruption of jihadism— were situated at opposite ends of the political spectrum shared by these descendants of postcolonial immigration.

Mohamed Merah and those who identified with him—the thousands who "liked" the Facebook posts and pages dedicated to him— tried to ravage the country where they were born by implementing the jihadist strategy of civil war whose battle plan al-Suri had drawn up and whose stages the Franco-Tunisian jihadist Boubaker al-Hakim outlined in his interview in *Dabiq*, ISIS's online magazine, in March 2015. And yet the vast majority of French Muslims wanted, by contrast, to participate completely in the political life of their country by taking up the duties of their newly acquired French citizenship.

The antinomy can be explained in part by the third coincidence that occurred during this tragic period: Merah's shooting spree at the Jewish school occurred on the fiftieth anniversary of the bilateral proclamation of the ceasefire that put an end to the Algerian War, on March 19, 1962. This emblematic date has provided more than a thousand street names in French communes, testifying to the importance in the collective consciousness of the day when conscripts returned home after a brutal war. Merah desacralized that day on the calendar by relaunching, as a jihadist, war against France. The French far right, for its part, mirrored him by desacralizing it in its own way, attempting to expel the date from republican memory because it considered the 1962 French withdrawal a national shame. Thus in March 2015, the

"19 of March 1962" Street in Beziers was given a new name by the mayor, Robert Ménard, a *pied noir*[1] who has been all over the political spectrum but who now supports the National Front. The street was rebaptized to honor Commander Hélie Denoix de Saint Marc, a participant in a putsch in Algiers in April 1961 and a supporter of French Algeria. As the mayor of the fourth-poorest city in continental France, where much of the housing in neglected neighborhoods is occupied by destitute immigrant groups and Roma people ("Gypsies") and where, according to his controversial remarks, "64.9 percent of schoolchildren are Muslims," Ménard sought by this symbolic gesture to efface the commemoration of what he and his political allies saw as a capitulation. Similarly, in Beaucaire, in November 2005, the FN mayor, Julien Sanchez, renamed a street "rue du 5-juillet-1962-Massacre of Oran" (July 5 Street—Massacre of Oran). On this emblematic date, several hundred French Algerians were massacred in that Algerian city, an event that precipitated a mass exodus of *pieds-noirs* to the France.

Merah, too, sought to metaphorically violate the fifty-year-old ceasefire that had ended the war in Algeria, like Khaled Kelkal, the Franco-Algerian perpetrator of the 1995 terror bombings in France. Merah was born into a family in which the hatred of France was extreme: when he took up arms, his acquaintances crowed that he would "bring France to its knees," and his sister So'ad declared that she was "proud, proud, proud" of her younger brother's acts. In this way he combined the undying anti-French bitterness of his milieu with al-Suri's new injunction to massacre apostates wearing the infidel's military uniforms. Merah was careful to confirm that his victim, a paratrooper of Moroccan origin named Imad ibn Ziaten, was in fact a soldier. Because Merah recorded the killing so that he could pass on images to Al-Jazeera and post them on social media sites, we know that while executing Ibn Ziaten, Merah declared, "That's Islam, my brother: you kill my brothers, I kill you!" The expression "my brother" testifies here to the intra-Islamic identification. It translates the dialectal Arabic expression *khouya*, which North Africans use to address each other and from which the French slang term *crouille* is derived.

However, nothing indicates that this impudent killer—in Arabic, *merah* means "cheeky, insolent, impudent, jovial"—deliberately

---

[1] A person of European origin or descent who was born lived in Algeria and who migrated to France after Algeria became independent. The nickname came from the fact that Europeans wore black shoes—hence *"pieds noirs"* (black feet).

committed the massacre in Toulouse on that particular day in March in order to bring to mind the fiftieth anniversary of the Évian Accords. On the contrary, his mediocre education suggests that he may not have known the precise chronology of the Algerian War. But whatever his perception of the real meaning of this date may have been, the symbolic power of the anniversary transcends the crime itself. It explains the link between the new strategy laid out by al-Suri's *Call* and French Salafism, which had strong ties to Algerian culture and was characterized by a visceral resentment against the former colonial power, particularly in the jihadist wing of the movement. It is the catalytic action of al-Suri's *Call* that explains why France, despite sixteen years of peace, gave birth to people like Merah, Nemmouche, and Kouachi, all of whom were Franco-Algerians or Algerians, and then to the largest European contingent of jihadists to have joined ISIS in Syria.

These events can be traced back to the 1990s, when two phenomena emerged simultaneously: the Algerian civil war, which brought armed Salafism to France, and the arrival in France of preachers of Saudi origin, which advocated a radical break with the values of infidel French society, though without violence. Al-Suri knew Algerian jihadist Salafism well; as a former fighter in Afghanistan, he had lent legitimacy to the Algerian GIA by editing its international bulletin, *Al-Ansar*. As Khaled Kelkal was in a sense the manager of Algerian Islamism north of the Mediterranean, the Algerian Islamists ceased to engage in actual terrorism in France after his death in 1995. However, this milieu continued to expand there through the illegal immigration of jihadists following the Algerian army's victory over the insurrection in Algiers and the eradication of resistance groups from most regions in the autumn of 1997.

These radical Islamist networks thus remained very much alive in France. As we have already seen, examples of this include Djamel Beghal and his accomplices' plot to blow up the American embassy in Paris, as well as the Buttes-Chaumont jihadist network in the mid-1990s. Chérif Kouachi's mentor, Farid Benyettou, who had been initiated into this doctrine by his brother-in-law Youssef Zemmouri, a former member of the Algerian GSPC, preached to young Parisians to persuade them to go to Iraq to join the local branch of al-Qaeda, which was then led by Abu Musab al-Zarqawi and from which ISIS would be born.

Unlike the Salafist movement that arose in Algeria in the early 1990s and quickly became politicized and militarized, the movement that arose in France at the same time was for the most part politically apathetic. The majority of its followers considered elections haram and refused to mobilize against the established powers, preferring to focus on proselytizing instead. The first preachers arrived at the beginning of the decade, at the time when their Saudi mentors needed to win back the hearts of Sunni Muslims throughout the world, especially immigrants in Europe, who enthusiastically supported Saddam Hussein during the Iraqi invasion of Kuwait in August 1990 and condemned the pro-American oil monarchies on the gulf. The strictly depoliticized and ostensibly pietist Islam of these Salafists was expressed by absolute obedience to the Grand Wahhabi Ulemas that support the Riyadh regime, which lavishly remunerateds them in return.

It was in Roubaix and on the outskirts of Lyon, which were bastions of the Algerian colony in France, that the movement took off. Those who showed inclinations toward this doctrine gradually left to be trained in the Salafist seminaries in Egypt or Yemen. Saudi Arabia granted only a few of these marginalized youths visas allowing them to study in its own universities. The kingdom's cautiousness increased after September 11 and then again after the attacks al-Qaeda carried out in the Arabian Peninsula between 2003 and 2006.

The authorities in Riyadh distrusted these fragile individuals who had been touched by grace but who were capable of suddenly turning against the monarchy and biting the hand that fed them by slipping into violence. However, they were willing to use these French Salafists to relay their message abroad, as part of their bid for hegemony over all of Sunni Islam. Thus the Saudi authorities repeatedly granted temporary visas for the pilgrimage season, especially since French Muslims did not fill the generous quota allocated to the Republic by Saudi authorities. This rite, one of the "pillars of Islam," which a pious believer must carry out at least once during his lifetime, was quickly transformed by French Salafists into an exercise in virtuousness that led their followers to go to Mecca each year, distinguishing themselves from co-religionists whom they considered worldly or too lukewarm in their faith. The multiplicity of meetings during the *hajj*, the permanent emulation, and the exemplarity helped structure a milieu that was to grow in numbers and in self-affirmation during the first decade of the twenty-first century.

Salafism, contrasting its alternative lifestyle with generalized "misbelief," explicitly situates itself in the most rigorous tradition of Sunni Islam, which reserves salvation for such an elect alone. But paradoxically, Salafism found a cultural opportunity that allowed it to flourish in the soil of a de-Christianized and post-leftist Europe. Sometimes it is also able to substitute for the secular models of utopian counter-societies incarnated by the "radiant ideal" of Communism and then by the nebulous "alternative" issuing from May 1968, from Larzac, or even from hippie communes or religious sects that made headlines at the end of the last century, from Mandarom to the Order of the Solar Temple,[2] before falling into oblivion. As for the jihadists, the terrorists of the French Action directe group,[3] the Italian Red Brigades, and the German Red Army Faction—movements that fell into abeyance around the year 2000—were their avowed forerunners on the Old Continent.

Thus in the Midi-Pyrénées region in the southwest of France, a neorural commune combining a return to the land and a return to religion, pigeon raising, and the indoctrination of followers served as the surprising soil that nourished Mohamed Merah.

ARTIGAT: FROM HASHISH TO SHARIA

In 1983, a Syrian Islamist preacher named Abdulillah al-Dandachi was granted French citizenship under the strangely Christian name of Olivier Corel. He was born in 1946 and came to France in 1973 to pursue a degree in pharmacy but was unsuccessful and made a living working in various trades. He came from the Sunni town of Tell Kalakh, which straddles the road between Homs and Tartous at the foot of the Krak des Chevaliers, a Crusader castle in Syria that blocks communications between the Alawite coastal area and Damascus—and that would be one of the first localities to take up arms against Bashar al-Assad's regime in May 2011 and thus one of the first to be subjected to the murderous bombardments of his air force.

Sheik Corel was a member of the Association des étudiants islamiques en France (AEIF, or Association of Islamic Students in France), the first group in modern French history that brought together students

---

[2] Larzac is an isolated region in southwestern France that was the site of protests against the expansion of a military camp (1971) and neoliberal trade policies (2003). It became a byword for communities of former leftists going back to rural areas and raising sheep. Mandarom is a temple in the French Alps erected by the "Aumism" sect to establish itself in the wilderness of the mountains. The Order of the Solar Temple is a secret society associated with a series of murders and mass suicides in 1994 and 1995.

[3] A French revolutionary group that committed a series of assassinations and violent attacks in France between 1979 and 1987.

with Islamist leanings. It was created in 1963 under the aegis of Professor Muhammad Hamidullah, the author of the very literal French translation of the Quran preferred by Salafists of all persuasions. The Toulouse branch of the AEIF, along with those in Paris and Strasbourg, was the most active, and Corel taught "total" Islam in the banlieues there. He acquired a certain aura among young French "natives," some of whom combined a taste for post-1968 utopias with a taste for hashish.

Sojourns in Morocco, particularly in regions where the cultivation and consumption of hashish were associated with the practice of popular religion and where trading the substance was profitable, favored some people's conversion to a faith that facilitated these transactions. But the same people, who later adopted Salafism and became followers of Abdulillah/Olivier Corel, rejected their earlier deviance with horror. Like the Prophet, who was himself a merchant, and following the ethos of Western alternative cultures that advocated a rejection of capitalism and a return to the land, the families of converts who followed Corel engaged in petty trade, making and selling pottery in southern France. In the summer, they supplied the bourgeois bohemian and the vacation home market, but as Salafism required, they declined to offer customers representations of animals, humans, or even garden gnomes that might be seen as idolatrous.

Savings made it possible to travel during the winter. Sojourns in Afghanistan to carry out "humanitarian and religious missions" gradually replaced tours in Morocco, especially among some of the strictest Islamist groups. At the beginning of the 1990s, as both their business and their flock expanded, several of these families bought a group of ruined farms in the hamlet of Les Lanes.

These families settled in the foothills near the village of Artigat (population five hundred) in the *département* of Ariège, less than an hour's drive from Toulouse. Their land was poor, supporting only chestnut forests and small flocks of sheep. It had been deserted during the rural exodus of the 1970s, but in the past, these foothills had sheltered other dissidents, such as the Protestant philosopher Pierre Bayle, born in 1647 just a stone's throw away, in the town of Le Carla. The nearby city of Albi had been home to a group of Catharist heretics, whose dream of a new society that would break with the values of the Catholic Church may remind us of the Salafists' break with contemporary French society; notably, both sects divided humanity into two groups: believers and infidels, the instruments of Satan, who were to be eliminated.

The village in which these families settled, Artigat, was briefly famous as the site of the Martin Guerre affair. This story of sixteenth-century identity theft was popularized by Daniel Vigne's film *The Return of Martin Guerre*, with Gérard Depardieu and Nathalie Baye, made in 1982, just at the time when Abdulillah/Olivier Corel was preaching Salafism in the housing projects of the Toulouse banlieues, where he was known as "the white sheikh" because of his light skin and his flowing silvery hair.

Abdulillah/Corel and his disciples bought sixty-two hectares (153 acres) of land and restored or built houses, creating a neorural community where women wore the facial veil, or niqab, and children were brought up with the teachings of sharia far from the infidels' secular public schools. In this way, after four centuries of obscurity, Artigat recovered a notoriety that was paradoxical but that still reeked of brimstone. This rustic Salafist commune became the little Mecca of southwest France, to which the faithful traveled not only from elsewhere in the region but also from the Paris banlieues—notably Les Mureaux and Mantes in the Seine valley, which were famous for their housing projects riots and for the mosques that were built there during the 1980s. Summer camps were organized in Artigat, where young people from the banlieues learned about the "total" Islam from a charismatic sheikh who expressed himself in an oriental Arabic that fascinated converts and North Africans who did not know the language well.

Among those who went to Artigat during these years we find the crème de la crème of radical Islam from all over the Midi-Pyrénées region. In addition to the Merahs and Sabri Essid, Mohamed Merah's Franco-Tunisian brother-in-law, the brothers Fabien and Jean-Michel Clain were there. In 2001 these two converts from Réunion, a French possession in the Indian Ocean, tried to take control of the Bellefontaine mosque in Toulouse, the main place of worship frequented by young people from the neighborhood of Mirail. In April 2015, the elder Clain, then living in Syria, was suspected of having sponsored the attack on a church in Villejuif for which Sid Ahmed Ghlam was arrested in Paris and later indicted. And on November 14, 2015, Fabien released a recording in which he read a statement taking responsibility for the massacres the day before in Paris and in Saint-Denis, while his younger brother sang the *anashid*—chants performed a cappella by men, the only ones permitted by strict interpretations of Islam—that preceded and followed the message.

Another person who spent time in Artigat was Thomas Barnouin from Albi, the son of teachers, who had been a Jehovah's Witness before discovering Islam in 1999. In 2001 he briefly attended the UOIF's training school for imams in Saint-Léger-de-Fougeret, in the *département* of Nièvre, but he was expelled from this institute, which leaned heavily toward the Muslim Brotherhood, a few days after classes began. Then he studied at the University of Medina in Saudi Arabia, for which French citizens could obtain study visas only if they had a strong local recommendation. This gave him not only the nom de guerre Omar al-Madani ("from Medina") but also a measure of prestige among apprentice jihadists in Albi's housing projects. In 2006, he left for Syria, where he rejoined Sabri Essid before they went on to fight in Iraq.

Barnouin and Essid were both arrested by the Syrian secret services in September of the same year. They were caught with weapons in an al-Qaeda hideout and were extradited in February 2007—at a time when the relations between Bashar al-Assad and the French minister of the interior, Nicolas Sarkozy, were very good. Indicted in 2009 along with other members of the "Artigat network" for "conspiracy to engage in terrorist activity," Barnouin was sentenced to four years in prison. He served his time and then, after a brief return to Albi—where he preached haloed with his twofold glory as a victim of the infidels and a scholar from Medina—he returned to Syria to take part in the jihad. He was now one of the main francophone religious figures affiliated with ISIS, and his "lessons" could be found online. In them he showed a perfect mastery of Arabic and of the radical Salafist corpus, as well as of the conflicts between rival groups on the Syrian-Iraqi battlefield. In particular, he used the holy scriptures of Islam, cited in the original and then precisely translated in excellent French, to justify the massacre of infidels and apostates, the seizure of their goods, and the enslavement of their women.

Another figure in this picture is Imad Djebali, one of Merah's childhood friends, who was for a time described by legal chroniclers as the head of the "Artigat network." In 2009, he, too, was convicted for his involvement in this affair. After his release from prison, he left for Syria in spring 2014 along with several men from Toulouse, including acquaintances of Merah's, and then made a surprising return to France in September of the same year. He had gone back to the battlefield for several months in the company of Abdelouahed Baghdali, So'ad Merah's second husband, and another convert, Gaël Maurize from Albi. The trio, even though they were well known to the police, landed in Marseille while the police were waiting for them at Orly airport near Paris. Subsequently they turned themselves in at the gendarmerie in Le Caylar, in the neighboring *département* of Hérault. Their lawyers told the press that they were returning to what they had once considered the cradle of depravity, having "seen the horror" where they had expected to find paradise.

Due to the arrests of members of the Artigat network in early 2007, the "white sheikh" was brought in for the first time by the police. Nothing concrete was proved against him, and he was allowed to return to Artigat, where he devoted his time to various agricultural projects. He dissociated himself from the affair, but from that time on, he refused to make any public statements—that is, until he had to respond to inquiries from the press after the attacks of November 13, 2015, when the voice of his former disciple Fabien Clain appeared in ISIS's video claiming responsibility for the attacks. Several months earlier, he had politely declined to be interviewed by the author of this book, on the grounds that he had to take his mare to be bred on the day originally set for the meeting. He said that he preferred to continue our telephone conversation in French—which he pronounces with a strong southwest accent—rather than in the Syrian dialect: "It has been such a long time, I've forgotten."

Around 2005, the original community was disbanded amid general acrimony, riven by internal crises over obscure issues in which financial and ideological stakes seem to have been closely interwoven. Around the small farm where the sheikh still resides, some of the buildings where the young people of Les Mureaux had prayed together have been taken over by brambles and vines. Thanks to skillful and discreet real estate agents, a few Salafists have managed to sell their former homes (which women left only when wearing the niqab) to English people who might have been nostalgic for Guyenne or to Dutch people who wanted more space. Today, these homes are mere vacation cabins that reek of stale beer. The stream of followers coming to stay with the master has dried up, but the patriarch is still there, pushing his wheelbarrow, wearing his plastic boots, and smiling under his long white beard, just as he can be seen on Google Images.

At that time, the network in Ariège operated in parallel with the Buttes-Chaumont network in Paris, from which the Kouachi brothers emerged. But unlike the impulsive young Paris emir Farid Benyettou, whom a court had found guilty of explicitly preaching jihad to his flock, his elder, forty years older, was well acquainted with *hiyal*, the sophistry of traditional Muslim scholarly circles. His case was once again dismissed.

As for Sabri Essid, he found time, between trips to Artigat, jail terms, and terrorist exploits, to visit Mohamed Merah in prison and to put him on the straight and narrow path of jihad. His influence over Merah was comparable to Djamel Beghal's influence over Chérif Kouachi and Amedy Coulibaly in the Fleury-Mérogis prison. In both cases, an experienced mentor succeeded in transforming vaguely Islamist boys from the banlieues into jihadist killers on French soil, following to the letter the modus operandi recommended by Abu Musab al-Suri.

The network provided the *tazkiyya* (recommendations) that the children of immigrants and other converts in Midi-Pyrénées needed to register in Middle Eastern religious training programs, despite their rudimentary knowledge of Arabic. Travels to the area, meant to toughen them up, were also crucial for the formation of connections between these "brothers." Between 2006 and 2011, Abdelkader and So'ad, Mohamed's elder brother and sister, intermittently stayed at the Egyptian Salafist madrassa for francophones, *al-Fagr* ("dawn," the hour when the first daily prayer is said), in the Cairo suburb of Nasr City. The future killer in Toulouse and Montauban visited them there in October 2010 during one of his journeys to be trained in jihad.

In addition to his role as a spiritual advisor, Abdulillah/Olivier Corel supervised the apprentice jihadists' private lives. He blessed the second marriage of the Merahs' mother—separated from her husband since he had been imprisoned in France for drug trafficking and then had been deported to Algeria—to the father of Sabri Essid, Mohamed's mentor. In December 2011, three months before the bloodbaths in Montauban and Toulouse, Corel also married Mohamed to a young woman he was to repudiate only two weeks after the *nikah* (the consummation of the marriage).

For all these reasons, Mohamed Merah can hardly be considered a "lone wolf." No matter what causal chain led to the massacres in March 2012, he was socialized in a milieu from which a number of key figures in French jihadism emerged. Between April and December 2010, he traveled—with the help of financing whose origin is still unknown but that greatly surpassed his official income, which consisted primarily of welfare payments and government subsidies—first to Algeria, where he sought in vain to meet underground jihadists in Kabylia, and then to the Middle East.

He used his Algerian and French passports to make a surprising journey that took him across the Syrian, Turkish, Lebanese, Jordanian, Egyptian, and even Israeli borders before he returned to Europe and then left again for Tajikistan and Afghanistan. In Afghanistan, he was intercepted by the American military, who suspected that he was a terrorist and put his name on the No-Fly List for passengers to the United States. While he was there, he contacted Islamist milieus and visited tourist sites, where he posed for selfies—in order, he said, to fool the French intelligence agents who would question him when he returned.

The extent of his travels, the funds at his disposal, and his network of relationships gave rise after his death to a conspiracy theory that saw him as an informer for the secret services, which were thought to have deliberately had him killed at the end of the siege of his home in Toulouse to prevent him from revealing the nature of their relationship. Between mid-August and mid-October 2011, he went to Pakistan, where in the local Taliban camps he was briefly trained in the handling of weapons. Merah completed his jihadist transformation on site, as Al-Suri recommended, and it included military training, no matter how basic it might have been.

Mohamed Merah's acts gave rise to a lively media debate on the poor performance of the French intelligence service, which was said to have failed to gauge correctly the danger posed by an individual on whom it had a file and whom it was monitoring. At the time of this writing, this debate cannot be truly substantive, because the evidence in the file remains confidential. As President Hollande's five-year term was reaching its end, the case had not yet been tried, though the affair took place at the outset of the campaign that would lead to his election and under his predecessor Nicolas Sarkozy. This favored the proliferation of conspiracy theories on social media ranging from the "Islamosphère" to the "Dieudosphère"—the large Web network that revolves around humorist Dieudonné M'bala M'bala and his mentor, Alain Soral.

Nonetheless, we can propose a hypothesis: the new model of Islamist terrorism had not yet been assimilated by national intelligence agencies. At that time, they were resting on their laurels, France having gone sixteen years without an attack as a result of their great effectiveness in the battle against the second wave of jihadism, that of al-Qaeda. They were caught off guard, unable to grasp the third wave's "software"—which had, however, been clearly outlined by al-Suri. Because the French government failed to understand that the phenomenon was not exclusively a problem of security, and because it treated only the symptoms while refusing to exhume their social, political, and religious roots and to devote the necessary means to determining their causes, the French political elite doomed itself to waiting for the next occurrence.

THE EXTENSION OF CYBER-JIHAD

Since 2010, alongside the establishment of underground jihadist networks that hardened an avant-garde of militants, there have been other warning signs that a certain kind of Salafist discourse in the public sphere and on the Web and social media was moving toward violence. The growing trend toward identity politics that appeared during that year increased the visibility of markers of Islamization in the banlieues. The object was to radicalize those on the fringes of the religion, galvanizing them by denouncing the oppression that Islam allegedly suffered in France, which was popularized under the name of "Islamophobia."

The October 11, 2010, law prohibiting the covering of the face in public spaces targeted the wearing of the niqab, which most Salafists consider an article of faith. This law provided a pretext for increasing radicalization on social media and for engaging in provocative acts of civil disobedience. In some banlieues, women, a number of them converts, deliberately walked about wearing full-body and face veils to taunt the police, compelling them to enforce the law. Such incidents were intended to arouse feelings of solidarity among other Muslims and to expand the circle of sympathizers. This was part of a larger strategy of increasing tension between religions that involved threats and violence.

In July 2013, during Ramadan, when the police checked the papers of a young Caribbean woman who was wearing a niqab on the street in the town of Trappes, one of the western banlieues of Paris, the situation deteriorated into riots. Images of these riots, broadcast by the Islamist site *Islam & Info*, decried a manifestation of Islamophobia on the part of the authorities. In this verdant town in the *département* of Yvelines, the high-rise housing project had been demolished on the recommendation of ANRU and replaced by attractive new apartment buildings. In addition, a mosque that could hold 2,400 worshipers had been constructed with the backing of the Socialist mayor.

Nevertheless, Rachid Benzine, a scholar of Islam and a native of Trappes, saw Salafization progressing rapidly there. He defined it as "the model that is easiest to follow, the set of solutions that has an answer for everything in times of trouble." This municipality of some thirty thousand people is the birthplace of the movie stars Jamel Debbouze and Omar Sy and the football player Nicolas Anelka, models of success in the American fashion and of the integration of children of immigrants into the society of the spectacle[4] during the first decade of the twenty-first century. Nevertheless, more than eighty residents are thought to have joined the Syrian jihad in 2015.

However, the movement that triggered this process of Salafist radicalization in the media proved ephemeral. It appeared during summer 2010 and was dissolved on March 1, 2012, by President Nicolas Sarkozy, who was running for re-election, two weeks before the Merah killings in Montauban and Toulouse. Named Forsane Alizza (Knights of Pride), it was organized by Mohamed Achamlane, who lived in Nantes, Brittany. The son of a Moroccan father and a Breton mother, he had four children and was living on public assistance. He called himself Sheikh Abu Hamza. Sarkozy issued the decree dissolving the group on the grounds that "because of its structured organization, the religious indoctrination dispensed to its members, and its practice of providing training in hand-to-hand combat and hostage-taking, it has the character of a militant group." This legal provision, enacted in 1936, was originally intended to fight the fascist leagues that had organized riots on February 6, 1934.

In particular, the decree noted that

> the de facto group "Forsane Alizza," by calling for the establishment of the caliphate and the application of sharia in France, challenges the democratic government and fundamental principles of the French Republic, which are secularism (laïcité) and respect for individual freedom; that by inciting Muslims to unite in order to take part in a civil war presented as very probable and by preparing its members for combat and armed warfare, this group's goal is to attack by force the republican form of the government [. . . and] that moreover, the ideology thus propagated has been further pursued in connection with public demonstrations.

For initiates, the name of Forsane Alizza has explicit jihadist connotations, as "knights" alludes to *Knights under the Prophet's Banner*, Ayman al-Zawahiri's manifesto advocating the strategy that led to September 11. The Arabic term for knight (*faris*, the singular of *forsane*) is habitually used in the jihadist educational videos from Syria to designate those engaged in the holy war there.

---

[4] An allusion to Guy Debord's 1967 book *La Société du spectacle* (*The Society of the Spectacle*).

As for Abu Hamza, the pseudonym of Mohamed Achamlane, it is the name of the Prophet Muhammad's uncle but is also the nom de guerre (*kunia* in Arabic) of the famous Anglo-Egyptian jihadist Abu Hamza al-Masri. Calling for the strict implementation of sharia in Europe and support for al-Qaeda, this London-based imam, who supported the Algerian GIA in the 1990s, succeeded Abu Musab al-Suri at the head of the magazine *Al-Ansar*. A veteran of Afghanistan, where he lost his right hand in an attack and replaced it with a hook, he was imprisoned in the United Kingdom and then extradited to the United States in April 2012. There he would be tried, in January 2015, for kidnapping and taking hostages in Yemen, then sentenced to life imprisonment.

Forsane Alizza sought to exercise its "right to legitimate self-defense" on behalf of those who had been "victims of Islamophobic aggression." Though it embodied in its own way the radical avant-garde that al-Suri called for, the group drew its inspiration and its mode of action from a variety of sources. The Salafist reference and the exemplary videos of armed jihad in Afghanistan, Iraq, and Palestine broadcast on its website were combined with agitprop and attacks that are reminiscent of the ultra-leftism of the Gauche Prolétarienne (Proletarian Left)[5] in the 1970s. However, the pictorial vocabulary of the videos came directly from comic books and the adventures of superheroes, in particular Marvel's X-Men.

The founder of the movement was first known under the pseudonym "Cortex," which he took from the animated television series *Minus et Cortex*, known in English as *Pinky and the Brain*. One of the two protagonists of this iconic show for members of Generation Y, Cortex, or Brain, is a highly intelligent laboratory rat who thinks up a new plot to conquer the world every day.

The group engaged in provocative *coups de main* that they duly filmed and posted online. One of them was the occupation of a McDonald's in Limoges—a city in the center of France—in June 2010 to protest against the ties between the company and "Zionism." Another, in August 2011, consisted of burning a copy of the French penal code in front of police headquarters in Aulnay-sous-Bois, one of the epicenters of the 2005 riots, in order to protest the law prohibiting the concealment of the face (and the wearing of the niqab) in public. This also recalled the 1989 burning in Bradford of Salman Rushdie's *Satanic Verses* by Sunni Islamists who viewed it as an insult to the Prophet.

---

[5] A radical Maoist group founded in September 1968 that led daring attacks and provocations against the "bourgeois" French state.

Forsane Alizza also specialized in fighting against its opposite numbers on the right, the anti-Islamist groups of Français de souche (French Natives) and Riposte laïque (Secular Response), by organizing, for example, a counter-demonstration on the occasion of the Assises de l'islamisation, an anti-Islamist gathering held in Paris in December 2010. Forsane Alizza's actions recall those of leftists fighting against the far right during the preceding decades. Some of these actions, intended to intimidate "infidels" in the name of "self-defense," often involved violence—especially verbal violence, but sometimes physical. They were often filmed and then posted on social media sites. Despite the histrionics of Achamlane/Abu Hamza, whose absurdity several of his adversaries in the Salafist movement mocked, Forsane Alizza was the first French Islamist group to display violence on the Internet, to systematically justify it, and to threaten repeatedly to inflict it—but without actually doing so.

Historically, Forsane Alizza played a pivotal role in the transition between the jihadism of the 1990s, a decade during which the Algerian civil war overflowed into France under the management of Khaled Kelkal of Lyon, and the new outbreak in the first decade of the twenty-first century in both France and Syria. Representatives of both generations were among the movement's members and sympathizers. One representative of the older generation was fifty-year-old Baroudi Bouzid, from Lyon, one of the co-defendants in the Forsane Alizza trial held in the spring of 2015, who was sentenced to six years in prison. The current generation was incarnated in the main video recruiter of jihadists for Syria, Omar Omsen, who came from Senegal, grew up in Nice, and left to fight in Syria with the al-Nusra Front, as well as in Émilie König, the daughter of a French gendarme who had converted to Islam and left for Syria in 2012. She was very active online, and in 2014, the United States placed her on its list of foreign combatants. In addition, journalistic sources indicate that in April 2011, a militant belonging to this group, which was also established in the Midi-Pyrénées region, may have paid a visit to Mohamed Merah in Toulouse.

On March 30, 2012, in the wake of Merah's death, and when the campaign for the presidential election was in full swing, a roundup in Islamist milieus targeted Forsane Alizza, especially in the Toulouse banlieue of Le Mirail. Mohamed Achamlane, alias Sheikh Abu Hamza, and a dozen of his close associates were incarcerated, though others quietly set out for Syria. One of the people picked up on March 30, 2012, and later released was arrested again in September 2014, carrying weapons in the banlieues of Lyon. Some of his siblings were suspected of having joined the jihad in Syria and having helped young French women to do the same. A girl of thirteen, religiously married to a jihadist, was found in their Lyon home, which also contained an arsenal.

The trial of the fifteen members of the movement who were indicted, seven of whom were in temporary detention, was held in Paris between the killings at *Charlie Hebdo* and the Hyper Cacher in January 2015 and the massacre at the Bataclan in November of the same year. The eldest of the accused, Baroudi Bouzid, was born in Algeria in August 1962, one month after independence. In the 1980s, he became the imam of a mosque in Givors, in the Lyon area, and during the following decade, he associated with a convert who belonged to the "Chasse-sur-Rhône network," an Islamist group based in a nearby derelict industrial town that was involved in the 1995 attacks, and whose trial was to take place four years later. Bouzid's children had been taken away from him by the courts because he had isolated them from French society and had refused to send them to school. In a video mentioned during the hearing, he declared that "the French state did not hesitate to do anything to destroy the imam who was disturbing the Republic." During his religious work, he had constantly called (*da'wa*) "to Allah, to the *Tawhid* [the uniqueness of God, the criterion par excellence emphasized by the Salafists], to jihad and to the caliphate." After he contacted Forsane Alizza, the group decided to make the loss of his parental rights an emblematic case of Islamophobia, and imam Bouzid became a kind of religious mentor for the faithful. When his home was searched, an elegy (*madh*) in Arabic, addressed to Mohamed Merah, "who has destroyed the party of Satan with Allah's help" and who was "chosen by Allah as a martyr," was found and presented at the hearing.

Earlier, in September 2011, a meeting had been held in Givors, attended by numerous members and sympathizers of the group from various regions of France, to determine the type of action to be undertaken in order to publicize the affair of Bouzid's children. The conclusions drawn were confused and the versions given by the participants contradictory, but one of them, who had just been released from prison, made himself the subject of much discussion for the next four years. Omar Diaby, known as Omar "Omsen" because he came from Senegal, became the French jihadists' main cyber-recruiter; his extremely popular videos consisted of an elaborated variation on the theme created by Forsane Alizza, to which they render ringing homage, making the group's "persecution" by the infidel French government a major argument for shifting the jihad to Syria.

OMAR OMSEN'S GRAND NARRATIVE

Having moved from Senegal to Nice with his family at the age of seven, in the late 1970s, Omar Omsen fell into delinquency in his adolescence. Though the famous Promenade des Anglais may be what comes to mind when one thinks of Nice, the Ariane neighborhood on the eastern periphery of the city, where he went to school, is its polar opposite (as the Bastille Day 2016 jihadist attack on the Promenade would remind us later). The former evokes the charm of an area famous all over the world for its tourist attractions, whereas the latter, which has a very bad reputation, calls up images of low-cost high-rise housing projects constructed below the highway, out of sight for the summer tourists, between the waste disposal plant and the cemetery. This is the dark side of the French Riviera, where drug dealers dominate the streets, marks of Islamization have been multiplying since the beginning of the twenty-first century, and Salafism has gained a following.

Armed robberies in Monte Carlo earned Omar Omsen a great deal of prestige in the underworld and several years in prison. And it was there that, like so many others, he mixed Salafist doctrine and his past as a violent gangster in an Islamist radicalization that retroactively justified his criminal behavior by reorienting it toward the pious goal of jihad. When he was released in 2011, he strengthened his ties to Forsane Alizza, several of whose followers had profiles comparable to his own. The group had a few important members in Nice, including the Franco-Tunisian "Osama," who took his converted girlfriend to Syria, as well as a telephone company employee who supplied the movement with the addresses of "infidels" against whom punitive operations could be launched.

Taking this group's audiovisual productions as his model, he began to cobble together a series of videos meant to tell the true history of humanity. This account was based on the premise that history leads to universal redemption through the Syrian jihad. He posted it on the Internet, where it became a very important tool for recruiting French youths, as is shown both by court cases and by interviews with the families of jihadists and those at risk conducted by the author of this book, as well as by journalists and by associations responsible for preventing such departures.

But in late 2011, Syria was not yet the magnet it would become the following year, when civil war would begin on a grand scale. For lack of opportunities in Syria, even Mohamed Merah had to complete his military training in the Pakistani tribal areas under the control of the

Taliban. A few dozen aficionados of Omar Omsen's first videos—in 2015, the videos had been viewed more than a hundred thousand times—decided to transform their imaginary world into a reality and met for that purpose in Nice, on Friday, December 9, 2011, two months after Omsen took part in the meeting with Forsane Alizza in Givors. They came from all over France, by plane or by train, to prepare themselves to depart for the jihad, which was at that time limited mainly to the "AfPak" zone (Afghanistan-Pakistan) and Yemen. The meeting's goal was to explain the scriptural basis for the permissibility of this hegira, or migration, to the land of Islam and to discuss practical considerations.

The members of the sect planned to go first to Tunisia, where the victory of the Islamist party Ennahda in the elections held in October of that year gave the Salafist jihadists greater latitude, and then to Libya, where the death of Colonel Gaddafi had effectively dissolved the state. Most of the Islamists from Nice were Tunisians, like most of the Muslims in Alpes-Maritimes, and they had numerous contacts there. According to the account his wife and friends posted on the main francophone jihadist site, *Ansar-al haqq* (*The Partisans of the Truth*), Omsen was arrested by the police at the Nice train station, where he had gone to meet "brothers" after the Friday prayers, and incarcerated on the pretext of a seven-year-old criminal charge. He was tried immediately and sentenced to a term of two years in prison, which he was still serving when Forsane Alizza was dissolved. One year later, in March 2013, he was released from prison and deported to Senegal the following month.

The police operation that caused the collapse of the plan for a collective hegira had its origin in the surveillance of the jihadist forums that summoned people to the meeting in Nice. In 2011, the limited number of these forums made this task still feasible. The profusion of dedicated Facebook pages later changed the situation, hindering the intelligence services' capacities. In July 2013, after having put the final touches on the videos and posting them online, Omsen joined the Syrian jihad, leaving Tunis on a ship bound for Istanbul, a voyage he filmed and used in the episode "Destination Holy Land." This episode was the apogee, in the form of a selfie, of the video series *19 HH, The History of Humanity*, which was centered on the person of the charismatic guru himself, and it proliferated all over the Web.

Once he arrived in the "land of Sham,"[6] as Syria and the Levant are called, he became the "spiritual emir" of a French *katiba* (phalanx)

---

[6] See pp. 125, for the Islamic significance of Sham to Salafists and jihadists.

of the al-Nusra Front, the local branch of al-Qaeda. The hegira of numerous French people is attributed to his influence, and no doubt it must be considered one of the reasons why the idyllic French Riviera has provided a contingent of fighters in Syria almost as large as that of Seine-Saint-Denis, representing about a tenth of all those from France. The prevalence of this radical contingent in the region perhaps also explains why Nice was the locus of the deadly attack of July 14, 2016, that caused eighty-six deaths.

In August 2015, the death of Omar Omsen was announced on social media sites, but this report was refuted by Omsen's appearance on a television broadcast in June 2016, in which he engaged in a critique of ISIS's strategy. After two years in the area, the original charisma of the jihad's main video maker had been blurred by the bloody conflicts between the al-Nusra Front, to which he had pledged allegiance, and its rivals in ISIS, who had attracted the largest contingent of French fighters. But he remained famous for his exceptional abilities as an online propagandist, a key vector for understanding the rationale of the French jihadist commitment, of which he had constructed the founding narrative.

The trailer for the three films in the series, beginning with *The Creation of the World* and ending with *The Final Confrontation*, was made in 2013, the year when its creator arrived in Syria to give his virtual characters a flesh-and-blood reality. The video passed on via Facebook in order to evade the potential censorship of file-sharing sites. It flourished far beyond the Islamist movement in the strict sense, penetrating in particular the Dieudosphère (Dieudonné's websites), a number of whose semantic codes it adopted. It can be found, for example, on the *Libre Penseur* (*Freethinker*) site of the Marseille dentist Salim Laïbi, who ran as a candidate in the parliamentary elections of June 2012 with the active backing of Dieudonné and Alain Soral. The video was posted on his blog with the note: "Here is a very interesting documentary on Islamophobic media manipulation. A must-see!"

The similarities between the grand conspiracy theory narrative that the videos on Soral's site *Égalité et réconciliation* (*Equality and Reconciliation*) rehearse at length and *19 HH*'s worldview are striking: their basic argumentation consists in deconstructing television news reports, which they present as a web of lies intended to enslave humanity to the American-Zionist "Empire," in the case of Soral, and to Ibliss (Satan), in the case of *19 HH*. They espouse a sort of Manichean conception of the Universe, viewing everything as a struggle between Good and Evil, which must be denounced at every opportunity. This situates the Salafist view in a much larger "antisystem" discourse whose rhetoric it shares and many of whose followers it has succeeded in capturing. Such a view was attractive even to people who were initially non-Muslims or simply not religious, thanks to its holistic structure and especially to the militant commitment to which it leads: the jihad to drive out Evil and achieve Good, as proclaimed by the Islamic motto *al amr bi-l ma'rouf wa-l nahi 'an al mounkar.*

19 HH is nothing more than a long montage of sequences telescoped in a quasi-professional style, making extensive use of special effects and slow motion. The videos alternate between synthesized images, news shows, interviews with "intellectuals" and experts both legitimate and dubious, and clips from films, nature documentaries, and even amateur videos made for the occasion.

This "mash-up," which takes its jerky delivery from the tempo of rap music, is narrated by the voice of Omar Omsen. He has the slightly guttural accent of the French spoken in Senegal, polished by his stay in Nice and given its rhythm by the choppy scansion that characterizes protest speech in the banlieues. He constantly challenges the viewer in the name of the Truth and urges him to question the dominant ideology of "atheism," basing his arguments on quotations from the Quran and hadith, the Prophet's sayings. The path to salvation is traced out by holding up jihadi combatants like Osama bin Laden as tutelary figures and the Syrian battlefield as the means of fulfillment *hic et nunc.* Lacking musical accompaniment—according to the Salafists, music is inspired by the Devil—the mesmerizing *anachid* (chants) of male choruses intoning Islamic hymns a capella is part of the almost hallucinatory dimension of this hour-long video.

The first twenty-five minutes make the point clear by conferring on French Muslims the quality of victims par excellence. This situates the video in the logic of the battle against "Islamophobia," the buzzword of the Islamist movement in general and the point of departure for the denunciation of Zionism, which allegedly usurps, through the lies of the media in thrall to the Jews, this same victimization in the name of the Shoah. It begins with a point-by-point review of the Merah case, which was the origin of the ultimate sequence of jihadism and of its shift to violence. Noting that it happened shortly before the 2012 presidential election, the voiceover explains that Muslims have paid the price for "the presidential election show." The video continues with images of the arrest of members of Forsane Alizza in late March 2012, of Omar Omsen in Nice in December of the preceding year, and of many "visible Muslims" (despite the fact that many of them were rapidly found innocent of the charge of belonging to terrorist movements):

So they set out to persecute disruptive Muslims, clearly in order to destroy their image among other believers, and so that the latter will *disavow* them and change sides [. . .]. Those who want to silence "disruptive Muslims" always use the same method: when these Muslims denounce falsehood and call for truth, they are systematically imprisoned, eliminated, and this happens all over the world. [. . .] Politicians have constructed lies about them, about us, and about other Muslims who are more anonymous, in order to make them into juicy media items.

Sometimes the voiceover is replaced by text that appears in capital letters on the screen to lend the authority of writing to the remarks made. The graphic codes used—metallic gray background, bordered with two horizontal bands striated in yellow and black—recall futuristic video games that were popular around the turn of the century, like *Unreal Tournament* or *Half-Life*.

Their control over the media gives them the power to show what they wish, how they wish, and when they wish, they can choose to change things and influence the masses in the direction they desire [. . .]. In the name of so-called security [. . .] propaganda against Islam has begun!

In the numerous illustrations of this theme, disparate scenes are shown in a continuous sequence for effect. Images of Israeli children in their school bus singing hymns urging people to kill Arabs are juxtaposed with a regional television report about the use of plastic explosives to blow up the homes of Arabs living in Corsica, thus suggesting a perfect congruence between the fate of French Muslims and that of Palestinians.

After a quotation from the hadiths condemning "those who fight against the religion of Allah," the video tells the viewer that the cause of the problem is the secular school system that teaches the false laws of evolution and not divine creationism. Another mash-up of images ridiculing evolutionism is accompanied by a voiceover spoken by a boy:

In school, the teacher taught us that man was descended from apes, and at home Mama told me that it was God who created us. [. . .] I always thought my mother was right. [. . .] Then I grew up, the world was on the wrong track, and when I looked more closely, I saw that it was people who were on the wrong track.

The proof is provided by a return to the montage of images taken from television news programs showing the then French minister of justice, Christiane Taubira, defending the law authorizing gay marriage, elected officials supporting surrogate gestation for gay parents, and extracts from a fictional film in which a husband and wife visit a doctor to order a son "with white skin, brown hair, and brown eyes."

The voiceover explains the cause and the consequences:

> That goes back to May 1968 [. . .]. The atheists were growing more numerous, as if they were the norm, as if it was they who had understood everything, who were the most intelligent, and everyone else was stupid. The Christians were the nice ones, the kind ones [. . .], everybody left them alone. The Jews, it was like they were porcelain dolls, they had to be protected. And the Muslims were not liked, they were on the fringe of society. Why were Muslims taken as targets? [. . .] The problem with Muslims was that their voices were not unified and that there were no bonds of fraternity among Muslims throughout the world, even though they are all brothers. When a problem occurred in a country, they didn't do anything. [. . .] I grew up between two cultures, and one of them was predominant, because of the context. My parents told me it was haram [illicit], without explaining religion to me. And then one day the world changed!

Images of the collapse of the World Trade Center on September 11 then take over the screen, showing the irrepressible emergence of Truth striking a major blow against the Satanic lies of the American-Zionist conspiracy.

When he or she gets this far, the viewer has become "an awakened one" (*éveillé*), to use the term found in Alain Soral's videos and Dieudonné's shows. However, here the fascist Internet community and its jihadist counterpart begin to diverge: whereas the first deviates toward French identity politics, the second leads to belligerent jihadist Salafism. But on the way to the latter, there are still obstacles to be overcome. There is a perilous bifurcation on the path of Islam: one path leads to error, the other to truth. The illusory path is the one that Omar Omsen's voiceover calls *minhaj salafiyya* (the path of Salafism), as its partisans espouse the view that "the hearts of believers have to be changed before society is changed." These are only "pseudo-Salafists," or *talafis*, a scornful nickname formed from the Arabic root *talafa* (to be degraded or corrupted). On the other hand, for those who follow the right path

> there is another solution: defensive jihad [. . .]. These are Muslims who cannot tolerate inaction when faced by men and women who are being killed as a matter of course!

Then the screen is filled with images of massacred Muslims, in particular the mutilated and bleeding bodies of children and babies killed in the course of bombardments attributed to the regime of Bashar al-Assad or to Israel. Confronted by such ignominy, the blind passivity of the "pseudo-Salafists" amounts to culpability. Then come sequences showing graying sheikhs in the Gulf States being praised by President Obama, which are contrasted with images of black-bearded jihad fighters carrying Kalashnikovs and trench knives.

The options open to Muslims "awakened" by September 11 are made explicit by a drawing in which one sees on the left of the screen a blindfolded face and on the right a man wearing a black hood, staring at the viewer. Fighting and defending oneself, the voiceover explains, is a *fard 'ayn*—an individual obligation for every aware Muslim. That is the path that believers must follow; today, they are lost, some of them calling upon "science and patience," whereas the others are passionately eager to act, as they should.

How can the lost be persuaded to immediately join in armed jihad? Through teaching. The indoctrination videos put out by *19 HH* are rewriting the true "history of humanity." The acronym *HH* stands for this term and at the same time represents the World Trade Center's twin towers, whose destruction marked the advent of the era of Truth. Thus it is possible to "understand why man was created, why Allah created a being named Ibliss (Satan) who fights us day and night." And this genealogical perspective can lead only to fulfillment through armed jihad.

All through Nicolas Sarkozy's term as president, French jihadism constructed a complex and interconnected world in which Mohamed Merah, Omar Omsen, the Artigat commune, and Forsane Alizza all played a part. Although the movement's genesis goes back to the 1990s, and although some of its oldest activists frequented the Kelkal network and transmitted the memory of the last occurrences of jihadist violence in France, it was really starting with the Iraqi jihad between 2003 and 2005 that was gradually restructured around a new generation, not yet numerous, of which the groups in Buttes-Chaumont and Arti-gat are representative. This generation shared the experiences of the Iraqi battlefield and of prison, and it was beginning to construct hero-icized figures that would serve as models for various types of young sympathizers.

Although proselytizers took full advantage of the prison milieu, this was not the only sphere in which they had influence. The congruence of the Salafist model with the demand for radical change formerly con-veyed by leftists, countercultural movements, and hippies was shown by, in particular, the example of Artigat. We have seen how that kind of Salafism, which was originally pietist, was able to harden under favorable circumstances, just as happened in the case of soft leftism and terrorist organizations such as Action directe and the German Red Army Faction.

However, the main change, which was qualitative as well as quan-titative, between the jihadist generation of the 1990s and the one that emerged in 2005 and literally exploded with the Merah affair, was caused by the digital revolution. It expanded to the whole world a battlefield that had previously been limited to particular regions, such as Algeria or Bosnia. It made it possible to give faraway con-flicts an immediate resonance, which explains the difference between French Muslims' experience of the conflict in Iraq between 2003 and 2005 and of that in Syria several years later. Above all, the digital rev-olution favored movement—in both the concrete and the symbolic senses—between spaces: French jihad was continued in Syria and vice versa.

This shows the importance of video production, and of control over it, to this process. We have seen how Forsane Alizza's videos served as a "dress rehearsal" for actual violence and how they simultaneously forged a connection with the earlier generation and used Generation Y's cultural codes to amplify their message in milieus that would oth-erwise not have been affected. The unprecedented number of converts and young women who have been won over by this ideology, and who have followed through with the commitment that it implies, testifies to that.

If the "comic-book" side of Forsane Alizza limited its impact and led some of its members into the nets of the police and the courts, the next step was left to Omar Omsen. His video series *19 HH* summed up the preceding elements in a convincing way by constructing a grand deductive and didactic narrative that also borrowed from the conspir-acy theory of the Dieudosphère to increase its attractiveness. Beginning with Allah's creation of the world to the evil spells of Ibliss (Satan), passing by way of the parousia of September 11, and then touching on the Merah affair and the Syrian jihad, Omsen was able to produce the narrative that would be the most effective vector of recruitment. It was powerful because it forged a view of the world that led to a commitment to overthrow that world through extreme violence in order to give birth to the Good and the True.

When Nicolas Sarkozy left the political scene at the end of a term of office that closed with the Merah affair, it was still impossible to untangle all this. It was only with the rush of events under his successor that the scenes of this drama began to fall into place.

PART II

THE ERUPTION

FROM HOLLANDE TO *CHARLIE* AND THE BATACLAN AND THEIR AFTERMATH, 2012–2016

The victories of François Hollande and of the Socialist majority in the parliament in May and June 2012 benefited, as we have seen, from a "Muslim vote" that seemed to foreshadow a reconciliation between these voters and the sphere of institutional politics after a five-year presidency during which Nicolas Sarkozy had accentuated divisions. The elections took place right after the massacres perpetrated by Mohamed Merah, when the deep ramifications and significance of the phenomenon could not yet be gauged and when its effects on third-generation Salafist jihadists were even less foreseeable.

Subsequent events during Hollande's term occurred under much less promising auspices. As the Nemmouche affair revealed, terrorism had taken root at the heart of French society. It reached a high point with the massacres at *Charlie Hebdo* and the Hyper Cacher supermarket in January 2015 and with the massacres at the Bataclan and in Saint-Denis in November, which had worldwide repercussions. These were followed by the strange circumstances of Sid Ahmed Ghlam's arrest in April of the same year, the decapitation in June of a CEO by one of his employees who had a radical Islamist past, and the attempted massacre in August aboard a train from Amsterdam to Paris by a Moroccan residing in Europe. This trend continued in 2016 with the stabbing of policemen and a Catholic priest and with the spectacular truck attack

on the crowd celebrating Bastille Day on July 14 on the seaside Promenade des Anglais in Nice—killing eighty-six. All of these events indicated the increasingly rapid rise of French Islamism and the growing
interpenetration of the jihad in Syria and the jihad in France.

Events accelerated after ISIS proclaimed the caliphate on June 29,
2014, at the beginning of Ramadan, only a short time before an Israeli
offensive against Hamas in the Gaza Strip. In France, this offensive
aroused violent protest demonstrations in the course of which the
themes of jihad and hatred of Jews blurred the message of the traditional opponents of Benjamin Netanyahu's policies, who belonged to
the progressive and anti-imperialist left.

These demonstrations were not the only ones that drove a wedge
between the Muslim population and Muslim voters on the one hand
and the majority of Socialist parliamentary majority presidential voters
on the other. The Manif pour tous against gay marriage, in which
many Muslim associations participated, and then the School Boycott
Days (Journées de retraite à l'école, or JRE) protesting the teaching of
"gender theory," contributed to this phenomenon.

The rout of the left in the municipal elections of March 2014 was
due especially to massive abstention in the banlieues, where many
Muslims live. In some cases, notably in Seine-Saint-Denis, the inclusion
of Islamist-leaning figures on the center-right lists helped the latter win.
Hardly two years after 2012, this circumstantial conservative alliance,
which turned on a common rejection of gay marriage, demolished the
accord between Muslim voters and the left.

The European elections of May 25, 2014—in which the National
Front, using a rhetoric opposing the "Islamization of France," performed extraordinarily well—took place the day after the massacre
at the Jewish Museum of Belgium, which Mehdi Nemmouche, a follower of Mohamed Merah from Roubaix who had returned from
the jihad in Syria, was suspected of having perpetrated. A week later,
Nemmouche was arrested in Marseille carrying a significant arsenal of
weapons. As during the 2012 presidential campaign, the interference
of jihadist terrorism in an electoral process crystallized and redrew
ethnoreligious cleavages that no longer coincided with the age-old
opposition between left and right: now it was Marine Le Pen's party
that reaped the benefits.

It was at the end of this process that the cataclysm of January 2015
occurred with the massacre committed by the Kouachi brothers and
Amedy Coulibaly. It was in line with the acts imputed to Merah and
Nemmouche and completed the interpenetration of the French, Syrian,

and global jihads. Like their predecessors, the January 7 conspirators killed Jews in accord with the recommendations of the *Islamic Global Resistance Call*, but they took Abu Musab al-Suri's precepts all the way by targeting "Islamophobic" opinion-makers in the editorial offices of a weekly satirical paper that had emerged from the post-1968 movement. *Charlie Hebdo* had drawn attention by publishing caricatures of the Prophet Muhammad but had always defended the cause of immigrants and integration.

This event brought to a climax the third wave of jihadism and represented a kind of cultural September 11—just as the "blessed double raid" against New York and Washington had brought the second wave, that of al-Qaeda, to its culmination. The immense protests it aroused on January 11, in which almost four million persons demonstrated in the streets of France, and which led many heads of state and government to come to Paris, were subjected to various interpretations—some reasonable, some impassioned. These interpretations would be tested by the indiscriminate killings perpetrated in Paris and Saint-Denis on November 13—and by their aftermath in the 2016 jihadist attacks.

4

FRENCH JIHAD, SYRIAN JIHAD

During the development of the Merah affair, a twenty-seven-year-old repeat offender, Mehdi Nemmouche, imprisoned in Toulon-La Farlède, a penitentiary in the Southeast of France on the Mediterranean where he was serving a fifth sentence, asked for a television set to follow—"with jubilation," according to the guards—the saga of the killer on a scooter. By an astonishing coincidence, in December 2007, Nemmouche's most recent conviction had been for an attempt to steal at gunpoint, from a Yahama dealer in Saint-Laurent-du-Var on the French Riviera, the same model of T-Max scooter that Mohamed Merah used when committing his murders.

At the time of this attempted robbery, he was still only an awkward petty delinquent who had been born in the Harki[1] milieu in Roubaix, a once famous mill town on the border with Belgium that was now the poorest of all French cities. His father was unknown; he was put in various daycare centers and then was placed in contact with his mother's family in La Bourgogne, a troubled neighborhood in Tourcoing, a city adjacent to Roubaix. Like Mohamed Merah and the Kouachi brothers, he was cared for by institutions charged with the responsibility of protecting young people, but he spent his childhood—again,

---

[1] *Harki* is the term used to describe Muslim Algerians who served as auxiliaries in the French army during the Algerian War from 1954 to 1962. In France the term is also used to refer to all French Muslims of Algerian birth repatriated to France after 1962 and their French-born descendants. Once in France, Harkis were typically ostracized by other Algerian immigrants. Many Harkis unable to leave Algeria for France after the war of independence were slaughtered by pro-independence forces.

like the perpetrators of the other two massacres—in a broken family world, with no father figure present. The subject of multiple arrests, indictments, and then terms in prison for theft and violence, he had showed no interest in religion before his last theft, which earned him five years behind bars, from December 2007 to December 2012. Unlike Mohamed Merah, for whom incarcerations served only to reinforce a radicalization that had begun in his family environment and in the Salafist environment of the Midi-Pyrénées, it did not seem, in view of the information available before the trial, that Mehdi Nemmouche had been approached by the Salafist movement in Roubaix, which was nonetheless very active in a city that had become a seedbed for Syrian jihad volunteers.

MEHDI NEMMOUCHE, DETAINEE AND JAILER

Nemmouche's Islamization occurred during the five years he spent in the prison incubator between the ages of twenty-two and twenty-seven. With no family ties that might have provided him with moral support during his detention, he remained isolated in the penitentiaries of the south of France. It is not rare, in a prison where Islam predominates, for an individual stigmatized for belonging to a minority or other deviant group to turn this stigma into a source of religious pride, if only to survive the pressure brought to bear by fellow prisoners.

For some young people from Harki backgrounds whose parents were viewed as "traitors" by the children of other Algerian immigrants, a scrupulous adherence to all the outward signs and rituals of Salafism served both as a source of pride and as a way to delegitimize the children of activists for the Algerian National Liberation Front (FLN), whom they associated with the "apostate" state in Algiers. In Nemmouche's native city of Roubaix in particular, Harki children are over-represented in the associative network and Salafist mosques.[2]

As a Harki son and as one who was doubly stigmatized by the honor codes of the disenfranchised banlieues as *ould al h'ram* (a child of sin, a bastard) because his father was unknown, Mehdi Nemmouche may well have sought, during his last incarceration, to exorcise his demons through an intense form of Islamization. In any case, this Islamization was achieved in the company of prisoners who were already militants, starting in 2009 at the detention center in Salon-de-Provence, where he was identified by the Department of Corrections intelligence service

---

[2] I pointed this out in my *Passion Française* (Gallimard, 2014).

as a radical Islamist, and then especially in the detention center in Toulon, where he was held from March 2011 until his release in early December 2012.

Eager for information about the most rigorous injunctions in order to throw himself headlong into a suddenly discovered faith, Nemmouche moved closer to a support group for Muslim detainees called Salsabil (Ear of Wheat). This group was founded in 2010 but would be dissolved in November 2016 by the French Ministry of the Interior, as it was suspected to have served as a network for jihadist inmates. He quickly grew a beard, started wearing a *djellaba*,[3] and engaged in ardent proselytizing among the other prisoners. But his aggressiveness toward the guards, whom he bombarded with projectiles, caused him to be placed in a disciplinary area and then in solitary confinement until he completed his sentence.

After he was released, Nemmouche went to Molenbeek-Saint-Jean, a town on the outskirts of Brussels and a seedbed of jihadism, where the November 2015 massacres in Paris and Saint-Denis would soon be planned. On New Year's Eve 2012, he flew out of Brussels, passing through the United Kingdom, Lebanon, and Turkey before finally joining the ranks of ISIS in Syria. The complex logistics and cost of this itinerary, like that of his return trip through Malaysia and Thailand, could not possibly have been managed alone by the ex-con Nemmouche, with his lack of foreign travel experience and his modest savings from his past career as a thief. He clearly required help—specifically, a network of contacts and financing.

Nemmouche's journey recalls Mohamed Merah's similarly complex peregrinations between Algeria and Tajikistan. But whereas Merah's jihadist training in the use of weapons ended abruptly in a Taliban camp in Pakistan in autumn 2011, the year when the Arab upheavals exploded, Nemmouche was able to benefit fully from training in warfare in Syria a year and a half later, when by 2013 the Islamists had begun to control a vast area in which they imposed strict sharia law.

We have firsthand testimony about his time in Syria. In a role reversal after five years of incarceration, the ex-con was transformed into a jailer, assigned to guard prisoners held in the cellars of a former hospital in Aleppo that had come under ISIS control. Among these prisoners were four French hostages, including the journalists Didier François and Nicolas Hénin, who had been kidnapped in June 2013 and who

---

[3] A *djellaba* is a long, loose-fitting robe widely worn in North Africa and elsewhere by pious Muslims.

would be freed in late April 2014—though not without having suffered abuse at the hands of a particularly sadistic French guard of North African origin. Didier François, a former member of the Communist Revolutionary League (the French section of the Trotskyist Fourth International), had been not only one of the founders of SOS Racisme in 1983 but also the inventor of the movement's pet slogan, *Touche pas à mon pote* ("Hands off my buddy"), which at that time always appeared alongside an illustration of a little yellow hand that combined the shape of the North African hamsa or Fatima's hand amulet—a protective talisman—and the color of the infamous yellow star that European Jews had to wear under the Nazi yoke. The terrifying paradox—that thirty years after *Touche pas à mon pote* the inventor of the slogan found himself held hostage in a Syrian dungeon by an Islamist group, mistreated by one of the children of these same "buddies" whose protector he had been—casts a particularly cruel light on the last quarter-century.

In September 2014, Didier François's fellow hostage Nicolas Hénin revealed publicly that he had recognized Nemmouche, who had been arrested in Marseille the previous May, as his jailer. The radicalized neo-Salafist had hummed French hit songs as he tortured the Syrian captives. In addition, Nemmouche taunted his compatriots François and Hénin by sharing with them his fascination with the famous television series *Faites entrer l'accusé*,[4] which tells the stories of various notorious criminals. This petty thief who had become an Islamist projected himself onto these negative role models while combining the political grammar of third-generation jihadism with the mental vocabulary of a French youth brought up on pop television culture, even though he refused to watch infidel television while he was in detention (except to follow the Merah affair).

This kind of hybridization, encapsulated in the title of Nicolas Hénin's book describing his captivity, *Djihad Academy* (alluding to the famous reality television show *Star Academy*), is the key to the success of jihadist mastermind Abu Musab al-Suri's plan to place European jihadists at the heart of his campaign. After conditioning them by means of high doses of indoctrination and military training, and after they had grown accustomed to inflicting violence in the name of Islam, as they interpreted it, on the dehumanized victims of ISIS, these jihadists would be primed to return to Europe, there to light the fires

---

[4] *Bring in the Accused*, a long-running French television series (2000–2017).

of civil war. In this sense, Nemmouche incarnates the ideal type of the third-generation jihadist in his exploits as well as in his limitations.

In addition, the ongoing judicial procedures reported in the press indicate that Nemmouche, far from corresponding to the pseudo-model of the "lone wolf" emphasized by some superficial analysts, is thought to have been assigned to the jail in Aleppo under the orders of Salim Benghalem, one of ISIS's highest-ranking French jihadists. Born in 1980 in Bourg-la-Reine, in the southern outskirts of Paris, into a family whose other members were perfectly integrated into society, at the age of seventeen Salim began dealing drugs and then was sentenced in 2002 to eleven years in prison for having committed murder in the course of a confrontation between rival gangs in the housing projects in Cachan, also on the southern edge of the capital city, where he lived.

Before his incarceration, Benghalem moved closer to the jihadist group based in Buttes-Chaumont park in the northeast of Paris, where he met the Kouachi brothers, thus attracting the attention of the French intelligence agency. Although he did not go to Iraq, he was in the same prison cell as Mohamed al-Ayouni, who had been arrested on his return from the jihad, in the course of which he had lost an eye and an arm in 2004 during the battle of Fallujah against coalition troops led by the United States. Whereas Ayouni was found guilty in 2008, along with Chérif Kouachi, Benghalem was released. Here again, with prison playing its usual role as an incubator of jihadist terrorism, Benghalem became a de facto member of the terrorist network that planned and executed the attacks of January 2015.

In July 2010, with Amedy Coulibaly and Djamel Beghal, Salim Benghalem was arrested in the attempted jailbreak of Smaïn Aït Ali Belkacem, the explosives expert behind a series of Islamist terrorist attacks on French soil in 1995. After being released from police custody, Benghalem flew in July 2011 to Oman and then to Yemen in the company of one of the Kouachi brothers in order to be trained in jihad under the auspices of al-Qaeda in the Arabian Peninsula (AQAP). After a brief return to France, he joined the Syrian jihad in April 2013, initially in the ranks of the al-Nusra Front, the local al-Qaeda franchise and a sister organization of AQAP, and then in ISIS, where he held positions in the movement's hierarchy.

On February 12, 2015, a month after the *Charlie Hebdo* and Jewish supermarket killings in Paris, Benghalem appeared unmasked in a video praising the perpetrators of these massacres, whom he knew well, and encouraging his co-religionists in France to imitate their example. "Kill them with knives, or at least spit in their faces, but disavow them!"

he exclaimed, thus translating, in a way, the recommendations formulated in 2005 in Abu Musab al-Suri's *Call to Global Islamic Resistance*. It was this high-ranking activist—Salim Benghalem—who took Mehdi Nemmouche as his acolyte at the jail in Aleppo. This is how a jihadist network took a socially disconnected, intellectual lightweight ex-con and weaponized him, propelling him out of the misfortune that marked his birth in Roubaix and into a worldwide jihad.

However, Nemmouche's fortuitous arrest during a routine customs inspection at the bus station in Marseille on May 30, 2014, where he was found with an arsenal of weapons used in his attack on the Jewish Museum of Brussels the week prior,[5] reveals one of the main strategic weaknesses of third-generation jihadism. The latter relies on delegating to unstable individuals the responsibility of choosing when and how to enact jihad.

In fact Nemmouche's fortuitous arrest was brought about by his decision to board a cheap bus that regularly made the run from Amsterdam to Marseille via Brussels. The police knew that this bus route was often taken by small-time hashish dealers going to buy their supplies in Dutch coffee shops, and it was almost always inspected by customs officials upon its arrival in Marseille. Nemmouche's error would never have been committed at the time of al-Qaeda, when the organization planned the September 11 attacks in advance with the meticulousness of a secret service. This same sort of amateurism made it possible to foil two other jihadist attacks the following year: an attack on a church in the southern Parisian commune of Villejuif being planned by Sid Ahmed Ghlam and a massacre that Ayoub el-Khazzani was getting ready to commit on board a train traveling from Amsterdam to Paris.

Here we see the operational limits of the slogan *Nizam, la tanzim* (a system, not an organization) that had been popularized by al-Suri and that distinguished his program of network-based jihadism from that of Osama bin Laden's pyramidal model. In the absence of testimony by Nemmouche, who was extradited to Belgium and who as of this writing has still refused to say anything, the precise reasons for his presence in Marseille with the aforementioned deadly equipment, and for why

---

[5] Nemmouche was also found with an ISIS flag, a video made after the attack taking responsibility for it, and a helmet with a GoPro camera mounted on it— reminiscent of the GoPro camera carried by Mohamed Merah during his killing spree in Toulouse and Montauban two years prior. In the course of his police interrogation after being picked up in Marseille, Nemmouche was reported to have remarked, "it's a shame that the camera didn't work."

he claimed responsibility for the Brussels attack by filming himself in front of an ISIS flag (as Amedy Coulibaly was soon to do on January 8, 2015, in anticipation of the hostage-taking and killing at the Parisian Hyper Cacher grocer the next day), remain unknown. But the connection between the two lands of jihad—the West's soft underbelly of Europe and the Syria of ISIS—between which a continuous back-and-forth flow of jihadists had been established, found in Nemmouche its first spectacular incarnation and its paradigm.

In the wake of Nemmouche's arrest, conspiracy theorists claimed, as they had after September 11 and the Merah affair, that the clumsy jihadist was in fact a provocateur manipulated by the French and Israeli secret services in order to "soil the image of Islam" and feed "Islamophobia"—a claim many Internet users found convincing. ISIS, for its part, resisted these conspiracy theories because they devalued the "heroes and martyrs of the jihad," whose praises it sang in its online magazine Dabiq as part of its ongoing campaign to maintain the flow of recruits into its ranks.

"OH, MY BROTHERS IN ALLAH FROM FRANCE!"

In July 2013, while Nemmouche had joined ISIS in Syria and was mistreating the prisoners he was guarding, a video in French was posted by this jihadist group, which was still, a year before its conquest of Mosul and the proclamation of Abu Bakr al-Baghdadi's "caliphate," only one of the factions vying for the dominant spot in the Islamic resistance to Bashar al-Assad's regime. Whereas its rivals in the al-Qaeda–affiliate al-Nusra Front seemed to be dominant and had many French nationals in its ranks (including the recruiter Omar Omsen, discussed in the previous chapter), ISIS's new video testified to its own international influence and, for the first time, expressed clearly the interpenetration of the Syrian and French battlefields.

This ISIS video featured two half-brothers from Toulouse, Nicolas and Jean-Daniel Bons. The elder of the two had converted to Islam at the same Bellefontaine mosque in the banlieue projects of Le Mirail in the southwest of Toulouse that Mohamed Merah was fond of frequenting. The main place of worship in the neighborhood, it is located next to a supermarket whose parking lot it takes over on Fridays when as many as three thousand persons converge there for services. Although its imam, Mamadou Daffé, a charismatic director of research in biology at the Centre national de la recherche scientifique (CNRS, or National Center for Scientific Research), advocates an all-encompassing form of

Islam, he does not define himself as a Salafist. And yet the stalls in the parking lot that distribute Islamic literature during the main prayer service offer the faithful only Salafist texts in both Arabic and French.

The elder of the Bons brothers, Nicolas, also known as Abu Abdel Rahman (his Islamic alias is one of Allah's ninety-nine names and means "father of the servant of the All-Merciful"), was brought up by his mother, a non-commissioned officer in the army who divorced shortly after his birth. He lived in a lower-middle-class environment, both in the cities where his mother was garrisoned and in a subdivision in a quiet town on the outskirts of Toulouse. However, this protected childhood, punctuated by sojourns in Guyana with his father and his half-brother Jean-Daniel, did not enable him to find a stable occupation, because his grades in school were not good enough. Seeking an identity, he converted to Islam in 2009 through contact with North African friends in Toulouse, where, as we have seen in the last chapter's discussion of the "white sheikh" Abdulillah (Olivier Corel), Islamic proselytizing was particularly common. Jean-Daniel Bons returned to Toulouse to live with their common grandmother and also converted under the influence of his elder brother shortly before they both flew to Syria via Spain in March 2013—after telling their friends and relatives that they were leaving for a vacation in Thailand.

In the aforementioned French-language video broadcast by ISIS, Nicolas/Abu Abdel Rahman Bons wears a red-and-white checkered *keffiyeh* knotted at the nape of his neck. His trimmed beard is almost blond, and there is a strange light in his eyes: he looks ecstatic. He appears alone in the first part of the video, where he expresses himself in the following terms against a black background and under a flag marked with the seal of the Prophet:

> I am your brother in Allah, Abu Abdel Rahman, I am French, of a French father and a French mother, and, uh, my parents are atheists, they have no religion, and, *Hamdulillah* ["Allah be praised"], Allah guided me, I converted to Islam almost three years ago, *Hamdulillah*! So the goal of this video, my brothers, is to invite you and encourage you to join us in the land that Allah has blessed, the country of Sham [the Levant]!
>
> Oh! my brothers from France, my brothers in Allah from France, from Europe, from the whole world, *in sha' Allah* ("Allah willing"), jihad in Syria, it is obligatory, the jihad in Syria, it is ob-lig-a-tory! As the Prophet, *Salallah 'aleihi wa sallam* ["peace be upon him," a eulogistic phrase attached to the name of the Prophet Muhammad

in Islam] said, the Ummah [community of believers] is like a single body: as soon as one part suffers, all the others come to its aid, so we are obliged to come to the aid of our brothers, our brothers who are in a very difficult situation. And we are also obliged to work for the restoration of a *Khalifah* [caliph] so that Allah's word may be the highest. And those who do not work for that are unfortunately in sin, they are in sin!

There are many Muslims on Earth, and we need you, *in sha' Allah*! Where are the men? Where are the men? Where are the men of the community of Muhammad, *Salallah 'aleihi wa sallam*? What will you say, what will you say to Allah when you are before Him and when the witnesses who come before you will be women who have been raped, children who have been killed, brothers who have been tortured in the prisons of these dogs?

In conclusion, I would like to send M. François Hollande a message: "Hey, François Hollande, convert to Islam, save your soul from the fires of Hell and disavow yourself of [*désavoue-toi de*] your Jewish and American allies! Withdraw the troops from Mali, stop fighting Muslims, stop fighting Islam! You want to fight Allah? But Allah is the greatest, He is the greatest, Allah, and you are [all] very tiny!"

Declaimed in a slow and monotonous voice, this exhortation appears to be the recitation of a text held below and to the right of the screen that Nicolas/Abu Abdel Rahman struggles to read, sometimes stumbling over the words and looking at the camera lens only in moments of dramatic inflection, as when he addresses the president of the French Republic. This metatext, of which he does not seem to be wholly the author, as his hesitating delivery suggests, is written in a hybrid style. It consists of bombastic adaptations of ready-made Arabic formulas, reinforced by expressions of gratitude to Allah laboriously uttered in the language of the Prophet. The bits of subtitling in Arabic, partly hidden by another, more succinct subtitling into English, suggest that the text was initially conceived in Arabic and then translated into French to be read.

This Salafist gibberish, Orwellian Newspeak of the Islamic era, is the vector par excellence of jihadist indoctrination, thanks to the mental formatting through which it conditions neophytes. It is structured around strange-sounding phrases like "so that Allah's word may be the highest"—a word-for-word translation of an Arabic invocation. More surprising is the incorrect transitive indirect construction of the verb *se désavouer de* (literally "to disavow oneself of")—which, moreover, is seldom used in its reflexive form—when François Hollande is exhorted to convert (calling on the leader of enemies to convert before combat has been obligatory in jihadist literature since the dawn of Islam). In reality, the expression *désavoue-toi de tes alliés juifs et américains* (literally "disavow yourself of your Jewish and American allies") is a locution that makes sense only in the Salafist rhetoric translated here. It refers to the doctrine of "alliance and disavowal" (*al wala' wal bara'a*), which requires of Muslims absolute submission to Islam in its most literalist understanding and a complete break with the non-Islamic environment, all of which is described as "disbelief" (*mécréance*).

This doctrine, which is found in classical Islamic thought in the works of the most radical authors, calls upon pious Muslims to close ranks and engage in an uncompromising battle against all their enemies, whether they are infidels, heretics, or apostates. The phrase *se désavouer de* (disavow oneself from) expressing this break is commonplace on francophone jihadist sites. We have already encountered it quoted in Salim Benghalem's exhortation, and it is found several times in the interviews conducted in 2013–2014 by the journalist David Thomson and reproduced in his pioneering inquiry, *Les Français jihadistes*.[6] It is used by one of Thomson's interlocutors, Yassine, a young Frenchman of Moroccan origin born and raised in Seine-Saint-Denis, to explain that the "fighting sheikhs of Syria" whose videos he watches on YouTube are "the most credible":

> They are more centered on jihad, on *Tawhid* [the uniqueness of Allah], on Alliance and Disavowal, which are the basis of our religion. Know who to ally yourself with and who to disavow yourself from. Know who your allies are and who your enemies are.

In his ISIS video broadcast, Nicolas/Abu Abdel Rahman juxtaposes these formulas, translated and taken mechanically from Arabic, with the relaxed style of popular spoken language, systematically repeating the subject of the sentences ("jihad in Syria, it is obligatory," "He is the greatest, Allah"). An unintentionally comic effect is produced when he addresses François Hollande: the president's name is preceded by the expletive "*Ho*" (hey), probably reflecting the vocative *ya*, whose use in Arabic is required. This is not the case in French, but in southern France, the expression is used among

---

[6] Éditions Les Arènes, 2014.

intimates. "*Ho, François Hollande,*" pronounced with a strong South-west lower-middle-class accent and followed by the use of the familiar second-person singular *tu*, is clearly intended to diminish the solemn respect with which the office of the French presidency is normally regarded, in accord with an Islamic tradition that seeks to puncture the pride (*istikbar*) of the powerful of this world and that insists on humility (*istid'af*) before Allah. The overall effect of the video is odd, recording via the medium of a jihadist cyberworld the offbeat locutions of a child of the Toulouse banlieues, lost on the Syrian battlefield where he was soon to die like a sacrificial lamb. (In another segment of the video, Nicolas/Abu Abdel Rahman is designated as a future martyr ready to be received into the felicity of Muhammad's paradise.)

The second part of the video featuring Nicolas/Abu Abdel Rahman shows him in combat uniform, a Kalashnikov strapped on his shoulder, alongside his younger brother Jean-Daniel, who looks like a boy wearing a cap worn backward in the hip-hop fashion, against a background of palm trees. Holding a Quran in his hand, he once again exhorts his "brothers" in Islam to make the hegira, the emigration to the land of Islam, to leave a country which is full of infidels and which attacks jihadists in Mali. He boasts of having carried out *da'wa*, Islamist proselytization, around him and thus to have received into Islam his brother, a "gift of Allah."

Nicolas/Abu Abdel Rahman explains that his desire for jihad came to him both from reading a multitude of Quranic verses that call believers to it and from viewing the videos featuring the Sheikh Abdallah Azzam (1941–1989). The mention of Abdallah Azzam is significant. This Palestinian Sunni theologian and activist in the Afghan mujahideen struggle against the Soviets in the 1970s was an ideologue of the first generation of jihadists. Using him in an indoctrination video was a way for ISIS to assert its "respectable" jihadist pedigree in the context of its rivalry with the then dominant al-Qaeda branch in Syria, the al-Nusra Front.

Being a propaganda instrument for asserting ISIS as the only legitimate jihadist entity, the video in its third part features a column of vehicles filled with men brandishing their weapons and ISIS's black flag, winding down a road typical of the Syrian landscape, among hills planted with olive trees, with a soundtrack of *anashid*. A banner in Arabic entitles the scene: "The joy of the jihadis at the announcement of the proclamation of the Islamic State in Iraq and the Levant."

Nicolas/Abu Abdel Rahman's younger half-brother died in combat during the month following the broadcast of the video in August

2013. Even if he was proud of the sacrifice of his younger brother for the jihad, he admitted that he was very shaken by his death, as his mother revealed in a later interview with this author. He telephoned her regularly, and she suggested that he not make any more propaganda videos. Like many other young Europeans judged to be insufficiently experienced for combat, and to avoid having another mouth to feed, he was finally assigned to a suicide mission—possibly after having been given Captagon, an amphetamine widely administered to ISIS militants that inhibits fear—on which he died on December 22, 2013. On January 7, his mother received a text message informing her of his death the previous month.

On September 30, 2015, almost two years after the event, a new jihadist site, *Furat* (Euphrates), appeared online featuring a video showing the last moments of Nicolas/Abu Abdel Rahman. Five minutes long and entitled after the Quranic verse "I have hastened unto Thee, my Sustainer, so that Thou might be well-pleased" (20:84), it consists of a montage of the final statements of the future martyr and images of the attack in which he died. Complementing his call for volunteers for jihad in Syria and in France and his exhortation to François Hollande to convert, it provides rare psychological insight into the distress and loneliness of a French youth for whom the conversion to Islam and subsequent departure for "the blessed land of Sham" were a quasi-therapeutic, and fatal, recourse:

> I send my greetings to all my mujahideen brothers all over the world. I send a message to all other Muslims: oh! my brothers, hurl yourselves into jihad, Hurl yourselves toward the paths to paradise. Oh! my brothers, I urge you to organize in every country where the governments fight Islam. I urge you to organize to carry out operations, [providing] a good example like what Mohamed Merah did in Toulouse. [. . .]
>
> A message for all the brothers of the *dawla* [the Islamic State, ISIS]. It is my true family. In France, people's hearts are closed, there is nothing in their hearts; they are nice at first, and then later there is nothing. Here, truly, people's hearts are open, there are smiles, all that, compassion, warm reception, truly I love you for Allah, really a lot, you are the best people I've ever met, and I thank Allah for having put me here with you.

The disparate profiles of Mehdi Nemmouche and Nicolas/Abu Abdel Rahman Bons illustrate the broad social and ethnic spectrum of the activists ISIS manages to catch in its net. At one extreme, we have the son of Harkis and an *ould al h'ram*—a "child of sin"—from Roubaix, buffeted by fate from the moment he entered the world, a multiple repeat offender, re-Islamized in prison and trained in Syria to put his "vice" in the service of jihad before his massacre of Jews in Brussels in imitation of Merah. At the other extreme, we have a young man born of a white family and brought up by a divorced mother in a provincial middle-class suburban enclave where opportunities for cultural enrichment and socializing had been replaced by solitary social media consumption in front of screens, tablets, and smartphones.

These at-risk and somewhat lost young people, both searching in different ways for an absolute, were hooked by Salafism online. It offered them, particularly in the atmosphere of intense Islamist proselytism that characterized Toulouse, the warmth of a peer group that ended their loneliness, a preliminary condition for the exaltation of an ideal destined to "change their lives"[7] . . . through involvement in the jihad to destroy Evil and establish the reign of the Good.

THE LUNEL PARADIGM

These same diverse ingredients were present in the small town of Lunel, located in the *département* of Hérault in southwestern France. In 2014, some members of the media started calling it the "capital of French jihad" because six men from there had died in Syria—a tenth of all the French jihadists who died that year (the fatalities more than doubled in 2015, and by the time of this writing in 2016, two additional men from Lunel had died there). Moreover, about twenty Lunel residents left for Syria—the exact number is difficult to determine, because unlike the families of converted young people, who immediately report their children's disappearance to the authorities of a French state with which they identify, some parents of immigrant origin remain silent in order to avoid disapproval or because they regard the infidel state with suspicion, fear, or indifference and do not want to attract its attention.[8]

---

[7] *Changer la vie*—a motto of the May 1968 movement and its aftermath, a quotation from the French 19th century poet Arthur Rimbaud.

[8] Since March 2014, a toll-free phone number set up by a social service branch of the French state (the Comité interministériel de prévention de la délinquance, or CIPD) for reporting cases of "radicalization" has received a disproportionate number of calls from the families of converts.

Because only about twenty-five thousand people live in Lunel, the proportion of jihadists who left for Syria suddenly became the highest in France in 2014 (the following year, it was overtaken by Trappes, a city of equivalent size in the *département* of Yvelines, near Paris, whence there were more than eighty departures). In addition to the media hype, which brought dozens of journalists from all over the world to this commune locally known mainly for its Muscat wine, for its bullfights, and, among scholars, for the cultural influence of its medieval Jewish community, the case of Lunel is exemplary of the motifs and processes through which jihadism attracts young French people from various origins.

Located about twenty kilometers from Montpellier and from Nîmes, the region's two main labor pools, Lunel shared the economic decline of the rest of the wine-producing southwest, of which Béziers offers another striking example. (In 2014 the citizens of Béziers elected as its mayor the far-right politician Robert Ménard, a noted journalist and former founder of "Reporters without Borders," who received the support of the National Front.) Lunel's economic decline led to a fall in real estate prices, a deterioration of its downtown, and a subsequent attraction into the area of destitute people with immigrant backgrounds, along with problems of crime and drug dealing. Local politicians and business leaders have responded to these circumstances by attempting to turn the banlieue of Lunel into an affordable bedroom community for Montpellier and Nîmes.

The population of Lunel has tripled over the last thirty years, and a second town, consisting of tracts of residential subdivisions, a few low-cost housing projects surrounded by greenery and industrial zones, and shopping centers amid enormous parking lots, was built alongside the old city, which has retained, in its round shape, the trace of its ancient ramparts. Recent immigrants are among many of the newcomers—12 percent, according to an agency of the French state responsible for the collection and dissemination of economic statistics.[9] Taking all nationalities together, the head of the local mosque has estimated that six thousand Muslims live in the city, for about a quarter of the total population. (For his part, the prefect of the region estimates that the population of North African origin represents a quarter to a third of the city total.)

This growing town with a birthrate above the national average nonetheless remains the twelfth-poorest commune in France. It has an

---

[9] INSEE.

unemployment rate of nearly 40 percent for young people from immigrant backgrounds, according to the head of the local youth cultural center (the Maison des jeunes et de la culture, or MJC), who has long served as their contact person and who himself comes from their ranks.

Lunel's unemployment situation affects not only the low-cost housing projects and the crumbling downtown area but also the residential area subdivisions. Residents' limited prospects for social mobility have led to disillusionment and the sort of deprivation that sociologists since Tocqueville have seen as one of the chief sources of protest movements.

Culturally, Lunel is caught in a vise. The nearby Montpellier metropolitan area, energized by the economic development initiatives of its former mayor, Georges Frêche, has drained the rest of the *département* of Hérault, and even the whole surrounding region of Languedoc, of its economic vitality. Lunel's educated classes—not only long-standing residents but also the children of immigrants who have completed their education—take advantage of the good train connections with Montpellier to move there. Having left Algeria along with many *pieds-noirs* in the wake of independence, North African immigrants, of whom today's *chibanis* (elders in Arabic) are the survivors, work in wine grape growing and market gardening. At first, they were migrant workers, but then they settled down and brought their wives, with whom they had children born on French soil.

Starting in the 1970s, Moroccans supplanted Algerians in the world of French agriculture. In the course of that decade, a large number of immigrants from Tiflet, a small Berber town not far from Rabat, began to settle in Lunel. Tiflet, known locally for its *souk* and its *pétanque* bowling tournaments as well as its cultural isolation and poverty, was also the site of a police roundup that took place in May 2012, revealing the presence of arms caches belonging to an Islamo-terrorist network. (Since 2010 Tiflet has had a high-security prison in which about fifty jihadists are incarcerated, including some convicted in connection with attacks in Casablanca on May 16, 2003.)

By the first decade of this century, Lunel's old city center had fallen into decay. Over the years, the lack of maintenance resulted in more and more housing becoming unfit for human habitation. Shopkeepers deserted the core area for urban development zones on the outskirts of town and were replaced by indigent people from immigrant—largely Moroccan—backgrounds. The increase in crime, particularly burglaries and traffic in hashish from Morocco, was one of the main reasons for the defeat of the left and the election, in 2001, of the right-wing mayor Claude Arnaud, who began his third term in 2014. Arnaud significantly increased the number of municipal police officers and then tried to find interlocutors in the immigrant population in an attempt to end social conflict and restore public tranquility. Noting the divisions and rivalries between this community's different components, of which the local Harkis' vote for the far right was a sign, he concluded that the mosque was the most unifying authority.

In 1987, a Muslim place of worship was established in a dilapidated building on a Lunel street near the mayor's office. The association that managed it was a wing of Jama'at al-Tabligh (the Society for the Propagation of the Faith), an Islamic pietist movement that was particularly active in the 1980s, when it played an important role in the battle against drug addiction among young immigrants. It was, moreover, identified as such by some French municipalities that found themselves helpless to deal with a problem that was affecting groups with which they had no connection. In Lunel, Tabligh's followers approached drug users who were shooting up in the Jean-Hugo park, in the city center, and tried to get them to stop using drugs by encouraging them to embrace a strict Muslim identity that would provide structure to their lives.[10]

Founded in India in 1927, Tabligh initially sought to preserve the Islamic identity of the politically vulnerable Muslim minority in the Hindu-dominated subcontinent. Worried about the adulteration of the faith in contact with a massively non-Muslim environment and without the coercive power of the state behind it, Tabligh engaged in itinerant preaching to "revive Islam in the hearts of the faithful."

Combining Sufi spirituality with the scriptural religion of the learned, Tabligh is known for its unceasing efforts to locate and save "lost" Muslims (and also, for the past half-century, for its proselytizing of non-Muslims). This mission work is a powerful socializing device in that the group's norms and values can be interiorized only in the framework of a community of religious faith and practice that serves to guide each act in everyday life. The movement likes to quote an Arab proverb according to which "the wolf [the incarnation of Evil] eats only the lamb he finds all alone."

Tabligh's missionizing field trips missions last from a single weekend to forty days or longer and are conducted by teams composed of both neophytes and confirmed sect members who are led by an "emir."

---

[10] I noted this phenomenon in my book *Les Banlieues de l'Islam* (Seuil, 1987), which appeared at the same time as the establishment of the first Muslim place of worship in Lunel.

Carried out on foot as much as possible, they allow the movement to literally "enmesh" the whole world. Today, Tabligh is the Islamic network that has the most followers worldwide, and its annual meetings at its headquarters in Raiwind, Pakistan, not far from Lahore, attract millions of people. In France from the 1970s on, it has played the leading role in the Islamization of Muslim immigrants and their children and has provided religious supervision for most of the main prayer centers.

This is the case in Lunel, where a new and bigger mosque was built on the outskirts of town between 2006 and 2010. Situated on a large tract of land in an industrial zone surrounded by parking lots, at the traffic circle named after Charles de Gaulle's famous appeal to the French nation of June 18, 1940,[11] and next to an equipment rental business and a Quick fast-food restaurant, the el-Baraka (Divine Blessing) mosque was inaugurated with great ceremony and in the presence of the mayor in late October 2010. It had been financed, according to some of those responsible for it, by contributions made by area Muslims, and it benefited by the volunteer work provided by members of the community in the construction industry.

The spacious new mosque could accommodate worshipers without causing the crowding and traffic congestion problems associated with the previous house of worship in the town center. But while the increased space solved one problem, it created another for the mosque's board of directors, which was ill equipped to supervise a large place of worship that attracted people from all over the region and that provided opportunities for proselytism by radical elements.

The growth of the local Muslim population in Lunel went in tandem with increased polarization between two communities that spoke little to each other. On the one side, the local immigrant Muslims were becoming increasingly identified with Islamist orthodoxy. On the other side, local non-Muslim residents responded by reasserting a regional identity as Pescalunes ("moon fishermen," in the local dialect), a name associated with an ancient poetic legend about a Lunel fisherman who tried to fish for the moon with a broken net.

The Pescalune identity is also associated with the culture of bullfighting that has been part of life in the adjacent Rhone delta region of Camargue for centuries. Advertisements for the annual

---

[11] De Gaulle's call to French resistance against the Nazi occupation, broadcast from London in June 1940, was a landmark moment in the history of French nationalism.

mid-July Pescalune Festival celebrate the pleasures of both *bouvine*, or Camargue-style bullfighting, and Muscat, a regional sweet wine. This annual celebration of animal and alcohol is anathema to "total" Islam, which regards such a festival as impious and pagan.

On one side of the physical and mental barrier between the two Lunels, in the heart of the medieval city, there is a shop for aficionados of Camargue-style bullfighting. It sells rosettes, tassels, and strings— all of which are attached to the forehead of the bull and which the *raséteurs* (the local-style *toreros*) have to try to pull off, using trickery to avoid being gored. The show takes place in the nearby arena, and the crowd mostly includes Pescalunes and tourists (even though the majority of the most famous *raséteurs* are now young North Africans).

On the other side, a stone's throw away, an Islamic dress shop sells veils, hijabs and niqabs, and concealing gloves for women of all ages. Socioreligious pressure has made the wearing of the veil by women from Muslim immigrant backgrounds ubiquitous. This shop is located on rue Sadi-Carnot, a street named after a French president assassinated by an anarchist in 1894. The street name is sometimes pronounced "Sidi Carnot"[12] by some of the recent immigrants, a pronunciation taken up ironically by locals unhappy with their presence.

This same street leads to the Place des Caladons, the arcades of which date back to the thirteenth century and are ornamented with the cross of the Templars, a symbol of a Christian order that played a major role in the Crusades. This square marks the border with the Muslim neighborhood. When entering the main square of the Place des Caladons, one finds oneself staring down the barrel of a pistol brandished by a bronze figure on a pedestal. It is the statue of Lunel's native son, Captain Charles Ménard, killed in combat in 1892 at the age of thirty-one during a French attack on the village of Seguela, in modern-day Ivory Coast.[13]

The bronze statue, a realistic and passionate work by the sculptor Auguste Maillard, a pupil of Bourdelle, presents the young captain a few moments before his death. His colonial helmet has fallen to the

---

[12] In North-African Arabic, "Sidi" is an honorific equivalent to "Sir."

[13] Captain Ménard's forces were defeated by those led by Samory Touré, one of the leading figures of the resistance to France's colonial expansion in West Africa and the founder of the Muslim empire of Wassoulou. He is still celebrated as the "Almamy," a shortened version of the Arabic expression *amir al mou'minin* (commander of the faithful). The famous reggae singer from Ivory Coast Alpha Blondy dedicated his hit song "Bory Samory" to Touré.

ground, at the foot of a cactus; his sword is at his side. In a final but desperate effort, he is pointing his pistol toward an imagined adversary about to kill him. (The statue is positioned such that Ménard's weapon is pointed toward the present Muslim neighborhood of Lunel. City officials moved it several times in the last century before it found its final site in this symbolic place.) On the base of the statue, there is a bas-relief representing an allegory of "Colonial France": Marianne, also wearing the colonial helmet, lands on a shore, holding out flowers in one hand and broken chains in the other, an allusion to the abolition of slavery (which at that time of the statue's erection in the late nineteenth century still existed in the Wassoulou Empire of West Africa).

The first round of voting in the spring 2015 regional elections took place after a spate of national press reports that portrayed Lunel as the "capital of French jihad," to the dismay of municipal officials and most of its residents. In the canton of Lunel, the candidates of the National Front received the most support: 41.59 percent of the votes (with a voter turnout of 52 percent, the residents of the North African immigrant neighborhoods having largely abstained from voting). The far-right party thus surpassed its score in Lunel in the May 2014 European elections, in which it had finished on top with 37.88 percent.

At the municipal level, however, the National Front has not succeeded in capturing the Lunel mayoralty. Since 2001 Claude Arnaud has led a list of diverse right-wing candidates that have consistently prevailed over the NF, and this despite the NF's ceaseless efforts to exploit public safety issues for political gain. These issues are not of the far right's invention. In Lunel, the rate of burglary is 8.32 percent, much higher than the national average of 2.7 percent, and the rate of assault is 7.84 percent. In 2015 a magistrate in Montpellier told the Paris newspaper *Libération* that "on average, each week a young person from Lunel ends up in prison for burglary, drug-dealing, or repeatedly driving without a license. When the only response is judicial, all this creates a very propitious seedbed for all kinds of extremism."

Many local residents have pointed to the absence of networks that could promote social contact between the diverse groups in Lunel. The same mayor who inaugurated the mosque in October 2010 closed the local Youth and Culture House in the summer of 2015. The one remaining site where those of different races and ethnicities come together under the aegis of secularism is Louis-Feuillade High School, located near the low-income housing project of Abrivados, where many of those who left for jihad in Syria lived. Run by a dynamic team of instructors, it is one of the rare places in the town where young women from Muslim immigrant backgrounds do not wear the veil, due to the restrictions imposed by the 2004 law prohibiting the wearing of religious signs in public schools. But there as elsewhere, many Muslim students have stopped eating in the school cafeteria, which is not halal. And when a "philosophical café" was organized to exchange views and lessen social tensions after the jihadist attacks of January 2015, a few students, like those in many other schools, posted the Twitter hashtag #jesuisCoulibaly to their Twitter accounts—a gesture of solidarity with one of the January 2015 jihadist assassins, Amedy Coulibaly—in response to the popular hashtag #jesuisCharlie.

As we have seen, the form of Islam practiced in Lunel was strongly influenced by the Tabligh movement. But here as elsewhere, the movement's proclaimed apolitical nature and its willingness to enter into dialogue with the authorities diminished its stature in the eyes of those who wanted to do battle with "disbelief" in the name of a strict and all-encompassing understanding of Islam. Such believers in "total" Islam considered Tabligh's pietism an unacceptable compromise. Whereas the Muslim Brothers have always found Tabligh useful as a reservoir from which to recruit followers who were already religiously "awakened," the Salafists are more inclined to see Tabligh as a rival and have set about stigmatizing it in their online sermons. Certain well-known Saudi Salafist scholars issued online fatwas condemning Tabligh's followers to Hell in the beyond and to death in this world, and the movement's reputation suffered as a result, particularly among the younger generation of French Muslims, who have supplemented their education in "infidel" public schools with this form of online instruction.

The impact of Tabligh's all-encompassing approach to religion on young people and its complicated relationship to jihadism can best be seen in the case of Houssem and his friend Raphaël. Houssem, born in France of a Tunisian family with three sons, was mostly brought up by his pious father, an employee of a security company, after his mother died suddenly when he was very young. It was Tabligh that helped Houssem as an adolescent to overcome this family tragedy and that dissuaded him from the petty crime into which he was sometimes tempted. In Louis-Feuillade High School, he had a friend named Raphaël whose father was of Moroccan Jewish origin. Raphaël lived in the residential area near the school, a stone's throw from the Abrivados housing project where Houssem resided. Raphaël, impressed by the way Tabligh took care of his friend and going through a phase of doubt as he came of age, embraced Houssem's consoling Islam in early 2010.

To the stupefaction of Raphaël's parents—his father is a computer scientist and his mother a psychologist—with whom he lived as a pampered only child in a house in one of the town's new developments, this athlete and guitarist who loved Led Zeppelin abandoned all the "profane" activities in which he seemed to be flourishing, his studies excepted. Raphaël resumed these after a period during which he assiduously attended the el-Baraka mosque, dedicating himself to his new faith with all the zeal of a neophyte.

In a town where the communities were so separate, the closed life of the local Pescalunes held no attraction for a young man like him, who was casting about for an identity. The Islamic proselytism of the Tabligh movement spoke to him. It brought this foreigner whose Jewish family was originally from Morocco into the Islamic culture of those who had, like him, come from North Africa.

Raphaël slowly gravitated toward jihadism over a four-year period by getting involved with a series of Islamic "humanitarian organizations" that encouraged him to volunteer abroad and fight for the cause of the Islamic State. At first raising funds to dig wells in the Sahel, he later joined a more militant group, the Wake Up Project, which fronted the money he needed to travel to Syria. (He reimbursed the group via his PayPal account.) On July 9, 2014, about ten days after ISIS's proclamation of the caliphate in Mosul, Iraq, he was invited by an older Islamist serving as his "guru" to read an ISIS communique in French translation (Raphaël did not read Arabic, despite his efforts at the mosque). It was a message justifying the Syrian jihad from the spokesman for the new "Islamic State," Sheikh Abu Mohamed al-Adnani, the nom de guerre of the Syrian Taha Subhi Falaha, born around 1978 and a veteran of the jihad in Iraq since 2003. Raphaël, replying to his guru's e-mail, included the following laudatory commentary:

Now that the caliphate has been established and that sharia is applied, there reigns a stability like that in the city of Raqqa where the brothers live who have left and whom we know [here he refers to his friend and mentor in Islam, Houssem and, more generally, to the first group of young people from Lunel who left for Syria]. In this city, the brothers and sisters can study. Some people have emigrated to obey Allah *Wa ta'âla* [the Highest—the transcription of the Arabic is faulty] and benefit the community by their knowledge, their scientific or religious knowledge. The state pays each resident a share, which means that no one is harmed and that they do not experience poverty. People don't ask: "But what if I have three or four children, how can I feed them?" Or say "I can't find work and no one wants to give me any because my name is Abdallah." The shops are closed all day on Fridays. The sale of tobacco, alcohol, and any form of illicit substance has been forbidden and destroyed.

This utopian description of a radiant Islamic life under ISIS clearly assumes that all problems of unemployment and discrimination faced by the young Muslims of Lunel can be resolved in a majority Muslim land that strictly applies Islamic religious law. It was Raphaël's last written testimony and was striking evidence of the extent of the young man's indoctrination.

After a final interview with his guru on July 21, 2014, Raphaël flew from Barcelona to Istanbul in the company of Sabri, Houssem's younger brother. (Houssem had left for the jihad a year earlier with his wife, Maeva, also a recent convert.) They were headed for the Syrian border, where another boy from Lunel was waiting to take them into the "caliphate." It was only after he arrived in Turkey that Raphaël notified his mother, reassuring her that the motives for his emigration were strictly humanitarian. Raphaël, Houssem, and Houssem's brother Sabri all were killed in the ranks of ISIS during a bombardment near the Syrian city of Deir ez-Zor in October 2014.

Raphaël's fate was especially perplexing in that his father's religion was Judaism, whereas the milieu into which he was gradually drawn was drenched in hatred of Israel and in many cases marked by a visceral anti-Semitism. And it was particularly ironic that his fate unfolded in Lunel, a town once nicknamed "Little Jerusalem" because of its importance in medieval times as a center for Jewish philosophy. It was in Lunel that Samuel ibn Tibbon translated Maimonides's *Guide for the Perplexed* from Arabic into Hebrew in the early thirteenth century. Scion of a family that had come from Andalusia to Lunel two centuries earlier, and perhaps the best Arabist in the territory that was to become France, Ibn Tibbon made possible the entrance of the first great Jewish philosophical work into European culture. (Later translated from its Hebrew version into Latin, the *Guide* became famous for a rationalism that is still controversial and even condemned by the most orthodox rabbis, who remain as attached to the letter of the sacred Jewish scriptures as are the Salafists in the Muslim tradition.)

The Tabligh movement has not been the only Islamist group present in Lunel and in the triangle that that town forms with Montpellier and Nîmes. Other Islamist organizations have contributed to the establishment of a milieu favorable to ISIS. In addition to the emigrant branches of most of the Moroccan Islamist movements—nationals and natives of Morocco constitute the majority of North Africans between the Petit-Rhône River and the Atlantic coast—the Montpellier area has also received activists of the Algerian GIA who took refuge there after their defeat in the civil war of the 1990s. These groups have extended their networks into mosques where supervision is lax. The great mosque of Lunel, inaugurated (as we have seen) at the end of October 2010, a few months after Raphaël's conversion, has been an ideal venue for proselytizing. Although Tabligh remains influential there, the size of the buildings and the crowds of worshipers make monitoring difficult. As in the "Stalingrad" mosque in Paris, in which Farid Benyettou recruited the future followers of the "Buttes-Chaumont park gang" a few years earlier, more militant conceptions of the faith made themselves heard in Lunel— if not from the imam's pulpit, then throughout the prayer facility, where groups gather before and after prayer around preachers/recruiters.

In Lunel as elsewhere, "Islamophobia" has become a convenient label for all perceived discrimination. In a social context in which many young Muslims with college degrees seeking work have considered themselves at a disadvantage relative to their "Gallic" counterparts with similar qualifications, Islamophobia has served as a convenient explanation, providing both an outlet for frustration and a cause. "I did a BTS [a two-year degree from a technical college] in accounting, and when we finished, all the native French people found jobs and the only two Arabs in the class did not," Hamza, Houssem and Sabri's elder brother, told investigators after he was arrested on January 27, 2015, on suspicion of having organized the networks for going to Syria, and then indicted for "associating with criminals planning terrorist activity."

The Islamophobia mantra and the victim mentality it reinforces makes it possible to rationalize a total rejection of France and a commitment to jihad by making a connection between unemployment, discrimination, and French republican values. The emphasis on Islamophobia also serves to rule out of bounds all critical reflection on Islam and to excuse any enterprise undertaken in its name, including the form of Islamic humanitarian activity that eventually led Raphael and many other young people to armed jihad. In this sense, Islamists use the term "Islamophobia" in the same way that right-wing Zionists attempt to use the term "anti-Semitism" to prohibit any criticism of the Israeli government and its treatment of the Palestinian people under its military rule.

This sort of reasoning was expressed bluntly in the remarks made by Lahoucine Goumri, president of the Lunel mosque's association. He had been strongly urged by the mayor, who was worried about his town's reputation, to make a statement about the departure of twenty young Lunel residents for Syria and the death of six of them. (One of those killed had been the son of the former president of the mosque.) The mayor, who had inaugurated the mosque four years earlier as a symbol of peaceful coexistence, now had to face the concerns of voters as support for the National Front in Lunel increased from 37 percent to 41 percent between the 2014 European elections and the 2015 municipal elections.

Goumri's much-awaited statement sent a shock wave through the town. The mosque president, who had long participated in the missionary outreach organized by Tabligh, had in recent years distanced himself from the movement's traditional inclination to seek out compromises with governments. Goumri was less interested in joining with Mayor Claude Arnaud to reduce social conflicts and cleavages than in maintaining a tight solidarity with members of his own religious community—an orientation undoubtedly shared by others in the mosque. Moreover, his statement was marked by the kind of argumentation that is characteristic of the "Islamophobia blame game."

Lahoucine Goumri's statement, made on December 13, 2014, three weeks before the *Charlie Hebdo* and Hyper Casher attacks in Paris, began with a response to an invitation to comment about why so many of the local youths who had left for the Syrian jihad had been regulars at his mosque. Goumri remarked that

> the mosque has nothing to do with all these departures. They are individual departures. They never connected with the imam or the mosque. The Muslims who come to the mosque are from Lunel, and there is no problem in Lunel. There is a problem 6,000 kilometers from here, and we don't want to bring it back here to Lunel.

The imam of the Bellefontaine mosque in Le Mirail, where Mohamed Merah and most of the local jihadists were regulars, Mamadou Daffé, told the same story. This sort of response to the authorities' insistent demand that mosque leaders denounce the participation of congregants in violent jihad reveals the extent of the gap between these congregations and a broader society in which there is a general consensus that jihadism is equivalent to terrorism. Once again, Goumri:

> It's their choice. It's not for me to judge them. Only God will judge them. If we have to condemn something, we have to condemn that which is condemnable. Why condemn these young people who left

in the name of an injustice in Syria and not the French people who left and who killed Palestinian babies with Tsahal [the Israeli army] last summer? Why would a mosque condemn, while other religions do not? [...] I don't see why I should issue a statement if ten persons left out of six thousand Muslims, or 0.04 percent [in reality, 1.7 percent if we use his estimates, and double that if we consider the most likely number of actual departures]? The other young people are not leaving. Why should I speak to the young? Not all the Lunel residents are involved in the Syrian madness.

From the outset, the president of the mosque refused to issue the condemnation that the authorities expected from him. He could not be counted on to associate his former congregants turned jihadis with terrorism in order to dissuade their co-religionists from emulating them. He would not do this, neither in his own name nor in the name of Islam—a persuasive register to which France's secular institutions and elected officials cannot resort. He thought it "their choice" and understood that they believed they could repair an "injustice"—namely, the repression being conducted by Bashar al-Assad's regime.

At this point in his statement, having produced the scandalous effect he sought (which elicited vehement reactions that led him to make a half-hearted recantation in a communiqué that appeared the following day), Goumri first elaborated a comparison between Muslims and Jews. Nothing forced him to denounce the young people who had enrolled in the jihad (provided that they were blameworthy) insofar as no one was asking Jewish institutions to condemn French Jews who joined the Israeli army in the summer of 2014, and all the more because they could not claim to be righting an "injustice," since they went "to kill Palestinian babies."

Here we have reached the heart of an Islamist line of argument that pitches Islamophobia against anti-Semitism and that challenges, *mezza voce*, the "double standard" that benefits Jews and disadvantages Muslims. This kind of reasoning is very common not only in the Muslim milieu but also among North African immigrants in general and, beyond them, in a part of French society in which, as we shall see in the following chapter, sympathies with one side or the other in the Israel-Palestine conflict divide public opinion into two approximately equal parts.

The second part of Goumri's argument stems from his observation that only a tiny proportion of the Muslim residents of Lunel have left for Syria and thus the mosque need not make a public statement, lest that amount to casting suspicion on all Muslims because of the actions of a very few. This "refusal to be lumped together" is a common Islamist response to this situation, as is the resort to statistics that tends to minimize the phenomenon—despite the fact that six congregants from the el-Baraka mosque had already died on the jihad battlefield.

In support of his refusal to condemn those who left for jihad on ethical-religious lines, Lahoucine Goumri evoked Raphaël's words, before his death, about the happiness of life in Raqqa. He mentioned in particular the situation of the young Maeva, who had converted and become Houssem's wife and then his widow and the mother of a child born in Syria:

> She no longer has any family here. Her parents threw her out when she converted. Over there, she will receive a widow's pension. Come back? Come back for what? Maybe she doesn't see how she would live better in France. No doubt her true family is over there, among Muslims.

In conclusion, he suggested that if anyone were to be blamed, it should be the president of the Republic:

> The biggest jihadist recruiter is François Hollande! In my opinion, these young people have been pushed to leave ever since March 2011, when François Hollande said that Bashar al-Assad is a butcher and a criminal. These young people left to fight an injustice. They have been bombarded by videos on the Internet. They have seen horrible videos. They have not accepted all that.

Calling the head of state the "biggest jihadist recruiter" aroused indignation and strong official reaction, but this provocation, simultaneously clumsy and too clever, reminded people that the president's office and the government had indeed early on favored the overthrow of the Syrian regime as a precondition for any solution of the conflict. The government's early position seemed to be encapsulated by Jean-Pierre Filiu, an ex-diplomat and politically *engagé* "historian" of the Middle East, who had the ear of President Hollande and his prime minister. Filiu's article in *Le Monde* on April 2, 2013, was entitled "Syria is our Spanish Civil War." Since the government did not follow up its strong rhetorical stance against Assad with any effective political or military action, the young French jihadists may have been encouraged to imagine themselves in a position similar to that of the International

Brigades of the 1930s. The jihadists in this analogy rushed into the breach, taking the battle to Assad in the absence of effective French state action just as the brigades had made up for the failure of the French Popular Front government in the late 1930s by going to fight General Franco.

In the weeks that followed Goumri's remarks, elections were held in the mosque's managing association that began a long period of internal crisis. The new president, a halal butcher born in Tiflet, appointed as his spokesman a loquacious director of a driving school, the brother of the next-to-last president. That spokesman was forced to resign after he participated, at the invitation of the district's Member of Parliament, the socialist Patrick Vignal, in a meeting held on February 25, 2015, in the neighboring village of Saint-Just. At this meeting, Vignal, accompanied by the rector of the Muslim Institute of the Great Mosque of Paris, Dalil Boubakeur, and a master of the Languedoc region chapter of the Masonic Grand Lodge of France—wearing his ceremonial apron in a hall where Freemasons had gathered in large numbers—called for brotherhood against terrorism. The hatred of freemasonry is extreme in the Islamist movement, and the pressure of a number of activists on the mosque's spokesman prevented him from continuing his work.

In March 2015, the Moroccan, non-francophone imam of the Lunel mosque finally decided, in response to many requests, to criticize from the pulpit the departure for jihad in Syria. This earned him death threats from other activists, some of whom had serious criminal records. In an interview with the newspaper *Midi libre*, one of these activists, speaking in the name of "French Islam," claimed that the imam's inability to speak French prevented him from understanding young people who had been born in France and who spoke only French. By the fall of that year, the imam was forced to resign after a stormy assembly meeting of his congregation during which he was accused of treachery with the *gaouris* (French, literally "non-Muslims"). This left the mosque association without a leader on the occasion of the Eid al-Kebir (Festival of Sacrifice) holiday, September 14, 2015, which took place in a particularly tense atmosphere. In mid-September, the court had handed down heavy sentences to the men who had threatened the imam. The sentences were suspended, but the men were forbidden to frequent the mosque. The imam left for the pilgrimage to Mecca, informing people that he would no longer exercise his ministry. He was replaced by an interim imam, also from Morocco, who held the position while shuttling back and forth between the two countries.

In 2015, Lunel was largely supplanted as the main French takeoff point for the Syrian jihad by the Parisian banlieue of Trappes, which had a comparable population but four times as many departures. Despite having lost this dubious honor, Lunel remains a useful case for understanding the genesis of contemporary French jihad.

THE ESCHATOLOGY OF JIHAD AND PSYCHOLOGICAL WAR

On March 26, 2011, in the first days of the rebellion against Bashar al-Assad's government in Syria, an eighteen-page booklet appeared online that had been written by Husayn ibn Mahmud, a Salafist sheikh who was famous in the "jihadosphere." Translated into rather good French under the title "Damas, la base du djihad sur terre" ("Damascus, the Base of Jihad on Earth"), it was posted online by the main francophone Salafist jihadist site *Ansar-alhaqq (The Companions of the Truth)* and was still accessible at the time of this writing.

The text gathers together narratives and advice for the departure to Syria and is part of a body of propagandistic prose that is now of considerable size and generally rendered from the Arabic by young, educated amateur translators. The level of written French on Salafist sites has noticeably improved in the course of a decade, thanks to the increasing numbers of motivated converts who have learned the Prophet's language by passing through the madrasas of Egypt and Yemen, as well as to the young bilingual college-educated North Africans who have gotten involved in francophone jihad.

Romain Letellier, an unemployed young man of twenty-six from Normandy who lives on welfare, is the aforementioned Salafist website's chief moderator. Born into an atheistic communist family, he converted at the age of twenty and henceforth called himself Abu Siyad al-Normandy. He was arrested in September 2013 and six months later was sentenced to a year in prison for "justifying acts of terrorism" and "provoking the commission of terrorist acts." He was accused of having posted on *Ansar-alhaqq* a translation of two issues of the anglophone online magazine *Inspire*, founded in July 2010 by the American-Yemeni jihadist Anwar al-Awlaki. Articles in these magazines called for "bloodying the heads of unbelief" and justified the "marvelous operation at the Boston Marathon" on April 15, 2013. With its three dead and 254 wounded, it was described as a "perfect example of investment at low cost" in line with the modus operandi of third-generation network-based jihadism.

According to the court, *Ansar-alhaqq*, which appears in most of the files on "self-radicalization," has more than four thousand subscribers who have exchanged a hundred thousand messages. It was through this efficient channel that Ibn Mahmud's writings reached francophone jihadists on the Web, providing them with arguments for dropping everything and joining the jihad in Syria—arguments that were presented as both irrefutable with regard to Islam's sacred texts and politically rational. Part of this text consists of a collection of the Prophet's hadiths extolling the "country of Sham" from an eschatological perspective. The latter is carried through jihad and ends up, beyond martyrdom, at the Hour of the end of time and the triumph of Islam on Earth. The second part concentrates its attacks on the impiety of the syncretic Alawite religious sect in Syria and calls for its extermination.

In the Islamic tradition, the mystique of Sham covers a vast spectrum whose usual French or English translation, "Levant," does not render its whole semantic and symbolic amplitude. In the ancient cosmography of Islam, organized along an east-west axis of which Mecca is the center, Sham, or "Greater Syria," designates the left or north (*shamal*), and Yemen designates the right or south (*yamin*). It is this sacred geography, and not the modern cleavage between Orient and Occident, that provides the Salafists' orthonormal reference points. For those who excitedly discover this cosmology on the Internet, be they recent converts or Muslims by birth who have been initiated into Islamist doctrine and who are eager for jihadist action, Sham presents a matchless attraction as the site of the decisive battle that will allow the universal triumph of Islam on Earth.

The departure for Syria to engage in jihad and undergo martyrdom there is the natural and concrete sequel of their virtual indoctrination. Other privileged destinations, such as Libya, which is after all an important geopolitical and military relay point for jihad against Europe, cannot rival it in terms of messianic expectation. The "Greater Syria" of Sham is the zone that extends from the lonely deserts of Iraq and Syria to the Mediterranean and that includes the territories of the modern states of Syria, Lebanon, Palestine-Israel, and Jordan. But the Arabic term also designates by metonymy the capital of this enormous symbolic region, the city of Damascus. Although standard written Arabic calls this city Dimashq, from which the French adjective *damasquiné* (English "damasked") is derived, together with the English "Damascus," ancient usage and the local dialect prefer instead the expression "Ash Sham" ("the Sham"). For French Salafist jihadists who have been only superficially Arabized, jihad, in the cities and countrysides from Aleppo to Homs, from Idlib to Raqqa and to Palmyra—where most of them were deployed in summer 2015—will acquire its full meaning only once Damascus has fallen into their hands, triggering the final apocalypse from which will emerge, after endless massacres, the worldwide triumph of Islam.

That is the message of Ibn Mahmud, made accessible through the *Ansar-alhaqq* forum for French neophyte jihadists, whose knowledge of Islamic history is normally so slight that they are inclined to take literally the quotations the author makes out of context and then to put them in action, making his short treatise a kind of vademecum. Its first six pages consist of a collection of the Prophet's hadiths. Arranged in a crescendo, they begin by praising the emigration of jihad to Sham and end with the eschatological promises opened up by the fall of Damascus.

A section entitled "The elite of warriors on the surface of the globe" introduces the reader to the sanctification of the battle in Syria by the Prophet himself. The hadith is reported by one of his companions, Abdullah ibn Hawalah, and, as is the custom in the transcription of Islam's Scriptures, people's names are followed by Arabic calligraphy (not translated by *Ansar-alhaqq*) that indicates that their remarks are sacred:

> You shall be led to raise armies: an army for Sham, an army for Iraq, then an army for Yemen. Then 'Abdullah said: "Choose one of them for me, O messenger of Allah!" Then he said: "Go back to Sham. And if anyone is not capable of that, let him go then to Yemen. For Allah the All-Powerful and Majestic has promised me the region of Sham and its people."

The land of knowledge and faith, Sham is also where the resurrection will take place on Judgment Day. "When the period of troubles comes, Belief will be in Sham," another hadith explains:

> At the end of time a fire shall rise up from Hadramawt [Hadramaut, now in southern Yemen, which was plunged into civil war between Shiites and Sunnis and fell under jihadist control in spring 2015], making all the people of that time unite. The Companions asked: "What do you command us to do, then, at this moment, O Messenger of Allah?" He replied: "Go to Sham."

A similar situation can only further increase the urgent necessity of beginning the emigration (hegira) to that country, especially since the peoples already there will suffer the wrath of Allah, who will consume them in fire along with monkeys and pigs:

> There will be a hegira [emigration] after the Hegira [the Prophet's original hegira from Mecca to Medina in 622], and the best people all over the world will then be those who will follow the Hegira that was that of Ibrahim (to Sham), and then there will remain on the face of the Earth the worst of its inhabitants, who will be driven out of their own lands.

The first part of the pamphlet ends with a reminder of the scenario of the end of time and the advent of the Hour, which will take place in Sham. The battle will begin in Dabiq, where the infidel armies and the Muslim armies will confront one another. In the Islamic Scriptures, these impious armies of Byzantium are those called "Roman," or *roum*, referring to the Roman Empire of the Orient, or designated by the metaphor *banou asfar* (sons of blonds), two terms that facilitate the identification of "infidels" with contemporary Europeans and Westerners.

A modest town now located between Aleppo and the border between Turkey and Syria, without any particular strategic importance, Dabiq fell under the control of ISIS in summer 2014, at the price of a large number of casualties in its own ranks, for the sole purpose of making sacred geography coincide with the battlefront. (ISIS would lose Dabiq to a coalition of Syrian rebels and Turkish special forces in October 2016.) The power of this symbol is recalled by the title *Dabiq* given to the English version of the ISIS "caliphate's" online magazine in summer 2014:

> The final hour will not come before the Romans have taken up positions at al-A'maq [a neighboring village] or in Dabiq. At that time an army composed of the elite fighters of the world will appear from Medina [to counterattack them]. [. . .] And the last third of the army shall be victorious; they shall not be further tested and they shall be the conquerors of Constantinople.

In Salafist thought, the conquest of Constantinople represents an ineluctable defeat of the West. According to al-Qaeda, the "blessed double raid" of September 11 was a continuation of the countless raids launched by Muslims against the capital of the Byzantine Empire until its final fall in 1453. In Ibn Mahmud's predictive narrative of the Syrian jihad, the terrestrial conquest undergirds an apocalyptic narrative.

It is in fact in Damascus that the "great massacre" that announces the Hour will be situated:

> The city of the Muslims on the day of the great confrontation [al-Malhamah] is located in a fertile oasis near a city called Damascus. On that day it will be the best of all places for Muslims.

This oasis, the Ghouta, was occupied by the rebels very early in the Syrian civil war, and in summer 2013, it was where the Assad government used chemical weapons to try to dislodge them. In 2015, it was ISIS's front-line position facing the capital, which was still held by the government forces and their Iranian and Shiite allies. From this point of view, the fall of Damascus would be seen in apocalyptic terms, Bashar al-Assad representing the *Dajjal*, the Islamic equivalent of the Antichrist, whose defeat will allow for the coming of the Hour:

> [The *Dajjal*] will emerge at the very moment that the Muslim troops form their ranks for combat. In all truth the hour of prayer will come, and it is at that moment that *'Issa ibnu Maryam 'Alayhi salâm* [Jesus son of Mary, may peace be on him] will descend to lead their prayer. On seeing him, the enemy of Allah will begin to melt away like salt in water. If *'Issa ibnu Maryam 'Alayhi salâm* left him [the enemy] that way he would be dissolved until dead, but Allah will make him perish at the hands of His messenger, who, after having killed him, will expose his blood to all, from the point of his lance.

The second part of the treatise returns to the present issues. If the people of Sham no longer benefit from Allah's bounties, that is because they have abandoned the path of jihad in favor of secular ideologies such as nationalism or Ba'athism. God has imposed on them "the worst elements of His creation: freemasons, Jews, and Christians. And the much hoped-for grandeur shall not return so long as the eternal banner of Islam is not yet held aloft." But the cause of all ills is the domination of the Alawite sect over the land of Sham.[14] After having adopted the Islamic polemical tradition with regard to the Alawites,

---

[14] Since the coming to power in Syria of Bashar al-Assad's late father, Hafez al-Assad, in 1970, the Syrian government has been dominated by a political elite composed largely of members of the Alawite sect.

a tradition notably illustrated by the famous thirteenth-century jurist Ibn Taymiyya, the spiritual father of Salafism and Saudi Wahhabism, Ibn Mahmud recommends the "final solution" against these "apostates more infidel than the Christians and the Jews."

Such a text explains what in our time the Syrian jihad offers to would-be jihadis based in France and elsewhere in the West, and we find an echo of it in the video made by Nicolas/Abu Abdel Rahman Bons. Ibn Mahmud situates himself in the direct line of a contemporary jihadist literature that defers to a canonical tradition with precise and incontestable references. He privileges literal readings and considers any effort at contextualization to be heresy or impiety. Out of a concern for efficiency, he wrote for an audience little versed in Islamic theology a treatise that is simultaneously easy to understand and in which the connection between prophetic injunctions and their execution is made in a didactic mode. As is customary in Salafist thought, his argument is based more on the Prophet's hadiths than on the Quran itself. In fact, the polysemy of the Quran, which was composed in an allegorical mode, opens the way to numerous interpretations that have maintained, over fifteen centuries of the history of Muslim civilization, a plurality of opinions. Inversely, the hadiths, to which the Salafists accord priority, are richer in explicit injunctions and close the path to interpretations of dogma.

In this respect Ibn Mahmud sheds light on the social crisis with which aspiring French jihadists are confronted and responds to their demand for meaning, of which we have one example in Raphaël's commentary on the proclamation of the caliphate in Mosul. Its most salient characteristic is the imposition of an intangible, sacrosanct norm, an indisputable response to the feeling of disorientation among the young people who go over to jihadism, no matter what their social background and ethnic origin. Through its many versions on the Internet and the captious seductions of a cyber-language that borrows from video games, television series, and cult films, this rhetoric produces a self-projection that systematically counters the anomie experienced by his readers in Lunel, as it does in such housing project neighborhoods as Le Mirail in Toulouse, L'Ariane in Nice, and L'Alma-Gare in Roubaix, among so many others. It is the doctrinal outcome of the deconstruction of a fallacious impiety and then of the edification, on dynamited ruins from Palmyra to Nimrod, of the Truth, a *parousia* of Islam through the Syrian jihad.

For third-generation jihadists and French people fed on Omar Omsen's *19 HH* and comparable grand narratives, the emigration to

Syria, elevated into a hegira to Sham, took on a polysemous dimension that fulfilled and federated diverse expectations. It immediately proceeded to carry out a "transvaluation of all values," to use the Nietzschean expression, which brings individuals uncomfortable in today's Western societies within a heroic process that leads to their individual redemption as well as the redemption of society. We have seen how the robber Mehdi Nemmouche, the son of a Harki, a "son of sin" and a convict, reversed, thanks to his stay in the land of Sham, all the stigma that had led him to prison.

Engagement in the Syrian jihad ultimately participates in two continuities. One, which is based on scriptural Islam, was abundantly used by Islamist authors to justify Hamas's suicide attacks against Israel, which are redescribed as "martyrdom operations." In a fatwa issued in 1996, the sheikh Youssef al-Qaradawi, the main international figure in the Muslim Brotherhood and the anchor of Al-Jazeera's flagship program "Sharia and Life," had exalted these operations as part of the "legitimate terrorism" (al irhab al machrou') that the Quran indicates in the words of the All-High: "And prepare against them [the infidels] whatever armament and horses on alert you can to terrorize the enemy of Allah and your own" (Surah 8, "Booty," verse 40). This very well-known verse has become the justification for the all-out "psychological war" being waged by contemporary jihadism. 19 HH's mash-up provides its overall narrative environment, and Ibn Mahmud's treatise "Damascus, the Base of Jihad on Earth" represents its contemporary outcome.

Another justification for this jihadist psychological war situates it in two opposite worldviews that come together to challenge the world order dominated by the West. Far-right radicalism sees in it a victorious battle against "Zionism," while far-left radicalism sees in it a continuation of the "anti-imperialist resistance" of the last quarter of the twentieth century. Two eloquent examples of this occurred at the very moment that Lunel found itself in the spotlight: on the one hand, Marc-Édouard Nabe, an inflammatory polemicist who was a fellow traveler of the "conspiracy theorists" Soral and Dieudonné before renouncing them to become ISIS's sycophant, and on the other hand, Illich Ramírez Sánchez, universally known under his pseudonym Carlos, the perpetrator of numerous attacks connected with the defense of the Palestinian cause during the 1980s.

In December 2014, the first issue of Patience, a periodical written and edited by Marc-Édouard Nabe, was published. Claiming that he was following in the path of twentieth-century French novelist

Louis-Ferdinand Céline—including even the latter's anti-Semitic 1937 *Bagatelles pour un massacre* ("Trifles for a Massacre")—Nabe, a writer and musician, is the son of the Italian-Greek-Ottoman singer Marcel Zanini (the performer of the 1970 hit "Tu veux ou tu veux pas") and was also a cartoonist for *Hara-Kiri Hebdo* (the predecessor of *Charlie Hebdo*) when he was young. For a time, he was a neighbor of the novelist Michel Houellebecq, whose success he envied. Wanting to be the *enfant terrible* of a Parisian media-literary world that is supposed to have marginalized him because of his anti-Semitism, he moved closer to Soral's anti-Zionist movement before sharing in the latter's implosion. He then promised to write a big book denouncing the compromises that the Dieudosphère and Soral's *Égalité et réconciliation* had made with Iran and with Bashar al-Assad's Syria.

The cover of *Patience* features a provocative photomontage reproducing the image of the beheading of the American hostage James Foley by the Palestinian-Briton Abdel-Majed Abdel Bary, in which the executioner's head has been replaced by that of the author, while Dieudonné's face is substituted for that of the hostage, and Soral's effigy, dressed in an orange jumpsuit, appears in a cartouche. But apart from its contribution to the petty wars recurrent in this extreme-right milieu, this sixty-three-page publication is distinguished by a panegyric to ISIS written in Nabe's characteristically ornate and vulgar style.

Patience, in which Nabe combines in his usual way abjection, brilliance, attacks on the memory of the dead, and exaltation, testifies in its own way to the bridges built between a Salafism about which the author understands nothing and political causes of all kinds of which he is willing to make himself the spokesman provided they seem to him to oppose a "system" that has failed to recognize his talent. The text is illustrated by about fifty photographs, most of which show scenes of execution and throat-cutting that are almost pornographic in their fascination with graphic violence. They also include some "girlie" photos that Hervé Gourdel (a mountain guide from Nice who was decapitated in Kabylia in September 2014 by local followers of ISIS) published on his website. In so doing, Nabe wanted to mock Gourdel—despite the fact that the latter's beheading caused great anguish in France.

In December 2014, Houssem's elder brother, Hamza, a member of the Lunel jihad milieu who would be arrested at the end of the next month, sent Raphaël's family a JPEG file reproducing the first issue of *Patience*, from which he had deleted, in accord with Salafism's requirements, the unfortunate Gourdel's erotic photos. He was seeking to justify Raphaël's emigration to the land of Sham and "martyrdom" by borrowing the eloquent words of a "white man" and a non-Muslim whose rhetoric in favor of ISIS was not religious and to which he attributed a power of universal persuasion that went beyond Islamic milieus.

Hamza had marked one passage. In it, Nabe begins by adopting a tone vaguely resembling that of Victor Hugo celebrating the epic of Napoleon's Great Army, then makes an attempt at sociology in the manner of Pierre Bourdieu:

> One cannot imagine the variety of mujahideen, converts or not, natives or immigrants, who constitute this vast army on the march! What mixtures! The caliphate is a pool as rich as the Foreign Legion. Baghdadi gives foreigners $1,000 a month [much less, according to most testimonies], and there are twenty thousand of them: do the math. It's better than welfare. [. . .] That's what the media don't understand: there are idealists and adventurers. No brain-washing on Facebook will provide a satisfying explanation of the impulse that leads these hordes of young people to leave to break the bones of the bad Muslim and his accomplice the Yankee. [. . .] To be unable to understand that at the age of fifteen one can be an idealist is to underestimate youth itself!
>
> What officials and *conspis* [conspiracy theorists, the Soral-Dieudonné movement] have in common is that they never believe in the sincerity of an act. For system people, the jihadist is necessarily manipulated by terrorists, and for anti-system people, he is also manipulated, but by the Empire [a reference to Alain Soral's book that designates by this term the Americano-Zionist forces of Evil]. But it's simple: they have experienced idleness and humiliation in their sinister housing projects, their hopeless schools, their miserable jobs, and they want to escape, thanks to Allah, the sadness of living in a colony: [. . .] the Arabs are still colonized by the French, but this time not in Algeria: in France!

In this short passage, Nabe's prose (from which we edited out the most obscene parts) is congruent with Raphaël's idyllic view of life in Raqqa ten days before his fateful trip.

Although ISIS thus found echoes on the far-right end of the political spectrum, it nonetheless also hijacked, as we have seen in the case of the community of Artigat, a certain trend on the far left that sought to "change life" in utopian communes. But these connections are part of a subjective continuity and have been neither theorized nor claimed by the social actors concerned. In the same month, December 2014, shortly before the terrorist attacks in Paris on January 7, 2015, it fell to one of the principal figures of violent Leninist revolutionism to make this filiation explicit. Carlos, captured by the French secret service in Sudan in 1994, sentenced to life imprisonment, and then converted to Islam during his detention in the early years of the twenty-first century, sent me, from the penitentiary in Poissy—a city in the outskirts of Paris where he was serving his time—a seven-page handwrittten manuscript entitled "La guerre psychologique" ("Psychological Warfare") and dated December 15, two days after the statements made by the president of the mosque in Lunel:

> The Palestinian resistance use sacrifice attacks chiefly for their psychological impact on the Zionist invader and his allies. Hijacking airplanes and boats and taking hostages to attract media coverage are high art in psychological warfare that will keep the Palestinian cause in the spotlight, and at the same time fill the coffers of the Fedayeen's organizations. The jihadists have followed this line of psychological warfare with great success in the media. The decapitations now carried out openly by citizens of countries that are members of NATO, transmitted over the Internet, are a magisterial media coup with immense, unparalleled benefits: the recruitment of mujahideen from all over and an increase in donations from believers throughout the world. Now the imperialist states will be subjected to reprisal attacks within their borders against which they cannot defend themselves, leading them to indiscriminate repression which will multiply the recruitment of volunteers for jihad. Ineluctably, NATO forces will intervene directly on land, where the mujahideen will be waiting to die as they kill the invaders.

Certain passages in this text, which interweaves the leftist and Islamist vocabularies in a symbiosis that its author himself realized by converting to Islam, recall Abu Musab al-Suri's predictions and the political dynamics he envisaged for third-generation jihadism. It was written less than a month after ISIS broadcast a particularly striking video showing the execution of eighteen Syrian pilots who had been taken prisoner, a scene to which Carlos referred. The execution was carefully staged and carried out by jihadists acting with their faces uncovered.

The dread was especially great in France when it became clear that one of the executioners was none other than Maxime Hauchard, twenty-two, who now called himself Abu Abdallah al-Firansi ("the Frenchman"). He comes from Bosc-Roger-en-Roumois, a dismal village with a population of 3,200 in the *département* of Eure that is situated between a picturesque Norman *bocage* and the Sotteville-lès-Rouen industrial zone. A residential project built around an ancient center where a few traditional Norman houses survive has allowed the village's population to triple in thirty years. Housing mainly employees and supervisors who work in the surrounding factories, it has enormous supermarkets, a bus station, and pizzerias. It reminds one of the residential neighborhoods in Lunel or the suburbs of Toulouse where Raphaël and Nicolas/Abu Abdel Rahman Bons lived. Like the latter, Maxime, a nice young man from a solid family who was known for his kindness and who was always ready to repair mopeds, converted to Islam at the age of seventeen after having assiduously frequented the appropriate Internet sites and viewed the corresponding videos on social media networks.

Disappointed by an initial journey to Mauretania, where the Islam taught did not meet his requirements, and having viewed images of children who had been killed in the bombing by Bashar al-Assad's air force, he left for Istanbul in the summer of 2013 with a plane ticket for which he paid 170 euros, crossing without difficulty borders fenced with wire mesh and guarded by soldiers. During an interview carried out through Skype in July 2014 by a twenty-four-hour news channel, he stated, from his barracks in Raqqa, that ISIS paid him $30 per month (far from the sums Nabe imagined!) and that he was part of a group of about forty combatants. He also said that he had radicalized himself alone on the Internet, that he was engaging in jihad in order to make Allah's laws applied on earth, and that he was prepared to accept martyrdom for the cause.

On January 4, 2015, three days before the bloodbath at the offices of *Charlie Hebdo*, Maxime Hauchard presented himself in a Twitter thread under his real name, using as a photo the famous picture taken from the November 2014 video in which he appears as one of the executioners of the Syrian pilots. He exchanged premonitory tweets with his interlocutors, among them the editors of the newspaper *Le Monde*:

#MaximeHauchard. I keep informed about the political, economic, and social situation in France the better to prepare the counterattack [. . .]. The French state must know that the war will not always take place in Muslim countries [. . .]. Thus one day you have to expect that it will be the Islamic army that enters France. And you will have well deserved it.

5

THE REVERSALS OF THE MUSLIM VOTE

The election of François Hollande in spring 2012 changed the political dynamics of France. If the intense distrust of Nicolas Sarkozy was reflected in a vote to punish him, the victory of the first Socialist president since 1988 was accompanied by great expectations in the economic and social sphere in a country that had suffered from the aftereffects of the 2008 economic crisis, rising unemployment, and job insecurity.

The left had mobilized during that presidential campaign, expecting to move beyond the Sarkozy years. For voters in the banlieues, Hollande's victory signaled the possibility of change in the government's policies toward the country's marginalized neighborhoods and their residents. Very quickly, however, the efforts of Jean-Marc Ayrault (Hollande's prime minister) to spur job growth reached their limits, thus weakening the president's position early in his term of office. Campaign promises went unkept, leading to deep disappointment. And whereas the pressing issues of the banlieues had been at the heart of French political debates during the electoral campaigns of 2002 and 2007, in the new socialist administration of Hollande, it seemed to be pushed to the side. As soon as it attained power, the left, in effect, turned away from this key constituency, put the issue of the banlieues on the back-burner, and reverted to its earlier tendency to take for granted the voters in these marginalized communities. For the new socialist government, it was almost as if the banlieue riots of 2005 and all the post-riot talk of the need for serious attention to these areas had never happened. (The Hollande government's security policy did include an urban component with the establishment of "priority security zones" in select cities to target crime hotspots. However, there was no concerted effort to attack growing inequality and poverty in the most troubled neighborhoods. The government's efforts, which without exception have been small-scale and piecemeal, have done nothing to attack the root problem and are far from meeting the heightened expectations of the residents of these neighborhoods for concerted action.)

The growing mistrust in government in the banlieues was shared by a second-generation cohort of young people raised in immigrant families, a cohort born and politically socialized in France that had always known the far-right National Front to be a significant political force. This is a generation with a different political frame of reference than the rest of the country, whose experiences have led in an unprecedented ideological direction.

THE RISE IN UNEMPLOYMENT AND INEQUALITY

High unemployment rates have remained a constant in France, before and after the 2012 elections. On the eve of Hollande's election on May 6, 2012, France's unemployment rate was 9.7 percent. Nicolas Sarkozy had succeeded, in the first phase of his term as president, in reducing it to less than 8 percent before the 2008 financial crisis put an end to that. In the fourth quarter of 2012, unemployment crossed the threshold of 10 percent, and in the second quarter of 2013, it neared the threshold of 10.5 percent—then finally crossed it in late 2014.

The government's image has suffered as a consequence, reflecting a growing mistrust of politics and politicians throughout French society. From 2009 to 2014, the number of people who believed that political officials did not care about voters rose from 81 percent to 89 percent. At the same time, the number of those who believed that democracy was not functioning leaped from 48 percent to 73 percent. The inability of successive governments to take effective action to increase employment transformed the political environment of 2012 into one of incipient crisis from which the National Front would reap benefits.

One can discern the crisis more clearly by examining the situation in the banlieues. According to the data provided by INSEE, the proportion of the population in the northeastern Parisian *département* of Seine-Saint-Denis that was between fifteen and sixty-five years old and unemployed increased from 12.2 percent in 2006 to 13.1 percent in 2011. To this we must add 11 percent of adults (not including students and retirees) who were without work. In May 2012, Seine-Saint-Denis had 125,700 unemployed. Three years later, there were 36,700 more. This hardscrabble area, until recently a bastion of political support for the left, has been struck by a rapid and deep deterioration of the labor market. The situation is especially bad for individuals of lower-middle-class and immigrant background. In Seine-Saint-Denis, 14.6 percent of French citizens born in France are unemployed, whereas the unemployment rates for French citizens who have acquired French nationality, foreign residents of North African origin, residents of sub-Saharan origin, and residents of Turkish origin are 19 percent, 31 percent, 27 percent, and 33 percent, respectively.

This disparity between the unemployment rates of different national groups is even greater in other urban *départements* such as Rhône and Bouches-du-Rhône—in the Lyon and Marseille areas, respectively—where the employment prospects of native French citizens are better in general. If a college degree provides some protection against unemployment, it does not reduce inequality among social classes or nationalities. The inequalities are maintained even when levels of education are the same.

Statistics typically understate the seriousness of the situation. A large number of young people in disenfranchised banlieues such as Seine-Saint-Denis cannot find their first job, so they appear in official government statistics only as "inactive" rather than as unemployed. Similarly, the official data do not record the unemployment and underemployment of illegal immigrants. The grim employment outlook has produced lasting effects, particularly among young, unemployed college graduates of immigrant background, who have grown disillusioned after having placed their hopes in the educational system.

This situation had immediate political repercussions for the Hollande government. Frustration with the left has been even greater in the disenfranchised banlieues than in the rest of the country, where Hollande's popularity was rapidly sinking. From July 2012 to September 2015, the president's approval rating fell from 55 percent to 13 percent. This 40-point drop is unprecedented in French political history. In November 2016, as the campaign for the 2017 presidential election began, only 4 percent of French voters approved of Hollande, an abyssal fall.

In the banlieues, the disillusionment with the left compelled residents to search for alternative solutions. For some young people, spirituality was the answer. Religious engagement offered them an opportunity to regain a personal dignity and social legitimacy unavailable through work—which was nonexistent—or political participation. While youth involvement in electoral politics in these communities has not vanished entirely, the plunge in the left's popularity has led to a marked withdrawal from the political arena as well as—among some—an increased willingness to explore new political options. In a time of disappointment with the established parties, some banlieue youth have asked themselves whether the painful prospect of a political coalition with the right might not be in the best interests of the French Muslim immigrant community.

FROM SOCIAL DESPAIR TO AUTHORITARIAN CONSERVATISM

Neither the riots of 2005 nor the sporadic revolts that have broken out since have offered a clear path for the political integration of the children of postcolonial immigration. On the contrary, we are beginning to discern a process of social disintegration marked by heightened mistrust of these young people, whose economic situation remains precarious and whose cultural and religious practices are marginalized or rejected outright by the cultural mainstream.

Faced with this mainstream shunning, some young people in the hardscrabble banlieues, in particular Muslims, are in turn shunning the mainstream. Their desire to get out of the 'hood is transformed into a need to dissociate themselves from France—to leave it and its republican institutions behind. These days, this distancing takes the form of an embrace of an all-encompassing, strict form of Islam characterized by careful, systematic, and religiously sanctioned efforts to exert control over all aspects of life, including gender relations and family life. The appeal of this authoritarian puritanism lies in its promise of a return to a "natural order of things" and a reestablishment of a form of social stability in which everyone knows his or her place.

This intersection between a self-righteous denunciation of inequality and injustice and the advocacy of authoritarian practices holds an undeniable attraction for some young people, even if those who embrace authoritarian solutions are few in number at present. The attraction is also felt by individuals who have not grown up in a Muslim family but who have shared the painful experiences of social exclusion. In groups destabilized by the experience of colonialism and migration, by job insecurity and poverty, by being made to feel inferior culturally and symbolically, the imposition on oneself and one's community of a set of rigorous religious norms can be seen as a way of restoring social stability and control.

In French Muslim populations, the tendency toward cultural authoritarianism can be combined with a different sort of conservatism issuing from the community's best-educated and most economically well-off members. Many members of this Muslim middle class, particularly those who are active in Islamic affairs as clothing manufacturers and retailers and as businesspeople in the halal food industry, are in principle receptive to the standard right-wing critique of the social welfare state, with its suggestion that generous public assistance fosters dependency and discourages entrepreneurship.

The sociopolitical configuration of the banlieues is far from homogeneous. Not all Muslims share the same ideological convictions, and the translation of religious conviction into political preference does not lead Muslim voters down a single path. The children of the second and third waves of Muslim immigration are following different trajectories in French society. While (for example) opposition to the largely anti-immigrant right wing remains strong, a conservative revival in this community has created a small but discernable political opening for the political right in the banlieues. This opening was discernible in the aforementioned Manif pour tous of January 2013—organized by largely Catholic groups to protest a law legalizing same-sex marriage—in which a notable number of Muslims participated.

THE EMERGENCE OF TRADITIONALIST ISLAMIC GROUPS

Another recent manifestation of a discernable conservative tendency in the French Muslim community is the mobilization of the Fils de France (Sons of France) collective, a group that purports to give voice to the "silent majority" of French Muslims who identify wholly with the nation. Launched officially in March 2012, its sponsors include conservative politicians, prominent media personalities, and other public figures, such as Nicolas Dupont-Aignan; Robert Ménard, then a host of Sud-Radio; Father Michel Lelong, a regular guest on the right-leaning radio station Radio Courtoisie; and Tareq Oubrou, the rector of the Bordeaux mosque. These figures gave Fils de France media visibility in the course of its first three years.

Operating primarily online, Fils de France has appropriated traditional republican iconography (its logo, a Gallic rooster, is an age-old symbol of French nationalism) and some of the far right's vocabulary, including in particular its rejection of globalization. It calls for a fusing or transcending of particularisms via a strong nationalism rather than via adherence to republican principles:

> We want to assert an obvious truth: a French Muslim can be a patriot just like a French Catholic, Jew, Protestant, agnostic, or atheist.

In an interview with the *Boulevard Voltaire* far-right website, Camel Bechikh, the president of the association, declared that it was "natural that French Muslims defend the traditional family." In the course of the interview, he also made clear his affinity for and affiliation with the Manif pour tous organization and its "exceptional" leader Ludovine de La Rochère. Bechikh is also close to the Parti chrétien-démocrate (PCD, or Christian Democratic Party), a right-wing, largely Catholic political group founded in 2009 whose leaders include Christine Boutin and Xavier Lemoine—the mayor of Montfermeil, an eastern banlieue of Paris adjacent to Clichy-sous-bois, where the 2005 riots started. On February 23, 2015, Bechikh published with Lemoine a joint interview conducted by Guillaume de Prémare, a member of two conservative Catholic groups, Ichtus and Civitas, whose members seek to harden the line of the Manif pour tous.

A very different conservative initiative had a more visible impact in the banlieues. The Journées de retrait de l'école (JRE, School Boycott Days) was a protest launched in December 2013 by a teacher, author, and activist of Algerian descent, Farida Belghoul, of the teaching of "gender theory" and the ABCD de l'égalité (ABCs of Equality [between boys and girls]) in French public schools. Belghoul denounced this curriculum for its supposed promotion of homosexuality and its challenge to traditional family values. The objective of JRE was to persuade parents to keep their children home from school one day a month in protest until the targeted programs were withdrawn. This initiative targeted Muslim parents in particular and enjoyed considerable success when it was rolled out in January 2014. On the first planned absentee day, 30 percent of students stayed home from school in those Parisian banlieues having large Muslim populations.

Farida Belghoul's career is emblematic of a certain postcolonial French elite that can trace its origins back to North Africa. Initially an activist of the left, Belghoul was present at the Marche des beurs in 1983. The following year, she organized the Convergence 84 demonstration, another antiracist initiative that attracted sixty thousand people to Paris and that took aim at the ruling Socialist Party for its hijacking of the antiracist movement. After a long period of withdrawal from political activism of any sort, in 2013, Belghoul was drawn toward the far-right message of author and essayist Alain Soral. She began posting her attacks on gender theory and its alleged propagation in public schools on Soral's *Égalité et réconciliation* website, an online forum also supported by traditionalist Catholic movements on the far right. She was delighted with the "Islamo-Catholic convergence" that her initiative created and declared victory when the decision was made, in June 2014, to halt the distribution of the ABCD de l'égalité program. But by then, her JRE had run out of steam, and she broke with Soral after a year of having been close to him.

Prospects for a more across-the-board Christian-Muslim convergence over values issues are uncertain at best. Traditionalist Christians and Muslims are on opposite sides of other issues, such as those connected with the much-contested French tradition of laïcité (secularism). Right-wing voters typically see laïcité as a shield against "Islamization" and brandish it as a weapon of resistance against Islamist activists' religious demands such as the right of women and girls to wear the veil in school or the niqab in public. Where there are political convergences between these groups, they tend to arise in communities in which Muslim families have decided to send their children to private Catholic schools in order to avoid the public schools in their district, which they may see as inferior or violent. In such cases, social proximity facilitates the development of communities of interest.

SECULARISM AS AN IRRITANT

Secularism (laïcité) is sometimes perceived in France as a discriminatory practice that targets Muslims and in this vein is regularly denounced as a pretext for monitoring and controlling their religious practices (clothing, swimming pool hours reserved for women, the consumption of alcohol, etc.).

In September 2012, Minister of National Education Vincent Peillon announced his intention to establish a program of instruction in "secular morals" (morale laïque) in French schools starting in the fall of 2013. The goal was to bring into the schools debates on fundamental moral issues important for the development of self-aware, thoughtful citizens. In Le Journal du dimanche, Peillon declared that "although these questions are not asked, reflected upon, and taught in the schools, they are taken up elsewhere—by merchants and by fundamentalists of all kinds," adding that

> the goal of secular morals is to allow each student's self-emancipation, because secularism's starting point is the absolute respect for freedom of conscience. To allow for freedom of choice, we have to be able to detach the student from all kinds of determinism, whether familial, ethnic, social, or intellectual, in order afterward to make a choice.

At the same time, a drama unfolded in the French court system involving a nursery school that shifted the debate over laïcité and "secular morals" away from the public sphere and into civil society. The case of the Baby Loup nursery school featured the director of a cooperative preschool being sued by one of her former employees. The former employee, who had been employed as a teacher, after having returned to work from a long maternity leave wearing an Islamic veil, was fired by the school when she refused to remove her veil to conform with legislation, passed in France in 2004, banning the wearing of "ostentatious" religious articles and signs in public schools. (The school in question is partly financed by taxpayers' money via local governments and is considered a public establishment.) At the end of a long series of hearings, the Final Court of Appeal decided in favor of the school director in a ruling handed down on June 25, 2014, reversing a Paris Court of Appeals decision which had ruled in favor of the employee. The final judgment defined "the conditions under which a private person, in this case an association, can restrain the freedom of its employees to display their religious convictions in the workplace." The court added that the principle of laïcité does not apply to all religious practices in private enterprises and that "the restriction of freedom to display one's religion [. . .] does not take the form of a general interdiction but [is] sufficiently precise, justified by the nature of the tasks accomplished by the employees of the association, and proportional to the goal sought."

The Baby Loup affair attracted the attention of the nation as a whole and triggered numerous reactions. This was understandable, because it is always questions concerning public schools—the institution through which individual fates and life chances are determined—that crystallize French society's tensions, divisions, fears, and uncertainties. While the organizations traditionally favoring laïcité mobilized resources to help with the defense of the nursery school director, Islamist associations in particular took the employee's side.

The laïcité issue became even more fraught and destabilizing after a government report on the French policy of integration, commissioned by Prime Minister Jean-Marc Ayrault in 2012, was released in December 2013. The report exposed disagreements between different factions on the left and within the government. One section of the document suggested reconsidering the 2004 law banning the wearing of the veil in the schools, thereby opposing the official position of the minister of national education. The authors of the 2013 report maintained that "it is important to reflect on the conditions of the development of an inclusive and liberal conception of laïcité, of a shared laïcité, sensitive to both the contexts and the consequences of its implementation."

The call for compromise and negotiation regarding the terms and modalities of applying the principle of laïcité fractured the fragile consensus within the government and bureaucracy. In a sign of smoldering confrontations, the report was taken down from the government's website in the weeks that followed its release. In the end, although one part of the left continued to demand "recognition" of France's "cultural diversity," the office of the president decided in favor of continuity with the 2004 law and with the policies of socialist governments extending back to the 1990s.

Less than a year after taking back the presidency and the National Assembly, the socialist majority appeared divided, contested by part of its base and in a compromised position. Whereas during the 1980s the defense of laïcité and antiracism had played the role of an ideological glue for the left after the adoption of Mitterrand's *tournant de rigueur*,[1] the years following 2010 led to a shattering of the consensus on how to regulate religious practice and combat racism.

Contrary to the situation that prevailed during the last quarter of the twentieth century, when the social ascension of many descendants of North African immigrants was accompanied by a secularization of behavior and their identification with radical and progressive French institutions such as the Communist Party, the CGT,[2] and even the Socialist Party, by the early twenty-first century, the influence of Salafism gradually changed the situation. An alternative model of rupture with the values of "infidel society" became a serious rival to the earlier model of social rupture with "bourgeois society." It is in the context of this shift that we can understand the rise of a professional class of college graduates, managers, and entrepreneurs who while embracing the laws of the free market and related right-wing values are also imbued with Islamic culture.

The intensification of Salafist identity politics was imported from Saudi Arabia and expressed by this professional class in how they behave and what they consider halal (permitted) or haram (not allowed). Salafists hoped to establish themselves among the disenfranchised young

---

[1] A radical change in economic policy adopted by President François Mitterrand in 1983 after the failure of the far-left program he pursued at the beginning of his first term of office.

[2] Confédération général du travail (General Confederation of Labor), one of the largest French trade unions; it has close ties to the French Communist Party.

people of the banlieues as "organic intellectuals" who had culturally "disavowed" infidel society. Success in this project in the name of their all-encompassing version of Islam would allow them to transcend class differences and contradictions between themselves and the marginalized young people whom they seek to lead and from whom they seek political support.

The campaign against gay marriage—something that is haram, understood as a cardinal sin in the eyes of Islam—appeared as a political gift to this Salafist cadre, which saw the issue as a means of breaking its target group's social attachment to the left. By having made permissible the sin committed by Lot (*Lout* in Arabic, from which is derived the colloquial Arabic epithet *louti*, or "faggot"), the Socialist party, in this Salafist view, now finds itself cursed as a "corrupter on Earth."

The most orthodox interpretations of the Islamic tradition insist that sodomy be punished with the greatest severity, even prescribing the execution of its practitioners. Thus in January 2015, the seventh issue of the online jihadist magazine *Dabiq* published an illustrated report on the Muslim purification of morals in the Syrian city of Raqqa, which had fallen under ISIS's control. In it we see a blindfolded "sodomite" perched on the top of a building before he is thrown off it. His broken body, lying on the ground, is then desecrated by the crowd. The article accompanying the images justifies this punishment in the name of the holy scriptures. In a similar video posted by ISIS, one can see the images of the stoning to death of a couple of homosexuals in Homs with the text of this hadith superimposed:

> The Messenger of Allah—may Allah's blessing and salvation be upon him—said "Anyone you find who acts in the manner of the people of Lot, kill the active and the passive!"

For those who consider gay marriage to be sinful, including both the imams who have railed against it from their pulpits and their like-minded congregants, the "marriage for all" bill signed into law by President Hollande in May 2013 posed a problem of principle. Indeed, in the eyes of some believers, the law in question gave the lie to the vaunted universalism of French law in its opposition to the application of Muslim marriage law. If, the Salafists reasoned, a well-organized lobby could succeed in using its political influence to legalize an immoral practice that used to be illegal (but that remains immoral), why couldn't they build an effective Islamic lobby to advocate for official recognition of Muslim marriages in accord with the rules of sharia? All it would take would be an Islamic lobby as effective as the gay lobby to give the force of universal law to the right this community demands.

Hollande's same-sex marriage law of 2013 had two related effects: it pitted a significant segment of the Muslim electorate against the Socialists, and it encouraged some Muslim citizens to organize themselves as an electoral lobby in order to ensure that they, too, win certain community rights. This development has favored the entry into politics of so-called "halal entrepreneurs" who, in the municipal elections of 2014, contributed to the rightward shift of cities with working-class traditions, such as Bobigny, the prefecture of Seine-Saint-Denis, or the large city of Aulnay-sous-Bois in the same *département*. In addition to the disaffection of the Muslim electorate in the banlieues, which in recent years has decided to punish the left for the government's economic failures, Islamic community leaders have begun to appear on right-wing electoral slates—in particular, those of the UDI,[3] led by the mayor of Drancy, Jean-Christophe Lagarde, that have captured a religious vote hostile to the Socialist "corrupters on Earth."

This recent phenomenon was still fairly limited in the 2014 municipal elections. Nonetheless, it was an unprecedented development and perhaps a harbinger of the future. Anti-leftist Salafist identity politics could play a central role in future elections. This would compound the massive rejection of the left already seen in the white "native French" working-class electorate, which has gravitated to the National Front. And the NF has a few Muslim elected officials—as well as a certain number of voters—who are carrying out its battle against "globalization" and the European Union, which they see as contributing to impoverishment and job insecurity.

MANIFS POUR GAZA AND JIHAD AGAINST THE JEWS

It was in this context of heightened identity politics and increasing social fragmentation in French society that certain events occurred in the Middle East that accentuated the rending of the French social fabric. The Islamic State in Iraq and the Levant (ISIS) seized Mosul on June 10, 2014, and proclaimed an Islamic caliphate several weeks later, on the first day of the Muslim holy month of Ramadan. At the same

---

[3] Union des démocrates et indépendants, a center-right French political party founded in 2012.

time, the intensification of the Syrian civil war, which threatened the regime of Syrian President Bashar al-Assad, led al-Assad to call upon the Lebanese Shiite militia group Hezbollah to supply aid by fighting the Sunni jihadists who had cut the road to Damascus, Homs, and the Alawite coast. With the blessing of Hezbollah's patron Iran, Hezbollah fighters crossed the Syrian border, using against the Sunnis the weapons originally provided by Teheran to fight the "Zionist entity."

Hezbollah's fighting prowess had been on display eight years prior to these events during the so-called Thirty-Three-Day War against the powerful Israeli army. But in the summer of 2014, the Shiite militia's decision to engage in the Syrian conflict left it short of troops on the Lebanese-Israeli front. Israeli prime minister Benjamin Netanyahu saw this as an opportunity to strike against Israel's other adversary, the Palestinian Sunni Islamist group Hamas, which was entrenched in the Gaza Strip. Hezbollah, bogged down in Syria, could not come to Hamas's rescue with its missiles, and Egypt's new president, Abdel Fattah el-Sisi, a former Egyptian Army head and an enemy of the Hamas-affiliated Muslim Brotherhood, maintained a tight blockade of Gaza's southern border. The Palestinian Authority in Ramallah, for its part, which was (and remains) a bitter rival of Hamas, did not look with disfavor on the prospect of its destruction at the hands of the Israelis. And to make a bad situation even worse for Hamas, it was also in the doghouse with Iran, whose Shiite clerical rulers were unhappy with Hamas's professed solidarity with the Syrian Sunni rebels opposing Bashar-al-Assad's Iran-friendly regime.

The context was thus favorable for an Israeli offensive against Hamas in Gaza, and the opportunity to strike was afforded to the Israeli prime minister by the kidnapping on June 12, 2014, of three teenaged West Bank settlers. Yeshiva students who were hitchhiking home to Hebron at the time of their abduction, they were found dead on June 30. Retaliating for the kidnapping, which was attributed to Hamas activists, a group of vigilantes from the Jewish settler community kidnapped, tortured, and burned alive a young Palestinian boy, an atrocity that triggered a Hamas rocket attack on Israel from the Gaza Strip. Thereafter the Israelis began seven weeks of military attacks on Hamas in Gaza, an operation dubbed "Protective Edge" by the Israeli Defense Forces. The 2014 Gaza war ended in late August of that summer with seventy-two Israelis and approximately two thousand Palestinian Gazans killed. The conflict further damaged Israel's international reputation as the Jewish state came in for strong criticism for its shelling of Hamas targets in civilian areas and for the disproportionate number of Palestinian dead. Hamas, for its part, survived the onslaught with its stockpile of missiles and other weapons diminished but not destroyed and its own reputation in the Arab world enhanced.

In France, the 2014 Gaza war both exacerbated social tension between the country's ethnoreligious groups and brought to a fever pitch the widespread dissatisfaction with the president of the Republic. Hollande's office stirred up a hornet's nest the day after the conflict began when it published a communiqué that drew on the president's conversation with Benjamin Netanyahu in the hours after Operation Protective Edge had begun:

> He [President Hollande] assured [Prime Minister Netanyahu] of France's support regarding the rockets launched from Gaza. He reminded him that France strongly condemned this aggression. It is the Israeli government's responsibility to make every effort to defend its population against these threats.

The French head of state, having thus given his blessing to the Israeli offensive in Gaza, was immediately accused of having betrayed France's balanced policy with regard to the Israel-Palestine conflict. Even though the very next day, in the course of a conversation with Palestinian Authority president Mahmoud Abbas, Hollande deplored the fact that Israeli military strikes had already caused many Palestinian casualties, the damage was done. The equivocation damaged the government's credibility and unleashed all kinds of protest demonstrations.

The subsequent mobilization in support of Gaza deepened the antagonisms in French society along cultural and religious lines. Since the first decade of the twenty-first century and the emergence of a new generation of French-born Muslims, solidarity with Palestine, and more particularly with Hamas, has given political visibility to Islamist movements seeking to offer Muslim youth in the economically hard-hit banlieues a universal projection of their social frustration. This had already occurred during the earlier military conflict between Israel and Hamas in the summer of 2006 and in 2010 and 2011, during operations intended to break Israel's naval blockade in the Gaza Strip. Support for Palestine was the glue that held French Muslims together. It represented a cause that was both anti-imperialist (a feature that also appealed to left-wing voters) and ostensibly humanitarian (which appealed to French society as a whole). Media coverage that summer of Israel's bombing of Gaza, which revealed the extent of the civilian casualties and which featured graphic video images of Palestinian children being killed on Gazan beaches by fire from Israeli warships, inflamed Muslim public opinion and led to protest marches on the streets of France.

In Paris, the marches on July 13, 2014—on the eve of Bastille Day—featured both the left and far-left movements and Islamist groups with ties to the anti-Semitic far right. Among the Islamist demonstrators, amid shouts in Arabic calling for Hamas's missiles to bombard Tel-Aviv, the Sheikh Yassin collective, named after the founder of Hamas, who was killed by Israel in 2004, led the crowd in chants of "Citizens, resistance! Hamas, resistance! Jihad, resistance!" Signs read "Israel Murderer, Hollande Accomplice" while cries of "Death to Jews" and "Death to Israel" rang out and a black-on-white Salafist banner bearing the twofold Muslim confession of faith now made popular by the ISIS flag stood out among the forest of Palestinian flags. Nearby, fans of the popular French comedian and militant anti-Zionist Dieudonné—those of the so-called Dieudosphère—were also taking part. The mixture of ideological registers between the latter and the Islamists could be seen in particular in a group of young people brandishing a cardboard Qassam missile and making Dieudonné's notorious *quenelle*[4] gesture, a photograph of which was published in the weekly magazine *Marianne*.

This demonstration signified the disintegration of the decades-old alliance between the humanitarian left and Islamic groups and the concurrent *rapprochement* between Islamists and radical elements of the Soralian far right, united by a common hatred of "Zionism." Jean-Marie Le Pen himself—distinguishing himself from the entourage of his daughter, who was eager to dissipate recurrent suspicions that the very recently proclaimed "leading French political party" was anti-Semitic—forcefully denounced the martyrdom to which Palestinian civilians were subjected.

Later that same month, two subsequent demonstrations took place that further inflamed relations between France's Jewish and Muslim populations. The first, on July 19, occurred on the boulevard Barbès, in a neighborhood with an especially high percentage of Algerian immigrants. The second, a day later, took place in the city of

---

[4] A hand gesture created and popularized by Dieudonné that has been interpreted as an inverted Nazi salute and an expression of anti-Semitism. A *quenelle* is a sort of sausage-shaped pâté, and the gesture also has similar connotations to "giving someone the finger."

Sarcelles, known for its less than successful postwar experiments in urban planning, which produced sterile and depressing public housing high-rises. Sarcelles is also a city in which a third of residents are Jewish, most of them from North Africa, and in which another third are Muslim.

In Barbès, where the demonstrators ignored police instructions to disperse, the tear gas grenades used by the riot police on defiant demonstrators were analogous, in the minds of the latter, to Israel's bombardments of Gaza. The vandalism committed by some of the demonstrators was similarly analogous to Hamas's resistance. This symbolism of confrontation metaphorically transplanted the conflict in the Middle East to French society, identifying the Palestinians oppressed by Israel with the children of North African immigrants oppressed by the postcolonial Republic. This comparison had already been made, a decade earlier, by activists involved in the 2005 riots. In this version of the clash of civilizations, the enemy is not the white nationalism of the far right but rather a French state administered by a socialist government and said to be in league with Jewish interests.

In the Sarcelles demonstration, the stakes were different. There demonstrators sought a confrontation not with a pro-Zionist French "colonial" state but rather with the local Jews, seen as the very incarnation of the despised Zionist ideology. Jewish stores in the shopping center located at the heart of the large housing project were targeted, whereas the Muslims' stores, especially those owned by Turks, were left untouched. Initiated by a local elected official who wished to represent "diversity," the Sarcelles demonstration was originally intended to protest what the demonstrators regarded as the excessive influence of Jewish organizations on the municipal government. The protests quickly escaped the organizers' control, particularly when Islamist groups from northern Paris banlieues arrived on the scene chanting "Allahu akbar!" as they confronted the lines of riot police blocking access to the neighborhood of the synagogues. Some of the young demonstrators took advantage of the disorder to start looting Jewish shops. In a metaphor that reversed the situation in Barbès, where the "colonial-Zionist" state besieged the Muslim neighborhood, in Sarcelles, the Islamist persecution of minority sects in Iraq by the "caliphate" in Mosul was replayed by demonstrators against the contemporary *mellah*[5] of the Jewish minority. Six months after this

---

[5] An Arabic word referring to a walled Jewish quarter in Morocco, analogous to a European ghetto.

protest aimed at Jews, the Jihadist gunman Amedy Coulibaly engaged in a deadlier protest against a Jewish business when he took hostage customers at a kosher supermarket and then began executing them.

Seen through the prism of Abu Musab al-Suri's *Global Islamic Resistance Call*, the incidents in Sarcelles on July 20, 2014, looked like skirmishes foreshadowing the "war of enclaves" anticipated by the theorist of jihadism once the success of the attacks carried out during the first phase had fractured European societies, made Muslim zones autonomous, and triggered a civil war on the basis of a confrontation between homogeneous ethnoreligious areas.

6

#CHARLIECOULIBALY

On January 7, 2015, France woke up to the publication of Michel Houellebecq's new novel, *Soumission* (*Submission*, a literal translation of the Arabic term *islam*). Houellebecq, who had won the Goncourt Prize—France's most prestigious literary award—for his previous book *The Map and the Territory*, is the most widely read and translated living French author. But he had to endure a rather hostile reaction in the press, some critics suspecting his novel of "Islamophobia." The action is situated in 2022, the year when Mohammed Ben Abbes is elected president of the French Republic. Ben Abbes, the son of a Tunisian grocer and a child of the Republican meritocracy educated at the elite École Polytechnique and École Nationale d'Administration, is the head of the "Muslim Fraternity." The plot describes France's fracture, at the end of François Hollande's disastrous second term as president, into mutually hostile identity-based factions in a derelict country where the National Front and the Salafists have become the opposing poles of attraction—a country fallen prey to rioters and armed gangs evoking the war of enclaves advocated by al-Suri.

The protagonist, François, a university professor specializing in the work of the nineteenth-century French novelist Joris-Karl Huysmans, teaches literature at the New Sorbonne's Censier Center—on the fringes of Paris's Latin Quarter—and endures the mediocre condition of academics in modern France, scorned by a state that pays them very little. Meanwhile, Saudi Arabia, which has bought the Sorbonne and wants to employ only Muslim instructors there, paying them at the market rate for great international universities—about three times the French salary—proposes a generous deal for professors who do not want to convert to Islam by offering them immediate retirement with the maximum pension, no matter their level of seniority. After considering this offer, the hero—persuaded by the new president of the university, an ex-identitarian far-right politician who has converted to Islam and who dangles before him the possibility of publishing an edition of Huysmans's works in the prestigious *La Pléiade* series and the opportunity to take additional wives—"submits" in turn and becomes a Muslim.

This dark fantasy about the future is sustained, like Houellebecq's two previous books, by an extraordinary talent for observing society and an ability to use fiction to heighten situations and passions to a fever pitch, in the spirit of Aristotelian catharsis. Confronted by such work, newspaper critics, normally inclined to damn in a knee-jerk fashion what they earlier praised in order to preserve their position as arbiters of taste, were disarmed by this kind of literary intensification of disturbing social and cultural phenomena. Invited to discuss *Soumission* on the France Inter radio station's live morning show on January 7, 2015, Houellebecq responded to remarks made by commentators and listeners, including the essayist Caroline Fourest, about whom he said:

I don't think I've read any of her books [. . .]. I did do some reading, though, but I relied chiefly on Gilles Kepel in my research.

A few minutes after the broadcast, I received text messages and e-mails from colleagues urging me to disavow myself from this "unsavory association" by issuing a communiqué designed to safeguard my academic honor. I did no such thing, and shortly afterward, in my university office at Sciences Po, I learned of the shooting at *Charlie Hebdo*. It brought to its culmination the sequence of jihadist terrorism that developed precisely in accord with the logic advocated by the *Global Islamic Resistance Call*, as had the Merah and Nemmouche affairs. The Kouachi brothers massacred the weekly's editorial staff "to avenge the Prophet" and then murdered an "apostate" policeman of North African origin. Amedy Coulibaly's subsequent murder of a policewoman from the French Caribbean preceded his killing of the hostages at the Hyper Cacher supermarket two days later.

The congruence between a work of fiction and a same-day reality that exceeded it has probably never been so flagrant: the number and the positions of the victims executed in cold blood in the middle of Paris made the event a genuine cataclysm whose symbolic import was tantamount to a cultural September 11. Much more than the Merah affair, whose unprecedented nature made it possible to hope that it would be only an isolated accident, the carnage in January 2015 was perceived as the climax of a series of attacks that sought to sap the foundations of the social and political compact that defines French society and, beyond it, European and Western societies in general. The objective of jihadist terrorism is to cause this society to implode by mobilizing behind its activists and "martyrs" the radicalized descendants of retro-colonial immigrants from the Muslim world. The perpetrators of this terrorism also target all the disaffected people who hate a system that excludes them, particularly vulnerable and confused young people for whom conversion to jihadist Islamism is connected with or a substitute for both far-left and far-right activism. In this sense, the mechanisms operating in the events of January 7–9, 2015, remind us of those fore-shadowed by Houellebecq. In the real world, however, French society proved to be more resilient, as was shown by the immense demonstra-tions of January 11 and the passionate reactions they elicited in turn. This response indicated that France was inclined to follow a differ-ent path—difficult but an alternative to the dazzling simplifications of Houellebecq's fictional work.

The massacre at *Charlie Hebdo*, the murder of the two police officers, and the shooting at the Hyper Cacher supermarket constituted the acme of a process whose concrete development in France we have followed from the Merah affair onward and whose genesis we have traced since the writings of Abu Musab al-Suri. But this was not all: the year 2015 was further darkened by the aftershocks of this tremor and then by the massacre of 130 people in November. The aftershocks began on April 19 with the incredible arrest in Paris of a twenty-four-year-old Algerian student named Sid Ahmed Ghlam, who held a scholarship granted by the French state and who lived in university housing—thanks, according to the weekly *Le Canard Enchaîné*, to the support of a student union that wanted to attract the votes of Islamist students. Having called emergency medical services after having been wounded by two bullets under unexplained circumstances—several sources said that he had accidentally shot himself—he was discovered to be in the possession of an arsenal and rapidly came under suspi-cion of having killed a young woman and of preparing an attack on a crowded church in Villejuif, following the instructions of French jihad-ists who had stayed in Artigat and had gone to live in Syria.

The suspect, on whom the police had been keeping an S (State Secu-rity) file since 2014 because he had shown signs of wanting to leave for the Syrian jihad battlefield, had gone to Turkey in February 2015, where he contacted a French jihadist from a family of Algerian descent in Villepinte—a lower-middle-class city in the northern banlieues of Paris—who was active in the ranks of ISIS and who is thought to have urged him not to go to Syria but rather to carry out attacks on French soil. Initial reconnoitering around the Villepinte suburban train station, the target his contact had originally designated, caused him to abandon it, because, according to extracts from the prosecution's files revealed by the press, the suspect noted that "there is hardly anyone but Arabs." In coordination with his "handlers," who told him how to pick up the arsenal he had at his disposal, the church in Villejuif was finally selected, perhaps because if the attack were successful, this place name would have glorified its perpetrators and commanders, to whom ignorant Islamist sympathizers might have attributed a victory over Israel, mistakenly taking Villejuif to be a city inhabited by Jews.[1] Amedy Coulibaly had, moreover, taken responsibility for exploding a car bomb in this same city (without causing any casualties) the day after the massacre at *Charlie Hebdo*.

Then, on June 26, in the *département* of Isère in the French Alps, after so many videos showing ISIS's decapitation of its hostages and prisoners in the Levant had been posted on the Web, the first beheading took place on French soil. A CEO's head was cut off by one of his employees, Yassin Salhi, and was displayed, surrounded by Islamist slogans, on the fence of a factory making chemical products, where the killer had also tried to trigger an explosion that could have contaminated the environment. Salhi, who also had a police file for Islamist radicalization, was in contact with a man close to the Forsane Alizza group and sent a photo of his victim, along with a selfie showing him alongside the latter, via WhatsApp to a contact who had left for the jihad in Syria. The date chosen, the second Friday of Ramadan, three days before the first anniversary of the proclamation of the "caliphate" in Mosul, also coincided with the massacre of "infidel" tourists sunbathing in swimsuits on the beach at a hotel in Sousse, Tunisia, committed by a jihadist Tunisian student named Seifeddine Rezgui. In addition, that same day was also marked by an attack on a "heretic" Shiite mosque in Kuwait in which many people died, as well as by ISIS's execution of more than a hundred Kurds in the Syrian town of Kobané.

---

[1] Villejuif is a suburb of Paris. It has no historical connection with Jews; the name is believed to be a corruption of a Gallo-Roman name, Ville Juvius, meaning "the villa of Juvius," but to a French ear it sounds like "Jewville."

Next, on August 28, 2015, Ayoub el-Khazzani, a young Moroccan from Tétouan who had emigrated to Spain, tried to use a submachine gun on passengers in the Thalys train from Amsterdam to Paris. El-Khazzani, a former drug dealer on whom the European intelligence services had an S file but who moved unhindered to and from France, worked briefly for a company specializing in selling telecommunications with North Africa and traveled to Germany and Belgium and on to Syria. Minutes before the attack, he had used his cell phone to watch a sermon calling for jihad. His weapon jammed, and he was overpowered by other travelers, including American GIs on vacation, who prevented the planned carnage.

The long list of attacks in 2015 reached its high point with the massacres in November and would go on in 2016. The pieces of this puzzle of third-generation jihadism fell coherently into place as the data, trajectories, itineraries, and accounts accumulated. This made it possible to reflect on the effectiveness of the model conceived by al-Suri: Would it be capable of deepening still further the cleavages within French and European societies and getting more and more young people to join its ranks, echoing the saga of ISIS in Syria and Iraq with an uninterrupted flow of departures toward the battlefield? Or, on the contrary, did it have fatal weaknesses that would lead its strategy to fail as the earlier jihadist waves had failed?

During the second jihadist generation, that of Bin Laden and al-Qaeda, the attacks on September 11, despite their spectacular worldwide dimension, did not succeed in achieving the goal set by those who organized them: seizing power in Muslim countries. One of the causes of this failure had to do with the political economy of terrorist activity. The increasing number of attacks after 2001, from Madrid to London and from Kenya to Indonesia, did not, in the end, destabilize the societies they struck; their primary effect was to exhaust the symbolic resources of terrorist violence—and to discourage potential sympathizers who were supposed to act. A weariness set in, comparable to the one that affected the first jihadist generation, when the indiscriminate massacres of civilians sounded the death knell of the GIA in Algeria and of the *Gama'at islamiyya* (Islamist groups) in Egypt by cutting them off from their bases of support among the people.

To gauge the similarities and differences between the two earlier phases and the third one, which is characterized by a "poor man's terrorism" in which some perpetrators have committed fatal errors but in which ISIS's "caliphate" has conquered significant territory, it is important first of all to review the development, logic, and consequences of the spectacular attacks carried out in 2015 and to put them in this overall perspective.

"MAY ALLAH CURSE FRANCE!"

Both the ethnosocial profile and the personal history of the three killers—the Kouachi brothers, Saïd and Chérif, and Amedy Coulibaly—seem to resemble those of the assassins in Montauban and Toulouse in 2012 and in Brussels in 2014. However, there are a few differences.

Attention has been focused on the Kouachi brothers, who acted first and who perpetrated the most significant carnage, in terms of both number of victims and symbolic value, with the twelve dead at the offices of *Charlie Hebdo*. The spectacular attack on a medium of communication gave its name to the whole event with the metaphorical slogan "*Je suis Charlie*," which rapidly spread around the world only to be contested by those who took it literally. The *Charlie Hebdo* attack obscured the rest of the operation, perhaps because soldiers, who were also from North Africa or the French Caribbean, had already been killed in Montauban and Toulouse, and the massacre at the Hyper Cacher supermarket followed those at the Ozar Hatorah school in Toulouse and at the Jewish Museum in Brussels.

In fact, Amedy Coulibaly stands out as the most important figure in the trio, the one who publicized his act with the greatest professionalism. Moreover, ISIS paid him vibrant homage through the eulogy in *Dabiq*, its glossy and gory anglophone online magazine, as well as in the second issue of *Dar al-Islam*, published by the "caliphate's" francophone media center. Appearing in the February 11 issue in a cover article featuring a low-angle shot of the Eiffel Tower guarded by a soldier, it was entitled "May Allah Curse France," hijacking the title of the rapper Abd al-Malik's book *Qu'Allah bénisse la France* (*May Allah Bless France*) and giving a nod to *Na'bou la France!* (*May France be Cursed!* in colloquial Algerian), published in 2002 by Farid Abdelkrim, the leader of the Jeunes Musulmans de France (Young Muslims of France). Incidentally, Abdelkrim has now recanted his former commitments and published, in autumn 2015, an essay entitled *Pourquoi j'ai cessé d'être islamiste* (*Why I Have Ceased to Be an Islamist*).

Like Merah and Nemmouche, Saïd Kouachi, born in 1980, and his younger brother Chérif, born in 1982, were difficult social cases. They came from a broken family of Algerian origin that had no paternal authority figure present, and their mother died, probably a suicide, in 1995, when she was pregnant with a sixth baby by an unknown father.

Her children were taken care of by special education and children's services, which sent them away to the provinces, far from the deleterious and violent atmosphere in the derelict neighborhoods. Despite the degrees they received—Saïd obtained a BEP (occupational training certificate) in hotel-keeping, and Chérif became a physical education teacher—they returned in 2000 to the housing projects in the nineteenth arrondissement of Paris where they had spent their childhood.

Their radicalization took place in the same manner as that of Merah, who passed through the mosque of Bellefontaine in Toulouse, the Salafist community in Artigat—a family milieu of total Islam, prison, and sojourns in the land of jihad. In the case of the Kouachi brothers, it was a long-haired Salafist "guru" named Farid Benyettou who, by means of his "lessons" in small groups after Friday prayer at the al-Da'wa (Call to Islam) mosque on the north side of Paris, redirected the violence of these troubled and embittered young people toward the sacred cause of jihad through the "Buttes-Chaumont Islamist network." By an irony of history, Benyettou, after serving a sentence for having sent his flock to Iraq in 2005, trained as a nurse and was present at the Salpêtrière Hospital in Paris on January 7, 2015, when the ambulances transporting the victims of his former disciples, the Kouachi brothers, arrived there.

Chérif, arrested in January 2005 when he was about to leave to join the jihad against U.S. troops in Iraq, was convicted and jailed, and it was in the prison incubator of Fleury-Mérogis that the threads were woven of the tragedy that was to take place a decade later. There he made the acquaintance of Amedy Coulibaly, who was then being detained for a bank hold-up and other armed robberies, and especially of Djamel Beghal. Although the latter was in solitary confinement on a floor above theirs, he easily communicated with them through the window or by the yoyo that moved between the bars, and he fascinated both apprentice jihadist and common criminal alike. Beghal, who had been trained by al-Qaeda and sent to carry out attacks in France, had been intercepted, thanks to tapped phones, in the United Arab Emirates as he was on his way to Paris. He incarnated the jihadist second generation and the way the intelligence services tracked it after hacking its "software." In this prison, resembling both in its architecture and in its population a banlieue housing project with bars on its windows, he served as a relay between the second and the third generations, between al-Qaeda's largely defeated pyramidal (*tanzim*) organization and the network-based "system" (*nizam*) in which the choice of terrorist action, if not its initiative, is largely delegated to the base.

While in temporary detention (along with Boubaker al-Hakim, alias Abu Mouqatel, now one of ISIS's most famous Franco-Tunisian fighters), Chérif Kouachi was convicted in 2008 of association with criminals with the intention of committing a terrorist act so as to "recruit terrorists to be sent to Iraq." After his release from prison when his sentence was reduced because of good behavior, Chérif, along with Coulibaly and his wife Hayat Boumeddiene, met again with Beghal, who had been placed under house arrest in a hotel in Murat (a small city in the south-central area of France known as Cantal). It was there that the discussions initiated between two floors in the Fleury-Mérogis prison three years prior were able to reach their conclusion, in full view of police telephoto lenses but unheard by the authorities, who were unable to record the conversations. In 2011, Chérif Kouachi visited Yemen, where he received further training under the auspices of al-Qaeda in the Arabian Peninsula (Aqap) in the company of Salim Benghalem, who would become a jailer in ISIS's prison in Aleppo along with Mehdi Nemmouche and one of the highest-ranking Frenchmen in the "caliphate." The brothers claimed to be followers of Aqap when they were on the run after the killing at *Charlie Hebdo*.

Chérif's elder brother, Saïd, who had also frequented the Buttes-Chaumont gang early in the first decade of the new century, followed the same activist trajectory but without serving time in prison. He was searched and held in police custody in 2010, as were Djamel Beghal, Coulibaly, and Benghalem, in connection with the investigation into Smaïn Aït Ali Belkacem's attempted escape. Belkacem was thought by the authorities to be the chief explosives expert for the 1995 attacks in France; he had been sentenced to life in prison in 2002 and incarnated the first jihadist generation. Connecting these people—all Algerians or descended from Algerians, except for Coulibaly, who had been Algerianized by his marriage—with one another shows the bridges and continuity between the individuals who had marked each of the three Jihadi phases. Beghal and Coulibaly went back to prison, but Saïd Kouachi was released from police custody and between 2011 and 2014 joined his brother with Aqap in Yemen. They were then located by means of tapped telephones; the Americans considered them terrorists and prohibited them from flying to the United States. The telephone surveillance carried out in France, which was considered inconclusive, was halted in 2014, a few months before the massacre at *Charlie Hebdo*.

While the Kouachi brothers acted in the manner of a Merah or a Nemmouche and provided another demonstration of the difficulty the police had in neutralizing potential terrorists whom they had identified and monitored some time before, Amedy Coulibaly presented a singular profile that gave him a much more central position in the apparatus of third-generation jihad. He had been born in 1982 in Grigny on the southern outskirts of Paris, where he lived in the Grande Borne housing project, and his family was originally from Mali and included ten children, of which he was the only son. This large sub-Saharan African family—whose model is still being perpetuated in the French banlieues, whereas families from North African backgrounds have already begun the demographic transition—was united and "happy," according to his sisters' testimony. However, when he was a junior in high school, he was already participating in burglaries and then got involved in drug dealing and engaged in violence. His hatred of society and the state is supposed to have had as its point of departure the death of an accomplice and friend who was killed in October 2000 by a policeman whom he had tried to run down with his car.

Coulibaly's itinerary reminds us of that of jihadist recruiter Omar Omsen, who lived in Nice's Ariane housing project, who had also committed multiple hold-ups, and whose family also came from the Sahel. Like Omsen, Coulibaly put in the service of his new vocation the criminal's habitus—violence, dissimulation, calculation, the substitution of means for ends, and a street-savvy intelligence. Arrested and convicted, he was imprisoned in Fleury-Mérogis, where in 2005 this confirmed criminal—whose family was in no way radical in its practice of the Muslim religion—met Chérif Kouachi and Djamel Beghal, as we have seen. This carceral happenstance put him in contact with the partisans of militant Islamism, who offered him the prospect of sacred redemption beyond hold-ups and drug trafficking while at the same time channeling his violence toward jihad.

Again like Omar Omsen, Coulibaly tried his hand at making videos—on a smaller scale than the author of *19 HH*, to be sure—and thereby acquired a little fame when he clandestinely made a film denouncing prison conditions, extracts from which were shown on television after his release and about which he was interviewed. A book inspired by his film and published locally in Grigny, *Reality Taule—au-delà les barreaux* (*Reality Jail: Behind the Bars*), which contributed to his profile as "rehabilitated," got this future opponent of the Americano-Zionist Empire a job with Coca-Cola when he was released from prison. His modest career as a video maker and actor ended with a bang in the film he made before committing the killings at the Hyper Cacher, against the background of ISIS flags, and which was to be broadcast after his death to claim this act in the name of the "caliphate."

July 2009 was particularly full and showed Coulibaly's ability to put together projects and relational networks. Rejecting his friends and family as *kuffar* (atheists, infidels), he married a young woman named Hayat Boumedene in a religious ceremony. A cashier from an Algerian background who had to quit her job because she was not allowed to wear a full-body veil, Boumediene, like the Merahs, Nemmouche, and the Kouachis, came from a broken family. At the age of six, she had been placed in foster families after her mother's death. This Algero-Malian couple formed a solid relationship that both framed their jihadist radicalization and gave them the strength to conceal their involvement, thus stabilizing the itinerary of these two damaged individuals by providing the goal that they had lacked from the start. Photographs taken beside the pool of a hotel in Southeast Asia show the slender, radiant wife in a swimsuit, nestled in her husband's muscled arms. This image of togetherness is also a model of *taqiyya*, the dissimulation advocated by jihadists. But when Coulibaly left Hayat Boumediene in the hands of the "brothers" who accompanied him to Syria while he prepared himself for the attack on the Hyper Cacher and his death, he wrote this text message:

I would like her to learn Arabic, the Quran, and religious science. See to it that she behaves [?] very religiously. The most important thing is *dine* [religion, Islam] and faith and for that she needs to be supervised. May Allah help you.

By another irony of history, in July 2009, the same month when he was married in a halal ceremony, on July 15, the day after the celebration of Bastille day, Coulibaly was received by President Nicolas Sarkozy at the Élysée Palace, where he was honored as a model of successful rehabilitation. This caustic wink from destiny, involving the consecration of the would-be mastermind of France's 9/11 in the very heart of the Republican pomp, tells us all we need to know about the inanity of the French ruling class and the French government's ignorance of and consequent lack of preparation for the challenges of the third wave of jihadism. The guest at the Élysée that afternoon was the same man who went every month to visit Djamel Beghal, under house arrest in Murat, and who pursued with this al-Qaeda missionary an indoctrination that he was able to keep secret. The photographs taken in the snowy mountains of Cantal in early 2010 show him in the forests, practicing the use of weapons. Hayat Boumediene, who had abandoned her bikini in favor of a niqab, appears in one photo in which she is aiming a crossbow at the camera, gazing through the slit in her facial veil. This jihadist superwoman was to inspire Hasna Aït Boulahcen, Abdelhamid Abaaoud's cousin, who posted this photo on her Facebook wall on August 3, 2015, three months before the massacres in November.

On May 23, 2010, this ideal "rehabilitated" ex-convict, Amedy Coulibaly, was arrested again, along with Beghal, for having planned the escape of the explosives expert Belkacem and was sentenced to five years in prison. He was released early, for good conduct, in March 2014; his electronic bracelet was removed in May, a few weeks before ISIS's proclamation of the caliphate in Mosul. The prison administration heaped praise on this exemplary prisoner who had completed a training program as, of all things, a first-aid worker. He was henceforth able to devote himself full-time to preparing the cataclysm that befell France in January 2015. Of the few months that preceded the killings we know mainly what Coulibaly himself said in the video he shot indoors on January 8, which was edited and broadcast by his accomplices after his death, along with additions and commentaries glorying his martyrdom. Another chance audio recording broadcast the exchange between Coulibaly and his hostages—without any of their knowing it—in the Hyper Cacher supermarket. Together, they form an exceptional firsthand document that gives us a precise picture of the jihadist third generation at a key moment in its history. The video reflects an amateur filmmaking activity that goes back the years when Coulibaly made his clandestine report on the conditions of detention in Fleury-Mérogis, but it also shows how easy it was for a descendant of ordinary immigrants to use audiovisual tools and the Web and to easily integrate himself into the network-based system whose potential Abu Musab al-Suri had foreseen in 2005.

The video confirms Coulibaly's major role in the events of January, making the Kouachi brothers appear, *a contrario*, to be subordinates given "a few thousand euros" to help do the killing at *Charlie Hebdo*. In text messages exchanged by Coulibaly and his probable mentor in Syria and leaked to the press in November 2015, the Kouachi brothers were, moreover, described as "*zigotos*" ("weirdos"). In fact, the principal perpetrator, the robber from Grigny, was not the sole planner of the Paris attacks. This is shown by his New Year's Eve car trip to Madrid, with Hayat Boumedene, who was pregnant and who was to fly to Syria via Istanbul on January 2. Ten other people also made the trip, including the brothers Mohamed and Mehdi Belhoucine, the latter of whom crossed the police barrier at the Istanbul airport alongside Coulibaly's wife. They came from Aulnay-sous-Bois and were the jihad's mathematicians. The younger brother, Mehdi, who was twenty-three years old at the time, was a student in electronic mechanics in Paris, at the Jussieu University campus, and the elder brother was a certified engineer at the School of Mines in Albi (the birthplace, as we have noted, of convert Thomas Barnouin, who had preached jihad there between two sojourns in Artigat and who was suspected of being Sid Ahmed Ghlam's handler).

In July 2014, the Islamist engineer Belhoucine was convicted of having participated in the conveyance of French jihadist fighters to the Afghanistan/Pakistan zone. Everything indicates that they were the group that supported, planned, and conceived the attacks and that they had gone to the "caliphate" as much to live their utopia there as to escape the police investigations to come. The following month, it was for the young widow of Abu Bassir Abdallah al-Ifriqi (the African), Coulibaly's jihadist alias, to claim and clarify the action in ISIS's name in an interview that appeared in the organization's anglophone and francophone online magazines. She situated the Paris attacks in the grand narrative of the "caliphate," following the example of the "blessed double raid" of September 11 against New York and Washington in al-Qaeda's golden legend.

The video, seven minutes and nine seconds long, opens with images taken from Coulibaly's report on the jailbirds: we see him walking in the Fleury-Mérogis exercise yard or doing push-ups. Then we can distinguish firearms lying on the floor while the famous passage from verse 8:40 of the Quran is first chanted in Arabic and then superimposed on the screen in French translation to justify "legitimate terrorism" (irhab mashru') against Allah's enemies. The whole Islamist movement has regularly cited this verse ever since the 1990s, when Sheikh Youssef al-Qaradawi of the Muslim Brotherhood used it in this way to support Hamas's attacks on Israel. The hero's birth name, Islamic nom de guerre—in white against a black background—and his position appear on three lines: "Amedy Coulibaly / Abu Bassir Abd Allah al-Ifriqi / Soldier of the Caliphate." In a voiceover, a woman recounts, in a neutral tone, the attacks of January 7, 8, and 9 while his three great feats are displayed, composing a virtual epitaph (reproduced here verbatim):

> Author of the blessed attacks of Montrouge where he killed a policewoman on January 8.
>
> The following day he carried out an attack at the Porte de Vincennes where he took seventeen people hostage in a Jewish grocery and executed five Jews [in reality, he killed four hostages].
>
> He also placed an explosive charge on the gas tank of a car that exploded in a street in Paris [in reality, in Villejuif].

The expression "blessed attacks" is a translation of the Arabic *gha-zwa mubaraka*, used in jihadist propaganda to designate September 11, which immediately placed the January massacres in this tradition. The third jihadist generation draws on the founding figure of Bin Laden (we will see hereafter how Coulibaly claimed to be his follower) while at the same time rejecting the hijacking of his heritage by his successor Ayman al-Zawahiri. The two factual errors that appear in the epitaph probably indicate that the editing of the video after his death was done in haste.

This introduction is followed by four questions in journalistic style that tend to objectify and neutralize the event in the manner of an interview with a politician, but they testify, by their use of the familiar *tu* and by their tone, to a closeness with Coulibaly: they are addressed to potential sympathizers and to Muslims in general, as is shown by the last question and response, which incite them to take action. The questions are displayed on the screen in a single format: white letters on a black background. Coulibaly expresses himself calmly, sitting on the floor in accord with the tradition of the Prophet, wearing four different sets of clothes, each adapted to the theme. At the beginning of the response, a summary of the content in a few words is superimposed on the screen. Coulibaly is designated only under his name Abd Allah, which is part of his nom de guerre and means literally "adorer [or slave] of Allah." Frequently used for converts or penitents, this name also provides a definition *a minima* of the Muslim: in this context, it indicates that Coulibaly represents any Muslim whatever and that every Muslim is called upon to identify with him and to imitate him. The written form takes care to systematically capitalize the word *Allah* to stress the respect due to the Creator:

> "To what group do you belong and who is your emir?"
> (Abd Allah states his allegiance to the Caliph Ibrahim.)
> "*As salam 'aleikoum rahmat Allah wa barakatouhou* [Peace be on you, Allah's mercy, and His blessing]. I am addressing first of all the caliph of the Muslims, Abu Bakr al-Baghdadi, Caliph Ibrahim. I swore allegiance to the caliph as soon as the caliphate was declared."
> [There follows a laborious reading, stumbling over the words, of the *bay'a*, or "declaration of allegiance," in Arabic, a language that Coulibaly reads haltingly.]

In this situation, Coulibaly was wearing a beige *djellaba* and a black scarf; an ISIS flag is affixed to the wall against which he is leaning.

The outfit resembles the one worn by fighters filmed on the battlefield in Syria and Iraq. The awkward recitation of the declaration of allegiance—a good minute long, it breaks the rhythm and rarely appears in the countless extracts from this video broadcast by the media—aims to make Coulibaly, in the eyes of sympathetic Internet users, appear to be a modest "soldier of the caliphate," as he is described. It places his act under the spiritual authority of the caliph for whom he is waging war against France, singling him out and exalting him in relation to earlier jihadist attacks.

> "Are you in contact with the brothers who attacked *Charlie Hebdo*?"
> (Abd Allah gives details of the operations.)
> "The brothers in our team, divided into two parts, did *Charlie Hebdo, Hamdulillah* [Allah be praised]. I went out a little against the police and then. . . . We did things a little bit together, a little bit separate, it was more so that it would have more impact, you know. . . . I helped him in the project by giving him a few thousand euros so that he could finish buying what he had to buy, and so, *Hamdulillah*, we managed to synchronize ourselves, to go out at the same time . . ."

Dressed for the occasion in a bulletproof vest in camouflage fabric, Coulibaly is filmed in a close-up, a three-quarter right-facing view. He uses the Salafist expression "go out against" (*sortir contre*), translated word for word from the Arabic *kharaja 'ala*, which means "attack," thereby showing his linguistic allegiance to ISIS. Here, "went out a little" probably refers to the assassination of the policewoman in Montrouge on the morning of January 8, which would date the video to that same evening. A cut in the editing prevents us from understanding to whom he handed over "a few thousand euros"—probably to Chérif Kouachi—but this admission serves to indicate his ascendancy over his accomplices and that of ISIS over Aqap. A video circulating on the Web claimed responsibility for the attack on *Charlie Hebdo* in the name of the latter organization and indicated that Zawahiri had given the command for it. With Coulibaly's declaration, such claims were revoked so that the "caliph" Baghdadi could take all the glory at the expense of his rival from the preceding jihadist generation.

> "Why did you attack France, *Charlie Hebdo*, a Jewish grocery?"
> (Abd Allah gives the reasons for the attacks.)
> "What we're doing is completely legitimate in view of what they're doing. Avenge the Prophet, *Sala Allah 'alayhi wa salam*

[Allah's prayer on him and salvation (the compulsory eulogy)], it's completely legitimate. *Ma sha' Allah* [Allah's will], it's been amply deserved for the time [. . .]. You attack the Khalifah, you attack the Islamic State, we will attack you! You can't attack and not get anything in return! So you pretend to be a victim, for a few dead, as if you didn't understand what was going on [in reprisal] [. . .] Whereas you and your coalition, only you at the head, almost, now, you regularly bomb over there, you've invested forces, you're killing civilians, you're killing combatants, you're killing [. . .] Why? Because we're applying sharia? Even in our own country we no longer have the right to apply sharia now? You're the ones who decide what's going to happen on Earth? Is that it? No! We're not going to allow that, we're going to fight, *In sha' Allah* [Allah willing]! We're going to raise Allah's word, *Sobhanohou wa ta'ala* [may He be exalted]."

To make this belligerent statement, Coulibaly put on his urban combat uniform: a black leather jacket, a black woolen cap, and a Kalashnikov at his side, leaning against the wall, where we can distinguish a bookshelf with the backs of four books that the video's poor definition does not allow us to identify. But the books strengthen the argument by suggesting that it is founded on sophisticated reasoning and not merely on the wild imaginings of a re-Islamized criminal. If we compare these remarks with those of Nicolas/Abu Abdel Rahman Bons or Maxime/Abu Abdallah al-Firansi Hauchard, quoted earlier, we can see that the script is very close.

Three days before the carnage at *Charlie Hebdo*, Hauchard announced that the Islamic State was going to attack France in reprisal for the bombardments of ISIS positions and that the attack would be "well deserved"—an expression we also find here. The invocation of the *lex talionis*, to which Coulibaly referred explicitly when talking with his Jewish hostages in the audio recording reproduced hereafter, was, in addition to a re-use of the Bible, the modus operandi of the milieu and the gangs in the housing projects of the banlieues. The classical register of victimization, in a version painted in the customary colors of Islamophobia, completes the statement: the West, with France "almost" at its head, is bombing the caliphate yet takes offense at "a few dead" on its own territory killed in reprisal. The Western double standard claims to have morality on its side, whereas true justice consists in applying sharia. Coulibaly emphatically denies the imagined Western claim that "even in our own country (*chez nous*), we no longer have the right to apply sharia."

The exact significance of Coulibaly's use of the expression "*chez nous*" serves here to reveal his identitarian projection. Literally it refers to the bombed caliphate, even though he had never set foot in it and was a French citizen. (Indeed, it was because of his French citizenship that Mali refused to accept his body for burial.) As a "total" Muslim, he wanted to be identified exclusively with this land of Islam, in accord with a mechanism that is not without parallels with part of French Jewry's identification with the land of Israel, where several victims of the attacks in France, from the Ozar Hatorah school in Toulouse to the Hyper Cacher, are buried. At a second level, Coulibaly's "*chez nous*" also designates the Islamized territories of the impoverished French districts from which he came and where the secular Republic wants to prohibit the wearing of the facial veil by "attacking our sisters," as we see in the fourth and last set of questions and responses:

"What is your advice for Muslims in France?"
(Abd Allah incites Muslims to combat.)
"I want to address my brother Muslims everywhere, and particularly in Western countries, and I ask them: What are you doing? What are you doing, my brothers? What are you doing when they fight directly against the *Tawhid* [divine oneness]? What are you doing when they directly insult the Prophet, *'alayhi as salam*, over and over? What are you doing when they attack our sisters? What are you doing when they massacre whole peoples? What are you doing when, right in front of you, our brothers and your sisters are [inaudible] by the *tawaghit* [demons, in the sense of oppressors]? What are you doing, my brothers? *Sobhanu Allah!*

Since I went out, I've moved around a lot, I've gone from one mosque to another, in France a little, a lot in the Paris region. They're full, *Ma sha' Allah!* They're full of men full of vigor! They're full of young athletes! They're full of men in good health! How, with all these thousands, out of ten thousand people, can there not be enough to defend Islam?"

For this last reply, Coulibaly poses leaning against a wall, sitting on the floor next to a flag of the Islamic State, a Kalashnikov at his side, in the same posture as during the first reply. But he has exchanged the beige *djellaba* for a white one, as immaculate as a shroud, symbolizing the purity of the martyr he is to become. And he wears, knotted over his skull, the checkered *keffiyeh* that represents Palestine, whose cause he will avenge by "executing five Jews." The video concludes with the chanting in Arabic of verse 4:84 of the Quran, with the French translation superimposed on the screen— "So fight, in the cause of Allah; you are not held responsible except for yourself . . ."—while images of the besieged Hyper Cacher pass by in the background.

It should be noted that the message is addressed to Muslims *in France*, not *of France*, as had been standard usage since 1989 following the UOIF's claim to make France a "land of Islam" for Muslims living there and holding citizenship. Even if the followers of third-generation jihad—who, like Coulibaly, were born and educated in France and grew up in neighborhoods where there are now many markers of Islamization—are ipso facto Muslims *of France* (or even exclusively French citizens, as in Coulibaly's case, since Mali does not recognize double nationality), he "disavows himself from" his French citizenship, to use the Salafist expression, having no allegiance other than to ISIS's caliphate. It was on the latter's terrain that his support group, brought there by the Belhoucine brothers and Hayat Boumeddiene, carried out the *hijra*, the emigration or hegira in imitation of the Prophet, who left idolatrous Mecca to go to Medina and there establish the first "Islamic State." For jihadist Salafists, there is no longer any reason to remain in an infidel land except to carry out acts of war there in the name of the caliph of Mosul—acts like those of January.

The dramatic intensity of this sequence is emphasized by the rhetorical use of two anaphoras: "What are you doing?" repeated nine times, and "They [mosques in France] are full," four times. The incriminating address to the Muslims of France, the goal of which is recruitment, is one of the recurrent themes in ISIS's discourse. Nicolas/Abu Abdel Rahman Bons had used it, as we have seen. Here the argument, once again, consists of riffing on victimization and legitimate armed self-defense against Islamophobia. The clichés are varied but on the same level, ranging from "the massacre of whole peoples" to "attacks on our sisters" and "direct insult to the Prophet," passing by way of the combat against the *Tawhid* and Allah's law—just so many vague formulas that provide a universal justification for violent jihad on French soil.

The call to action addressed to the faithful who fill the mosques in the Paris region and in France is preceded by the ambivalent expression "since I went out." This could refer to Coulibaly's release after his incarceration in the affair of Belkacem's attempted escape in March 2014 or, if we take the expression in the Salafist sense, translated from Arabic ("attack"), to the shift to armed jihad that led to the massacres in January. In this latter meaning, the tour of the mosques mentioned here is revelatory of a strategy implemented by the jihadists. We have seen how at the "Stalingrad" (also known as Ad da'wa) mosque Benyettou proceeded to fill out the ranks of the Buttes-Chaumont network—and what was done in the Bellefontaine mosque in Toulouse or the el-Baraka mosque in Lunel to guide young people toward Syria. The goal was to identify, hook, and indoctrinate worshipers who were likely recruits. Besides, the observation that the mosques were full of strong young men—beyond the deliberately frightening dimension it acquires when used by Coulibaly in this belligerent context—is entirely correct; it contrasts singularly with the churches of the Paris region, whose pews are seldom full during services and most of whose worshipers are female and elderly.

Coulibaly's statements in this video—which was carefully staged, as the changes in costume show, and then edited and broadcast after his death—leave a certain role to his own expression through the diction characteristic of a "young man from the banlieues." But it nonetheless follows ISIS's general script, of which the declarations made by Nicolas/Abu Abdel Rahman Bons, who put the stamp of his strong southwest France accent on the text to be read, provided a foretaste. Coulibaly's style, which makes use of the themes of victimization and the permissibility of vengeance, is familiar among the young people in marginalized neighborhoods, even non-Muslims, who are the video's main target. The killings had a twofold function: arousing panic in Western "infidel" societies and recruiting sympathizers who would perpetrate further murders. Their goal was precisely to justify the January attacks for those who would commit the next ones, in November.

This "staged" discourse was, like the images of Coulibaly's last moments or the incredible conditions of the Kouachi brothers' flight, the object of generalized suspicion on the part of the conspiracy theorists (conspis), for whom the Soral-Dieudonné networks supplied most of but not all the footsoldiers. We have seen that the latter are violently denounced by ISIS and even by the inflammatory writer Marc-Édouard Nabe, because they deny jihadists any authentic commitment and see them as agents manipulated by the "Empire." The ties of the conspis with the Syrian and Iranian regimes, like those of the far right in general with Vladimir Putin's Russia, which supports Bashar al-Assad, nonetheless have facilitated their lambasting by the jihadists. But by attributing the paternity of the attacks to the Americano-Zionist Empire, they have helped strengthen the obsessive and confused feeling of victimization and Islamophobia among young people in the disadvantaged neighborhoods. It is not without importance that six months after January 2015, Coulibaly's whole video was available, after a routine search of YouTube, only on a *conspi* site, Alterinfo, which warns the Internet user against a Zionist fabrication of which it is supposed to represent the ideal type, rebroadcasting as proof of evidence the version appearing on the site of *Haaretz*, the Israeli daily, bearing the paper's Hebraic initial letter. The video is thus *mise en abyme*, helping to blur the interpretation of the events of January 7–9 that has fed, as we shall see, the perplexity of more than one well-established French intellectual.

To complete the confusion, we have an audio document acquired by chance—a recording of the conversations between Coulibaly and his hostages. When the radio station RTL called the Hyper Cacher's telephone number on January 9, the entrenched jihadist picked up but said nothing, then failed to hang up the phone properly. The dialogue that ensued was heard through this phone. It was a kind of cat-and-mouse game between the heavily armed Coulibaly and Jews caught in the trap, four of whom were killed by him after he had verified their membership in the Jewish community, according to the retranscription of the sound track of the GoPro camera he was wearing, in a manner similar to Merah and Nemmouche. The exchange heard over the telephone let Coulibaly speak as he really was: in contrast with the staged and calibrated video, he talked without a script, starting with ISIS's ideology filtered through the screen of his idiosyncrasy. Coulibaly's composed tone as a "soldier of the caliphate" is replaced by the jerky rhythm of young people's lingo in the banlieues, pushed to a paroxysm by the adrenaline of the tense situation as he held his submachine gun in his hand, with four bodies lying on the floor in front of him.

The recorded extract begins with the argument that justifies the taking of hostages: the French have elected a government "that has never hidden the fact that it was going to wage war in Mali or elsewhere," and they pay taxes to finance it—an argument Bin Laden used after 9/11 to justify killing Westerners. To which a hostage retorts: "We have to!" Coulibaly's response: "But I don't pay my taxes! [. . .] You have a choice, you can go live in Israel! [. . .] Demonstrate to make them leave Muslims alone!" But the decisive point is the *lex talionis*, in which an allusion to the Jews' holy scripture is mixed with a reference to the Quran against the background of gang culture in the projects, this hybridization being summed up in the *chez nous* that raises the subject:

> No, among us [*chez nous*] it's the law of eye for an eye: you know that very well! That means, Allah, He said it in the Quran: If they transgress, then there will be equal transgression. That means: if our

women are touched, if our fighters are touched, if our old people are touched, we have to attack the men who are fighting us, now, I'm telling you, your army, there, they won't succeed in setting foot over there! They will never be able to defeat us, because Allah is on our side!

There follows a special message for his Jewish hostages:

As he said, Osama bin Laden—you know?—Osama bin Laden *Rahimo Allah* [May Allah grant him His mercy], he said: you will never be able to make peace! We're the ones who will make peace in Palestine [by destroying Israel]!

The war that ISIS is waging against France thus takes place mainly on French soil, because the "caliphate's" territory—apart from the bombing it has been subjected to—has been turned into a sanctuary by Allah. French soldiers cannot take the fight to there on the ground. The hostages, as voters and taxpayers, are in this case substitutes for the French soldiers, who deserve to be killed. The fact that Coulibaly's hostages are Jews who, as such, in his view, necessarily support Israel condemns them even further. The caliphate's spokesman, Sheikh Abu Mohamed al-Adnani, emphasized this by adopting the strategy advocated in 2005 by the *Global Islamic Resistance Call*: the French infidels have to be ceaselessly killed, wounded, humiliated, and insulted. And that strategy is just what pushed the third-generation jihadist incarnated by Amedy Coulibaly to commit such an extreme act.

TO BE OR NOT TO BE CHARLIE

Abu Musab al-Suri's strategic objective, to be achieved through the multiplication of terrorist actions, is, as we have seen, the implosion of society by a gradual process of wars between enclaves that would lead to the destruction of the West—starting with Europe, which constitutes the latter's soft underbelly. From this point of view, it is of primary importance to sow discord among the ethnocultural components of European societies while homogenizing a Muslim community that disavows the overall society and that enters into combat against it. One of the main political resources for achieving this "disavowal"—a translation of the Arabic *bara'a*—is the highlighting of victimization, of which the intensification of "Islamophobia" is the most effective instrument. By constantly denouncing Islamophobia, by making it a congenital defect of European societies, and by substituting it for anti-Semitism as the West's cardinal sin, the Islamists seek to establish barriers between cultural communities that are insuperable for all Europeans of Islamic descent, in order to transform the latter into exclusive members of the community that the jihadists aspire to lead.

Nonviolent Islamists have similar goals, though they use different means to achieve them. The pietists of the Tabligh and the Salafists want to make this closed community a socioreligious resource and use it to manage social peace (and, for the Salafists, to prepare the hegira out of "infidel" France). The Muslim Brothers want to make it a political instrument as well, using it to construct pressure groups that were first active in the recurrent and systematic campaigns, between 1989 and 2004, for the right to wear the hijab in schools. Since the Manif pour tous against same-sex marriage, this closure around a morally conservative definition of Muslim identity has begun to take the form of community-based voting in some elections, especially municipal elections, in a pragmatic alliance with various right-wing political parties.

In contrast, Islamists who are "Salafist jihadists" elaborate on the basis of this rupture between communities a move toward violence that takes several forms. The first consists in carrying out the hegira, like the earlier pietistic Salafists, except that whereas the latter left France simply to live in accord with "total" Islam in a Muslim country where women could wear the niqab, and so forth, the jihadists leave to engage in armed combat on the battlefields that have succeeded one another since the 1980s: Afghanistan, Bosnia, Pakistan, Iraq, and— principally since 2012—Syria, and then once again Iraq, with a few incursions in Mali, Libya, and Tunisia. The second form of violence is exercised on the territory of the *kuffar* (atheists, infidels . . .), whose "blood is licit," according to the Quran. The Merah affair began this process. It may be combined with violence on the external battlefield, as we have seen during the events of January 2015.

To produce this separation and polarization, whatever its purpose, whether socioreligious, electoral-religious, or violent jihadist, all the Islamist actors construct the victimization of their co-religionists by making the battle against Islamophobia a primordial resource. Since 2005 this discourse has acquired such influence in France that even a "moderate" Muslim institution such as the French Council of the Muslim Faith (CFCM) has had to create an office for the struggle against Islamophobia in order not to be accused by its Islamist rivals of being lukewarm in the defense of Muslims confronted by various attacks during the public expression of their faith. Going further in the battle against Islamophobia has thus become a stake in the competition for sway over the community that no competitor can ignore without being disqualified.

Finally, the deepening rupture between communities makes it possible to put strong pressure on persons of Muslim culture or descent who live their faith without making it a primordial or exclusive element of their identity and, still more, on the great number of those in France who are agnostics or atheists. In the impoverished banlieues where the signs of Islamization are patent, it has become socially difficult or even impossible to break the daytime fast in public during Ramadan if one "looks like" a Muslim. The jihadists have pushed this secession to its apex by making "apostates" their chief targets, their killing being intended to terrorize "bad Muslims" and dissuade them from leaving the closed community. Following al-Suri's recommendations, Merah, the Kouachi brothers, and Coulibaly took care to kill French people who "looked like Muslims" (*musulmans de faciès*) or who were supposed to look like them (notably those of their victims who came from the French Caribbean) and who were wearing the uniform of the army or the police—a clear sign of apostasy according to the jihadists, whose punishment could be only death.

Taken all together, these mental and cultural systems form the context in which the events of 2015 took place and in which the reactions and the counter-reactions were structured. Failing to take them into account makes it impossible to analyze the issues that have subsequently crisscrossed French society.

The great protest marches on January 11 were an event as spectacular as the attacks to which they replied—but they were expressed in a different sociopolitical repertory. The magnitude of the demonstrations—never before attained in the history of France, if we accept the estimate of about four million people in the streets—as well as the cortege of numerous foreign heads of state and government or members of the latter who came to Paris specifically for this purpose and the demonstrations of solidarity in many cities worldwide, are all unprecedented phenomena. By their wish to include everyone disgusted by the terrorist acts, they expressed the refusal of the fragmentation of society along ethnoreligious and community lines, the mechanism by which third-generation jihadism seeks to provoke civil war in Europe and the destruction of its civilization.

This protest demonstration of unequaled magnitude constitutes, a priori, the most powerful response to the strategy implemented by al-Suri's epigones. Just as the Algerian and Egyptian civil societies distanced themselves from the abuses committed by the GIA and the *Gama'at islamiyya* in 1997, leading to the decline of those terrorist groups, and just as the societies of the Muslim world have not followed the example of September 11 and have not mobilized to bring al-Qaeda to power, so the mass of French civil society blocked a handful of terrorists and reasserted—in this way guiding other European societies—the secular and integrative social compact that incarnates its original grand narrative.

This "spirit of January 11" was intended as a reaction of civilization confronted by jihadist barbarism, but dissonances soon appeared. They were crystallized by the slogan "Je suis Charlie," created in the emotion of the moment by Joachim Roncin, thirty-eight, the artistic director of the free magazine *Stylist*, and put online at 12:52 p.m. on January 7. It instantly went viral throughout the world and restored with a single click the lost universality of the French language and even the nostalgic illusion of the resilience of its values. Thus it is a visual artifact issuing from Generation Y that responds to the massacre perpetrated by other members of the same generation. A product of the Web, simultaneously a logo and a slogan, borne both by image and sound, it is the vector of an extraordinarily powerful message: confronted by a slaughter that was obscure and at first incomprehensible for ordinary people, it responded to a massive expectation of meaning by affirming a globalized subjectivity—that of the Internet user in front of his screen. The assertion "Je suis Charlie" associates the first-person singular subject pronoun (which on the Internet everyone appropriates individually) with a predicate designating a polysemic object. And it was for the great demonstrations to use a mouse click to federate these innumerable *I*s in a collective *we* that is real and physical.

Thus the protest marches that took place on January 11, 2015, were probably the first in history to mix the virtual universe with that of the street: "Charlie" became the name of the mass of people who rejected jihadist terrorism. The phrase "Je suis Charlie" puts it precisely: It does not in fact mean that "Charlie" is the subject's name. The French language would say that by using the expression *"je m'appelle Charlie"* ("my name is Charlie"); the copula *"suis"* (am) links the subject *"je"* (I) with a new communal identity—named "Charlie"—whose appearance in the public sphere on January 11 is its collective birth certificate. The challenge, then, was how to define the borders of this sovereign people when its adversaries were trying to diminish it. Although it is clear that "the people" of the January 11 mass demonstrations did not include the jihadists—since the demonstrators assembled against them—what is less clear is whether the reassertion of French Republican values on that day allowed those assembled to extend its embrace even to the young people of the banlieues—those of immigrant background and of Muslim cultural origin. Here we arrive, as we shall see, at the limits of the relationship between online political activism and abstract citizenship in a postmodern society.

If "Charlie" obviously refers to the title of the weekly whose editorial staff was massacred by the Kouachi brothers, and whose typography was adopted in the logo, the term deploys a much broader register. The meaning of this figure and its semantic contours were at the root of a polemic in which, confronted by a mobilization denounced as "Islamophobic" by Islamist activists and their fellow travelers, the hashtagged phrases #jenesuispasCharlie (I am not Charlie) and #cheh ("well done!" in North African Arabic) flourished while Dieudonné made headlines with a #jesuisCharlieCoulibaly (I am Charlie Coulibaly). The "Charlie" incarnated by the demonstration was first of all Charlie Brown—the hero, along with his dog Snoopy, of the famous comic strip *Peanuts*, created by Charles Schulz in the 1950s. This timid and introverted little boy, overwhelmed by the incomprehensible events in the world around him, represented the innocence of childhood on the threshold of the cruel world of adults. It gave its title to the French satirical weekly in 1970, when its predecessor, *Hara-Kiri Hebdo*, which claimed to be "stupid and nasty" (*bête et méchant*) in the wake of the spirit of 1968, was closed down by the minister of the interior, Raymond Marcellin, the persecutor of leftists, because of a front page published after the death of General de Gaulle that was considered blasphemous. (With the headline "A Tragic Dance at Colombey: One Dead," the cover amalgamated the general's death at his home in Colombey-les-Deux-Églises with a fire at a dance hall in Isère—a *département* in the French Alps—that caused 146 deaths.)

The "Charlie" of the January 7 slogan was first of all, for the universal community of Internet users—most of whom knew little or nothing about *Charlie Hebdo*—the Charlie of *Peanuts*, a figure of innocence faced by barbarism. Its creator, Joachim Roncin, has also mentioned that on that day, he happened to be looking through, with his little boy, a volume in the famous series of books for children by the British author Martin Handford, *Where's Wally?*[2]—which appeared in French

---

[2] Commonly known in North America under the title *Where's Waldo?*

translation under the title *Où est Charlie?* (Where is Charlie?). Handford's books ask their readers to find a miniscule figure bearing this name in the midst of an immense crowd. The slogan's extraordinary success initially owed a great deal to these connotations of "Charlie." At the same time, the image conceived by Roncin uses the graphic codes of an obituary notice with the colors reversed—white letters on a black background. Thus it is the protest against the death of innocents, and not support for the weekly's editorial stance, that elicits the initial reflex of identification.

For the French audience, there was also the exceptional popularity of some of the victims, with whom diverse generations and sensibilities were identified. The *Charlie Hebdo* cartoonists Wolinski and Cabu, killed at the ages of eighty and seventy-six, respectively, created characters—Mon beauf, the adjutant Kronenbourg, Catherine—who had helped shape the vernacular history of France during the past half-century since May 1968. In the minor mode of the comic strip, they incarnated a facet of the contemporary identity, that of popular culture. The economist Bernard Maris, murdered in the same attack at the age of sixty-eight, was a left-wing activist, a former "alter-globalist" (*altermondialiste*), and an editor at *Charlie Hebdo* as well as a commentator on radio and television and an admirer of Michel Houellebecq, about whom he wrote the essay "Houellebecq économiste" (Houellebecq as an economist), published in fall 2014. His violent end was like a capstone of the divorce between a secular progressive tradition, which had fought for decades in defense of immigrants' rights, and the very different orientation of some children of these immigrants who have become caught up in Islamic identity politics.

This divorce is of a piece with the previously noted rupture that occurred during the demonstrations in favor of Gaza in July 2014 between the usual "anti-imperialist" supporters of the Palestinian cause and the zealous partisans of Hamas and ISIS. It was also reflected in the emblematic Nemmouche affair, in which Mehdi Nemmouche, a radicalized jihadist French citizen of Algerian origin, fighting on the side of the Islamic State in Syria, took part in a hostage-taking in Syria of four French journalists, including Didier François, the creator of the famous antiracist slogan of the 1980s, "*Touche pas à mon pote*" ("Hands off my buddy"). Thus did the child of one of the "buddies" prized by Didier François and his colleagues in the group SOS Racisme turn on his parents' progressive defenders. This *Kulturkampf* within the French left, which destroyed political solidarities that had previously been structural, crystallized around the question of the caricatures of the Prophet published by *Charlie Hebdo* and opened a fault line that further weakened the consensus desired by the January 11, 2015, protestors chanting "Je suis Charlie."

Anticlericalism was a component of the spirit of 1968 illustrated by the weekly, which was in tune with its readers when it ridiculed the Catholic Church or Protestant pastors associated with the defense of a moral order and social hierarchies that the leftists detested. In the early 1970s, Islam was still completely foreign to French political debate, which it was to enter only at the time of the Iranian revolution of 1978–1979. Michel Foucault, who was then the guru of the far-left intelligentsia and at the same time an emblematic figure who made a powerful contribution to the legitimization of the gay community's demands and opposition to the normative universalism inherited from the Enlightenment, also developed an acritical fascination with the Islamic revolution in Iran and Ayatollah Khomeini.

In the course of the following decade, Marxists for whom Islamist organizations—some of which succeeded in assassinating Sadat in October 1981—amounted to nothing more than a "regressive fascism," to use the Orientalist Maxime Rodinson's formula, began to consider an anti-imperialist rapprochement with them. In the manner of German Protestant messianic movements, such as the anabaptists led by Thomas Münzer, they saw in groups that recruited many of their adherents in disadvantaged milieus an objective ally in their battle against the bourgeoisie. The traditional criticism of religion as the "opium of the people" was set aside in order to retain access to the masses that were deserting communist parties, whose death knell was sounded by the fall of the Berlin Wall at the end of that decade. For some people, the "proletariat" as the leavening of humanity's radiant future was replaced by "the Muslims." The latter became the figure of the oppressed par excellence, an equation that the intellectual Ali Shariati had already attempted before the Iranian revolution. In his translation of Franz Fanon's *Les Damnés de la terre* (*The Wretched of the Earth*) into Persian, he translated Fanon's Marxist concepts of the "oppressed" and the "oppressors" by using the Quranic terms *mostadafin* and *mostakbirin*, which mean, respectively, the "weakened" and the "arrogant"—categories in which the moral and religious dimension is more important than the sociopolitical meaning.

The permeability of the boundary between Islamist discourse and leftist discourse was seen in 1994 in *The Prophet and the Proletariat,* written by Chris Harrman, the famous leader of a British Trotsky-ite movement, who believes that it is possible to come to terms with the Islamists under certain circumstances. It found its counterpart in France in the support given by the leftist monthly *Le Monde Diplomatique* and by Alain Gresh, who had long been an influential organizer in the French Communist Party, to Tariq Ramadan at the European Social Forum in 2003. From this point of view, the beliefs of these new allies were not open to criticism on pain of breaking the ties that had been laboriously restored between the Marxist old guard, whose own popular support had dwindled, and the impoverished masses of the banlieues, which they saw as now being ineluctably Islamized. Between these old men touched by the grace of Tariq Ramadan and former left-wingers who remained anticlerical, a break concerning values became inevitable, and the debate about *Charlie Hebdo* pushed it to the extreme. It concealed the nature and meaning of jihadism by limiting it to a purely ideological confrontation suited to produce many virulent editorials, superficial roundtables on television, and ephemeral best-sellers written by a French intelligentsia that had reduced its analysis of a society it no longer knew to a series of contradictory incantations.

In this matter, *Charlie Hebdo*'s editorial line did not follow a rectilinear itinerary. In 1982 the weekly closed its doors, for lack of sales: the antiracist, ecological, and antimilitary periodical had lost its tonic effect, part of its staff had left, and it had gotten out of step with respect to the *air du temps* in the Mitterrand years. Its old caustic humor then turned into a generalized scatology that disconcerted its readers. It was revived ten years later under the guidance of the humorist Philippe Val, who directed it until 2009, when, under Nicolas Sarkozy's presidency, he was appointed as the head of the France Inter public radio station. This shift toward the right on the part of old left-wingers—notably in reaction to the influence of the Islamization of discourse among the lower classes—was pushed to the limit during the same years by the *Riposte laïque* website, founded by an ex-Trotskyite and now a National Front supporter, and by the itinerary of Robert Ménard, also a former Trotskyite and the founder of Reporters without Borders, who was elected mayor of the small southern French city of Béziers in 2013 with the support of the National Front.

At *Charlie Hebdo*, it was in the wake of September 11 that the cleavages within an editorial staff still dominated by the radical left grew deeper on the occasion of a laudatory review of Oriana Fallaci's book *La Rage et l'orgueil* (*The Rage and the Pride*), whose virulent statements opposing Islam in general went beyond a critique of the Islamists and of al-Qaeda, triggering a vast polemic. In 2003, *Charlie Hebdo* stood, like part of the secular far left, against Tariq Ramadan's participation in the European Social Forum meeting in Saint-Denis, a Paris banlieue that had once been a communist citadel and that now was an Islamist stronghold. The battle against "Muslim fundamentalism" then became one of the weekly's focuses and crystallized tensions. The latter exploded in February 2006 when it reprinted the caricatures of the Prophet that had been published in the Danish daily *Jyllands-Posten.* The UOIF and the Mosque of Paris brought a legal action against the paper, but the case was dismissed. However, *Charlie Hebdo*'s reputation for "Islamophobia" was now well established in the Muslim milieu and in the parts of the left and far left that prohibited criticism of Islam for the reasons mentioned earlier.

After Philippe Val left to join France Inter, the editorial staff, under the guidance of the cartoonist Charb, found itself once again confronted by decreasing sales and financial problems and was struggling to find its audience. In November 2011, after bringing out an issue of which it claimed that "Muhammad is the editor-in-chief," on the occasion of the electoral victory of the Islamist party Ennahdha in Tunisia, the offices of *Charlie Hebdo* were seriously damaged by arson, and its website was hacked to display images of Mecca and the Quran. In September 2012, in reaction to the polemic that arose from a video hostile to Islam that was made by a Copt in California, *Innocence of Muslims*—a video that provoked riots in some Muslim countries—the weekly published a new series of caricatures under the title "Muhammad: A Star is Born." The headline drawing was particularly shocking. It showed a naked figure prostrate in prayer, wearing a turban, in a three-quarter view from behind, exposing his hairy testicles and his dripping penis, a yellow star stuck into his anus.

A few days after the appearance of this issue of *Charlie Hebdo* on the newsstands, I was invited on a morning radio program on the network France Inter to discuss the matter. During the program, I argued that this caricature was no longer part of the register of criticism of a religious dogma but rather constituted an obscenity infringing the human dignity of every Muslim practicing his faith. Following this interview I was sharply attacked on the radio by the weekly's lawyer, Richard Malka, and subsequently received a few hate-filled e-mails.

The tenseness around *Charlie Hebdo* polarized all matters of opinion and conduct pertaining to the question of the media's image of Islam in France. In the autumn of 2013, in the soundtrack of a film that was made on the occasion of the thirtieth anniversary of the March of the Beurs in 1983—a film subsidized by Paris's City Hall—the singer Nekfeu rapped:

> Anyway there's nothing more square than a racist
> These theorists want to shut Islam up.
> What's the real danger, terrorism or Taylorism?
> My people get up early, I've seen my buds work.
> I demand an auto-da-fe for those dogs at *Charlie Hebdo*.

These remarks scandalized people, but they were significant in several ways. We can see the distance that has been traveled from the civilized vocabulary of the old battle "for equality and against racism" to the punch line of a contemporary rapper who was born Ken Samaras in La Trinité-sur-Mer in 1990—seven years after the march—into a middle-class family and who claimed to be a great reader of Milan Kundera and Jack London. (After the events of January 2015, this blond young man with a pleasant smile and good manners declared online to the *Parisien* that in retrospect he thought he'd been "stupid," adding that he "didn't belong to any religious community." He explained he'd wanted to defend "the one he thought was the oppressed" in a "context that had reeked of Islamophobia since September 11.") The stanza preceding the verses in question reveals the incoherence between the various social demands issuing from the vocabulary of the far left. It moves from the denunciation of Taylorism (a term that is hardly an everyday part of rap's lexicon) and the mention of "buds" (*potos*) who get up early to work (*taffer*—a slang term) to an evocation of across-the-board oppression by "theorists [who] want to shut Islam up." It is the phrase *potos taffer* that elicits, by assonance, the expression that scandalized people: "auto-da-fe."

This figure of the oppressed incarnated by "the Muslims" is a stereotype of French rap and French popular culture more generally as conveyed by its performing artists, many of whom define themselves through a similar religious membership. An eminent example of this is Médine Zaouiche, a rapper of Algerian descent from Le Havre who was born in 1983. He uses his first name as a stage name—it is the name of the city in Arabia (Medina) where the Prophet created the Islamic State after his hegira from the idolatrous Mecca in the year 622.

Médine has a long beard and a shaved head, a "hipster" variation on a Salafist theme. In October 2012, he published *Don't Panik!*, a book co-written with the versatile author and specialist in geopolitics Pascal Boniface, the director of the Institut de recherches internationales et stratégiques (Iris), a socialist think tank. Médine has also performed with the antiwhites movement Indigènes de la République (The [French] Republic's Natives), for which he sang—with Dieudonné for a time and then, in fall 2014, with the black supremacist Kémi Séba (the founder of the Tribu KA, a league dissolved in 2006 after committing violent anti-Semitic acts), whose work *Supra-Négritude* appears in the images of the clip from Médine's song *Don't Laïk*. The latter, put online on January 1, 2015, a week before the killings at *Charlie Hebdo*, includes certain words that rapidly aroused a polemic:

> Let's crucify the ultra secularists [*laïcards*] like at Golgotha [. . .]
> Your beard, *rebeu*,[3] in this country it's a *don't like* [*don't laïk*]!
> Your veil, my sister, in this country it's a *don't like* [*don't laïk*]!
> They have no God and no master except for Master Kanter[4]
> I saw off the tree of their secularism before putting it down
> Marianne's [symbol of the Republic] a tattooed feminist, "Fuck God" on her tits [. . .]
> Religion for freemasons, catechism for atheists
> Secularism is only a shadow between the enlightened and illuminated
> We are the Republic's scarecrows
> The elites are proselytes and ultra-secular propagandists
> Allah's all I need, I don't need to be secularized!

As a curtain-raiser for the tragedy that France was to experience a week later, this rap became a hit as soon as it was posted on the Web. It was viewed more than 500,000 times on YouTube at the time of the protests on January 11 and more than a million times by the end of the month, marking the cultural fault lines that undermined from the outset the spirit of unanimity sought by those who protested in the streets in the name of the slogan "Je suis Charlie."

---

[3] Backslang for beur, a person of North African descent.

[4] "Maître Kanter," a restaurant chain formerly associated with the Kronenbourg brewing company.

In May 2015, the demographer and public intellectual Emmanuel Todd published an essay entitled *Qui est Charlie? Sociologie d'une crise religieuse*."[5] The book was put on sale when the broad post-traumatic emotional consensus of January 11 had been replaced, four months later, by existential questions as to whether it was possible for the French to live together. These questions bear on the presence within France of cleavages of a religious character that jihadism pushes to extremes but which are based on a collection of everyday symptoms that the media echo. They mix the projection into France of the atrocities committed in the Middle East—whose topicality was recalled by the terrorist aftershocks of the cataclysm that occurred in January 2015—with the translation into an Islamic vocabulary of social conflicts or phenomena of exclusion among marginalized young people.

In particular, the refusal of some Muslim students to participate in the moment of silence in the schools to honor the victims; the ruckus and foot-stamping that prevented it from taking place in some cases; and the cries of "I'm not Charlie," "*Cheh!*" and even "Allahu akbar!" sometimes shouted in protest were interpreted as a profanation of the Republican sacred, which had been suddenly re-established by decree in order to communicate in a society reconciled in the face of terrorist violence. These events raised numerous questions, widely reported in the press, among teachers unable to cope with the reactions of some of their pupils—most of whom were, however, French citizens—that expressed the supremacy of the parallel culture of the rappers and the mosques over the secular values promulgated by the Republican school system.

In this context, Todd's essay seeks to oppose the *doxa*, the common opinion, on the basis of his own social science interpretation of the facts. According to him, the spirit of the demonstration on January 11 was the precise contrary of a general re-foundation of the Republic in reaction to terrorist violence. He sees in it instead the emanation of an aggressive secularism under the banner of "Islamophobia." The French elites are supposed to have mounted an ideological operation manipulating the middle classes and persuading them to engage in street protests stigmatizing a scapegoat, the Muslims. The latter are now called upon to blaspheme their Prophet in order to demonstrate their status as French citizens, in the same way that the Inquisition compelled the *marranos*, the Iberian Jews forced to convert after the *Reconquista*, to

---

[5] *Who Is Charlie? Xenophobia and the New Middle Class*, trans. Andrew Brown. Cambridge: Polity, 2015.

eat pork to be sure that they had really abjured Judaism (the term *mar-rano* comes from the Spanish word for pig, which is itself derived from the Arabic *mahram*, "illicit with regard to sharia," haram):

> The Republic that was supposed to be re-founded placed at the center of its values the right to blasphemy, and its immediate point of application was the duty to blaspheme regarding the emblematic figure of a minority religion associated with a disadvantaged group. In the context of mass unemployment, discrimination in hiring young people of North African descent, and an incessant demonization of Islam by ideologists established at the summit of French society, on television and in the French Academy, it is impossible to emphasize enough the repressed violence of the January 11 protest.
>
> Millions of French people rushed into the streets to define as the primary need of their society the right to spit on the religion of the weak.

The uproar elicited by these paradoxical theses, which evoke, behind their disciplined sociological phrasing, the furious punch lines of Médine's *Don't Laïk*, ensured that Todd's *Qui est Charlie?* would become a best-seller. Nonetheless, although Todd was playing his academic role by deconstructing the fragile consensus of January 11, and although the contribution he made to the debate on the fracture lines in French society is acceptable as a welcome approach by a critical intellectual, the occultations on which his argument is based pose a problem. From the outset, he presupposes that "to take this month of January 2015 seriously," it is important to "place French society's emotional reaction, and not the massacre on Wednesday, January 7, at the center of the investigation. [. . .] The demonstration on January 11, which was a moment of collective hysteria, provides us with a fantastic key to understanding the mechanisms of ideological and political power in contemporary French society."

But this refusal to take into account what happened on January 7—and also on January 8 and 9, since Coulibaly took over from the Kouachi brothers and made explicit in his video the reasons for the massacre—in order to focus solely on the demonstrations on Sunday, January 11, prevents us from understanding what is going on in France today. Concealing the cause of an event and attending exclusively to its effects instead of thinking about the interaction between the two leads Todd, in the case of so grave a subject, to fail to perform his function. Obviously, the analysis of jihadist and Islamist phenomena is complex; it requires knowledge and competencies that include learning Arabic and studying Muslim cultures, as well as fieldwork in the impoverished banlieues (where the marks of Islamization now stand out amid the social decay) and patiently listening to and interpreting what their residents say. This footwork from the Middle East and North Africa to the neighborhoods of our housing projects is harder than the sociohistorical acrobatics carried out between maps of France allegedly localizing the "zombie Catholics" who reject Islam (the supposed shock troops on January 11) by correlating them with priests who voted against the Civil Constitution of the Clergy in 1790 or with people who voted to approve the Maastricht treaty devolving in 1992.[6]

Interviewed on the morning edition of France Inter radio on May 14, 2015—an interview as tense as the one on January 7 with Michel Houellebecq but in the opposite way—regarding the publication of *Qui est Charlie?*, Todd claimed that his approach was based not only on his work as a demographer but also on his "Judeo-Bolshevik" heritage. Using this expression in the second degree, with the humor that Ashkenazi culture calls chutzpah, he explained the double posture that provides, through his personal history and his commitments during the past half-century, an important key to reading his text.

"What worries me most is anti-Semitism," Todd notes in a catchphrase adopted as the title of the podcast. In fact, by projecting the memory of French anti-Semitism onto Islamophobia, by suggesting that the "zombie Catholics" of the January 11, 2015, popular demonstrations are unconsciously transferring their old Christian anti-Semitism to Muslims, Todd is obfuscating what is happening today in France. He is deflecting attention from jihadism and the jihadis' attempt to confiscate the political agenda of French Muslims and to incite young people to acts of terrorism.

---

[6] During the French Revolution, in some areas in France that were the most Catholic, priests opposed the civil constitution of the clergy—and Todd insisted that the January 11 marches brought more demonstrators in those same regions. To his eyes, the Maastricht treaty submitted French identity to European market forces, and he also tried to correlate regions with high rates of approval to high numbers of January 11 demonstrators.

All of this leaves the analyst of the successive political demonstrations from 2013 to 2015 perplexed. As we have seen, the anti–gay marriage Manif pour tous demonstration made possible a new kind of conservative coalition between Catholics and "total" Muslims on the basis of a consensus regarding moral and family values opposed to gay marriage, which was reflected at the polls in a Muslim vote for the right in the 2014 municipal elections. From that point on, this Muslim vote began to substitute itself for the left-wing vote of sociological Muslims that had contributed to François Hollande's victory in May 2012. As for the demonstrations in support of Gaza, hardly six months before the demonstrations on January 11, they expressed the porous nature of the boundary between anti-Semites and the far right—the conspiracy theorists inspired by Soral and Dieudonné on the one hand and Islamists galvanized by ISIS's proclamation of the caliphate in Mosul on the other. This worked to the detriment of the traditional alliances between the French left and far left, which were anti-Zionist out of solidarity with the suffering of the Palestinians and postcolonial immigrants' children. They culminated in the attack on the synagogues and the looting of Jewish and Chaldean shops in Sarcelles, which revealed the persistence of a popular anti-Semitism that in this case was not connected with "zombie Catholics." Putting the politics of these pre–January 11, 2015, street protests into perspective gives us a better handle on the situation than Todd's transhistorical fantasies afford.

The old Bolshevik heritage claimed by Todd, who was a militant communist when he was young, leads him, like part of the French left and far left, disturbed by the disappearance of Communism—the former messianic midwife of humanity's radiant future—and by the shift in the working class vote, toward the National Front, to transfer the virtues of the former "proletariat" to "Muslims." In the expression "the religion of the weak," which he uses to describe the Islam on which the demonstrators of January 11 are supposed to have the "duty to spit," we find the persistence of the substitution of the moral-religious for the political that was already present at the root of the Iranian Revolution in 1978–1979: the term "weak" (a translation of the Quranic *moustadafine*) had been used, as we have seen, by the ideologist Ali Shariati to translate into Islamic categories the "oppressed" of Marxist rhetoric.

We have also seen how *Charlie Hebdo*'s caricatures created a deep gap between the "secularist" and "Islamophile" parts of the left. This obscure war within the media-oriented and academic intelligentsia led the champions of the two camps to joust in an audiovisual tournament in which, paralyzed by their mental armor and blinded by their ideological helmets, they no longer had any view of the society around them other than an outdated and fantasized representation that they vainly tried to impose on reality.

EPILOGUE

BETWEEN KALASH AND MARTEL: THE NATIONALIST HAMMER AND THE JIHADIST ANVIL

On September 21, 2015, the municipal council of Lunel-Viel, a residential village adjacent to the town of Lunel, announced that the commune was prepared to accept a family of Syrian refugees and that the latter would be lodged in the presbytery, a building that had recently been vacated. On that first day of autumn, the flow toward Europe of millions of people fleeing the wars that followed the Arab upheavals or seeking a better life divided public opinions and states, which were torn between solidarity with human distress and the fear that a new social burden would further slow the depressed economies of the Old Continent. At the time of the jihadist attacks, two of the terrorists at the Stade de France were Syrian and Iraqi refugees. Most of the refugees were Muslims, as is indicated by the multitude of women's headscarves in the crowds who were waiting at the borders and whose images were broadcast every day in television reports—thus providing fodder for the National Front, which was leading in the opinion polls for the December 2015 regional elections.

In the Lunel area, in this emblematic year, the symbolic contrast between the arrival of the family of Syrian refugees that would be settled on humanitarian grounds in an apartment made available by the dechristianization of France, on the one hand, and the twenty or so members of a brand-new mosque a few blocks away—who had been born in France but who left the land of religious laxity to carry out jihad in Syria and who might return to massacre the inhabitants—on the other hand, is striking. This contrast, along with the shock of the January 2015 attacks in Paris followed by the jihadist aftershocks perpetrated on French soil, described earlier, strengthened the progress of a political far right that denounces the "Islamization of France." This hyperbolic language of religious antagonism and of the clash of civilizations also crystallizes social and racial confrontations that are likely to have repercussions in future elections.

Before being marginalized by his daughter Marine and granddaughter Marion, the founder of the Le Pen dynasty, Jean-Marie Le Pen—who has a weakness for striking, inflammatory phrases that are often in poor taste, occasionally condemned by the courts, but always effective in giving voice to the discontentment and frustration of a growing segment of the French electorate—came up with an ultimate hashtag following the January attacks. Faced by the #jesuisCharlie chanted by the demonstrators of the Republican marches of January 11, 2015, who had banned the National Front from their ranks—a point Emmanuel Todd failed to note—and by the #jenesuispasCharlie and #jesuisCoulibaly found on the Facebook walls of some young people in the banlieues, Jean-Marie Le Pen made the hashtag #jesuisCharlieMartel the final spasm of a long life in politics. This invocation of the founder of the Carolingian dynasty of French monarchs and the unifier of the Frankish kingdom, who put a stop to Andalusian governor Abd el-Rahman's jihadist "blessed raid" in Poitiers in 732, exactly a hundred years after the Prophet's death, is a commonplace of National Front rhetoric. (In 2002, the year that saw the party's head qualify for the second round of voting in the presidential election, his supporters had rallied around the slogan "Charles Martel 732, Le Pen 2002.")

In the 2002 presidential runoff, Le Pen ultimately won only 17.9 percent of the vote against Jacques Chirac, whose clear victory inaugurated without glory the first five-year term (*quinquennat*) of the Fifth Republic (which had had seven-year terms since its inception). Fifteen years later, on the eve of the presidential election of 2017, his daughter and successor as head of the party, Marine Le Pen, is projected by most polling organizations to have enough electoral support to qualify for the second round of presidential voting. What is more, and in contrast to her father, she is expected to lead all other candidates in the first round. Previously the traditional parties of the right and left succeeded in managing the challenge of the far right through various means. During his first term in office (1981–1988), the Machiavellian François Mitterrand demonized Jean-Marie Le Pen, thus dividing the vote and making possible his own re-election in 1988. Nineteen years later, in 2007, Nicolas Sarkozy siphoned off Le Pen's electorate by adopting his rhetoric, thereby easily winning an election in which the voters were still traumatized by the great riots in the impoverished immigrant banlieues in autumn 2005. Thus did the leaders of the traditional political parties, each in his own way, exploit its far-right adversary to conquer or recapture the presidency.

More recently, and under the leadership of Marine Le Pen and her advisor, Philippe Péninque, the National Front has succeeded in "de-demonizing" itself. Indeed, in the wake of the terrorist attacks of 2015, it is clear that jihadism has displaced the National Front in the role of the archetype of evil that must be destroyed. Now all the presidential candidates accuse their adversaries of being either accomplices of the jihadists or impotent in face of the jihadist threat. This displacement has been to the great benefit of the National Front. The presidential standard-bearers of the "Republican" left and right are reduced to fighting for second place *behind* Madame Le Pen in the first round. None of them imagines that he might come in ahead of her.

Since the 2012 election and the Merah affair, the political approach to terrorism in France has had contrasting effects on the government and the opposition parties. During his 2012 campaign for re-election, Nicolas Sarkozy failed to take advantage of this; on the contrary, the electorate blamed him for poor police management of Merah, who was well known to and closely followed by intelligence agents in the months before his terrorist acts. The winner of the 2012 presidential contest, François Hollande, received a boost in the opinion polls when he acted the role of statesman on January 11, 2015, and marched at the head of the demonstrators on the boulevards of Paris, surrounded by the top leaders of the planet. But this boost was quickly erased by the structural parameters of his unpopularity; his approval rating in opinion polls plunged to 13 percent just before the attacks in November 2015—and would reach a historical low with 4 percent in late 2016, so that he finally drew the political conclusions of his staggering unpopularity and decided not to run for re-election in 2017.

The National Front then seemed in a position to benefit almost automatically from the population's anxiety connected with terrorism. Each time a jihadist with a Kalashnikov threatens to massacre innocent people on French soil to the cry of "Allahu akbar!" more fodder is provided to those who obsessively denounce the "Islamization of France" or demand the closing of the borders. And this is only strengthened when the state appears incapable of suppressing a phenomenon almost all of whose actors in 2015 were known to the police or to the courts, from the Kouachi brothers and Amedy Coulibaly to Abdelhamid Abaaoud and the 2016 killers Larossi Abballah, who slew two married police officers at their home, and Adil Kermiche, who stabbed an octogenarian Catholic priest during mass in his church. They had antiterrorism files and had even been previously imprisoned, whether they fell into jihadism through the prison incubator or had already been sentenced and served their time for that offense.

The establishment's incompetence has its origin in a cultural particularity that is not unrelated to the fact that France holds the absolute record for exporting jihadists from the European Union. This has to do in large measure with the ways in which France's political elite is recruited. These combine the peer networks of the obsolete parties from which they come—which maintain pseudo-experts who block public financing for in-depth research that would expose their imposture—with the stranglehold of high-ranking bureaucrats who are omniscient but incapable of learning anything about national security that the curriculum of the elite schools of public administration had not trained them for. Other comparable European states, the United Kingdom and Germany in particular, have a much more inclusive approach to choosing the political elite, to which are added members of civil society and professionals selected for their experience and competence. They do not hesitate to seek—and find—advice on the complex questions of contemporary Islam provided by experts from the university community.

By contrast, France has precipitated the decline of the field of Islamic studies (in which it was considered world-class for more than a century), particularly during Sarkozy and Hollande's presidential terms. The country of Louis Massignon, Jacques Berque, and Maxime Rodinson, orientalists and scholars known all over the world, can no longer offer training in the field of Islam to the best and the brightest. The most talented of the younger generation of Islamicists—and Arabists—in training must now go abroad for advanced studies, threatening the very continuation of the production of knowledge in a country where the domestic stakes related to Islam and Muslims have become central.

Neither is innovative thinking to be found at the top of the highly hierarchical French security apparatus, which would need to be retooled in order to grasp the shift in jihadist organization from pyramidal structures to an unprecedented model in which the actors operate in swarms. The price to be paid for this voluntary blindness and deliberate deafness is already great, and it will be still greater for politicians who are not up to the job, who now lack solutions to the challenges of jihadism, and who are also incapable of responding to the National Front's tirades in this domain.

In fall 2015, the coincidence of the jihadist attacks with the new influx of migrants from the Middle East, a pretext for disparate, emotional, and embarrassed responses on the part of European Union states, provided Marine Le Pen's party with an electoral gift when the campaign for the regional elections on December 6 and 13 began. Encouraged by favorable opinion polls, it aspired to win two important fiefs, Nord-Pas-de-Calais-Picardie and Provence-Alpes-Côte-d'Azur, where Marine and her niece Marion Le Pen were the respective heads of the lists. Even though the party eventually failed in that attempt, its unprecedentedly strong showing in the first round made the extreme-right National Front the pivotal party in French politics. Visiting Calais on October 2 of that year, where some three thousand migrants were crowded under precarious conditions in the "jungle" around the entrance to the tunnel under the English Channel, trying to enter clandestinely the British paradise of black market work, and where a lack of security and an absence of hygiene had become the obsessive concerns of part of the population, the leader of the National Front warned against "being submerged by migrants" and "Islamist terrorism":

> Calais is a city under siege, in the literal sense of the term. The residents barricade themselves in their homes. [. . .] I don't accept seeing French people feel like foreigners in their own homes. Don't give in. Don't forget that we are at home here!

These remarks are all the more striking in a city whose very name has been associated with capitulation and humiliation for generations of French schoolchildren. Calais was the site of a siege by the English army of Edward III in 1347, and upon its capitulation the city was forced to hand over six of its leading citizens in their shirtsleeves, their heads bowed and a rope around their necks, in order to lift the siege and spare the lives of its inhabitants. The city was subject to English rule for the next two centuries. This historical episode, somewhat fictionalized in later retelling, was elevated to the status of founding myth under the French Third Republic (1871–1940), and the famous bronze statues by Auguste Rodin depicting the six citizens were installed in front of the Calais City Hall in 1895.

Even if only a small proportion of the National Front's potential electorate believes in the vague and inapplicable solutions proposed by its heralds—from France's exit from Europe and the euro to the exclusion of residents who are not French citizens from welfare and family benefits—the party of the Le Pen dynasty has finally been able to recover, since the advent of Jean-Marie's daughter, the "tribune function" that the late professor Georges Lavau attributed in the 1970s to the Communist Party alone. The National Front's electorate is much more differentiated socially than that of the "workers' party" of old, but it has mobilized the support of voters to whom it gives the sense that it is voicing a "truth" hidden by the "establishment," just as the French Communist Party used to articulate the alleged truth of the "class struggle" masked by "bourgeois ideology." The constitution of mythical "plebs" of which the National Front is supposed to be the tribune is adding votes to what is already a record level. In Lunel, after the scandals connected with the local jihadist seedbed and the statements made by the president of the mosque, the left-wing candidate in the March 2015 departmental elections was able to defeat the National Front in extremis, by a mere 0.64 percent of the votes, only by soliciting votes . . . in this same mosque, among other places.

This small-town squabble in the age of French jihad is emblematic of a country in which Islamism and its multiple political uses are now able to become an important variable in elections. But the polarization between the Kalash of the jihadist and the *martel*[1] of the National Front, the outcome of the strategy Abu Musab al-Suri advocated in his *Global Islamic Resistance Call* as a premonitory symptom of civil war in Europe, went so far as to draw nourishment, in its very inspiration by the founding myth of Charles Martel, from an almost perfect mirror effect.

Interested Web users can consult a YouTube video, about fifteen minutes long, entitled *Lorsque l'État islamique était en France* (*When the Islamic State Was in France*). Posted by various sources that present themselves under the names of "True History," "French Taliban," or "*Dajjal* [Antichrist] Magazine," it recounts the great feats of an earlier, pre-modern jihad that ravaged France in the first half of the eighth century until 759, when Pepin the Short, Charles Martel's son, took back Narbonne, a city in southwest France which was the Saracens' advanced stronghold (*ribat*, in Arabic). From this stronghold, they had been launching "blessed raids," some of which reached up the Rhône Valley as far as Burgundy. I discovered this video in an appendix to the website of Salim Laïbi, candidate in the Marseille Parliamentary

---

[1] A reference to Charles Martel, whose byname "Martel" (Latin *Martellus*) means "hammer."

elections of 2012. A dentist from the seaside town of L'Estaque and for a time a conspiracy theorist along with Soral and Dieudonné, he later quarreled with them, in a contest of anathemas that is customary in the "fachosphere," and moved closer to the sycophants of "fundamentalist Islam."

The video reminds us, in its form and message, of Omar Omsen's *19 HH, L'histoire de l'humanité* (*The History of Humanity*), which was, as we have seen, one of the principal vectors of recruitment for jihad in Syria: it featured a haunting soundtrack based on warriors' hymns chanted a capella by male voices, a montage of images hijacked in the manner of the mash-up, onto which an ideological content is superimposed, and so forth. Although here, too, the goal is also to "reveal the hidden truths of history," the aim is no longer to project jihad toward the "land of Sham" but, inversely, to reconstitute this precedent, which is supposed to have given rise to the Islamic conquest of "a vast region that corresponded, for two hundred and seventy-five years, to half the current territory of France." Such a "truth" is said to have been concealed by Islamophobe official history, whose bards "hastened to make all traces of the Muslim presence in France disappear."

To do that, the jihadist video focuses, as does the far right, on the founding myth of Charles Martel. But contrary to the National Front, which appropriates that name in order to glorify it, the video deconstructs it by reducing the Battle of Poitiers in 732 AD to a simple, inconsequential incident, drawing on the revisionism of some historians to enlist academic knowledge in the service of jihadist propaganda. In Islamic historiography, the Battle of Poitiers is reduced to the rank of a skirmish and is designated only by the name of "the Road of the Martyrs," because Abd el-Rahman, the governor of Andalusia, was killed there.

The material used begins with extracts from a low-quality film produced by a Canadian Islamist entitled *The Lost Kingdom: The Story of al-Andalus*, which feeds a prolific and nostalgic line deploring the loss of Muslim Spain and presenting the *Reconquista* as a paragon of Islamophobia that is all the more unacceptable because, according to the doctrine, the whole territory that was once under Islamic control must remain Muslim for eternity. The video was made under the auspices of Sheikh Waleed Abdul Hakim, a preacher and lecturer with Salafist tendencies in Toronto who is omnipresent on the anglophone Internet.

The sequences used come from the section entitled "The Fierce Clash with France," and viewers are warned that now "history is repeating itself." The sequences are mixed with portions of film that are shot in the same style as that used for the Muslim epics produced in abundance by television channels in the Arab world to exalt the story of the expansion of Islam in its first centuries but that bear the logo of the French-German cultural television channel Arte. The video ends with a still shot of General de Gaulle, accompanied by the famous quotation extracted from his radio interview on March 5, 1959, with Alain Peyrefitte, which prepares this confidant of the head of state to defend Algerian independence against the supporters of French Algeria who want to integrate it into France:

If we integrated them, if all the Arabs and Berbers of Algeria were considered French, how would we prevent them from coming to settle in the metropole [the European part of France, as opposed to the colonies], where the standard of living is so much higher? My village would no longer be called Colombey-les-Deux-Églises (the two churches), but Colombey-les-Deux-Mosquées (the two mosques)!

This is followed by two shots of press conferences given by presidents Sarkozy and Hollande expressing their concern regarding the confrontation between Islam and the West and the diffusion of terrorism to the Sahel and to North Africa, thus threatening France.

The video presents the Islamic conquest of southern France in the eighth century as a strategy originally intended to take Constantinople by attacking it from the rear and to reach Damascus, then the capital of the Muslim Omeyyad Empire, from the northern coast of the Mediterranean. For spectators in 2015, this fantasized Islamic geopolitics of an earlier age acquires an "excessively topical" color: it was the French jihadists who found their "road to Damascus," whereas the Syrian refugees fleeing the war followed it in the opposite direction, and the Constantinople of old was transformed into the Istanbul of modern Turkey, the hub where their opposed trajectories intersect. As for the geography of the France subjected to Islam in the eighth century, its citadels were Toulouse ("*Talousha* for the mujahideen," a deformation of the Latin *Tolosa*, and we have seen what a jihadist seedbed it became), and Nîmes, in the lower Rhône valley, famous these days on the Islamist Web, where there is a photo showing how jihadists from the down-market housing projects in that city have sprayed walls with graffiti bearing the name of their neighborhood buildings in Ramadi in Iraq, under the auspices of the ISIS caliphate. This astonishing anticipation of a cartography of the strongholds of contemporary French jihad ends in the city of Sens, "a hundred kilometers [south] from Paris, the farthest point in France reached by the Muslim army."

Citing the crowd psychologist Gustave Le Bon, the author of the romantic *Civilisation des Arabes* (Civilization of the Arabs) published in 1884, in support of its minimization of the importance of the Battle of Poitiers, the video "reveals the hidden truths of history" in an insert that is superimposed on images of triumphal cavalry charges by turbaned horsemen cutting down soldiers with shields bearing the sign of the Cross:

> You can clearly see that, contrary to a received idea, Charles Martel's battle at Poitiers did not put an end to the *Ghazawât* [raids] of the mujahideen [soldiers of the jihad] in southern France, quite the contrary!

The subsequent conquest of Narbonne by Christian troops is treated as a calamity for the peoples of the south. It is illustrated by scenes in which Crusaders tear a child away from its veiled mother, anticipating the "Islamophobia" of our own time. Finally, "the corsair Hayreddin Barbarossa's conquest of Nice" in 1543, which lasted only one year, is presented as the acme of this first glorious phase of the jihad on French soil. If the video can make the link, almost half a millennium later, with the robber, jihadist, and video maker Omar Omsen, thus placing *19 HH* in the ideological and mental tradition of *Lorsque l'État islamique était en France*, the historical reality of the siege of 1543–1544 and the trace it has left on the local memory are more complex than this document suggests. The surrounding and attacking of the city was a joint operation by the armies of King Francis I of France and Sultan Suleiman the Magnificent against a stronghold belonging to the Duchy of Savoy.

In Nice, this episode, immortalized by the cannonballs shot by Barbarossa's galleys, still present in many façades in the old city, is celebrated especially through the heroic and mythified figure of Catherine Ségurane. This laundress, subsequently enthroned as the popular patron saint of Nice's folklore, is supposed to have run up to a janissary who had climbed on the rampart on August 15, 1543, the feast of the protectress Holy Virgin, and clobbered him with her laundry bat, which in this case had become an avatar of the *martel* (hammer). According to the legend, this virgin with a sad face, as is indicated by her dialectal epithet *Maufada*, wrenched the banner marked with the crescent of Islam away from the dead Turk. Then, disrobing and displaying her "fleshy parts" from the top of ramparts, she wiped them with the flag, restoring courage to the besieged, who ended up repelling the Ottoman invader and his French ally.

On September 13, 2015, two months to the day before the massacre at the Bataclan, the far-right identitarian group Nissa rebela organized, as it had each year for six years, a parade in *oumage a Segurana* (in homage to Ségurane) in the port neighborhood. It took place in a tense context, in which immigrants and refugees who had crossed the Mediterranean were piling up at the Italian border at Menton, thirty kilometers to the east, and trying to enter France. The Nissa rebela movement demanded their expulsion in the name of the "remigration" it advocates. The preceding year, on September 8, 2014, the parade, preceded by children in traditional costume, surrounded by red smoke bombs, testified that "the reference to Catherine Ségurane is not a matter of folklore but of memory." According to the head of this identitarian group, Catherine is the "guiding light"—"the path." "It is she, the laundress, reminding us that in Nice as elsewhere it is always the people that rise up when governments betray or surrender," he told the press, making a transhistorical allusion to Francis I's compromise with the sultan. The allusion becomes more precise when the Ottoman invader of yesteryear is replaced by "one of these thousands of 'French' jihadists, dozens of whom have left Nice and are now fighting in Iraq or Syria but who will end up coming back here to continue their war."

*

In the same month, September 2015, the philosopher Pierre Manent published the most structured, painful, and, in many respects, paradoxical reflection on the events of the previous January. His *Situation de la France (Situation of France)*, a title reminiscent of the religious and nationalist writer Charles Péguy (1873–1914), begins by treating these events as a symptom of the country's moral and institutional decay—in particular the failure of secularism, which has become, in Manent's view, its civil religion. He advocates a new type of national compact in which the "customs of Muslims" must be accepted and endorsed by the law on a community basis, in "friendship" with the customs of Christians and Jews.

This proposal, made by one of the main French Catholic philosophers—a disciple of Raymond Aron, co-founder of the review *Commentaire*, and a resolute supporter of political liberalism—aroused reactions that were as passionate as they were contrasting. Lauded by

La Croix and *Le Figaro*, as well as by the website *Islam & Info*, which conveys "total Islam" propaganda, it was reviled by other publications as a "capitulation" to sharia, which would thus be granted legitimacy in France. Although Pierre Manent's work, like that of Emmanuel Todd, makes room for what Nietzsche calls, in *Beyond Good and Evil*, "philosophers' instincts" (that is, the moral ideal that precedes the intellection of the world)—Manent conceiving France within Catholicism, Todd conceiving it on the basis of his self-definition as a "Judeo-Bolshevik"—the import of the two reflections inspired by the events of January differs in nature.

Todd refrains from a serious analysis of the killings perpetrated by the Kouachi brothers and by Amedy Coulibaly, being obsessed instead by the demonstration on Sunday, January 11, 2015, which he sees as propagating an Islamophobic ideology that now serves as a substitute for the atavistic anti-Semitism attributed to an earlier generation of French elites. Manent, by contrast, is not interested in this demonstration, which was overtly secular in character, but instead considers the whole sequence of events from January 7 to January 9 as a significant entity that has to be taken seriously:

> A war is being waged, and it has been declared on us. A war in which sometimes Jews alone are targeted [. . .], sometimes along with Christians, blasphemers, police officers, and in general the authorities and institutions of Western nations, and sometimes, finally, they are targeted not only with the latter, but also with "apostate" Muslims.

Manent's argument consists of both a diagnosis and a prescription. The diagnosis points to the moral and institutional decay of a nation that has become "weak" by its dilution in an evanescent European Union and by the substitution of the secular ideology of human rights for the social bond that was founded on the Christian religion, even though Europeans "have refused for two generations to raise the political question and the religious question outside which the life of Europe loses all its meaning." And this emptiness has led to the irruption of a "strong" Islam within contemporary France, of which the massacres in January are the hyperbolic manifestation. Manent's prescription advocates giving this Islam a legitimate place in the Republic as a community of its own, so that Muslims, without having to betray their attachment to their dogma, might become full-fledged members of the French nation. In this compact, Manent sees an opportunity to detach

Muslim citizens of the Republic from radical influences and financing coming from the Arabian Peninsula, and he convinces himself that they will thus accept reasonable arrangements without coercion, voluntarily giving up both the wearing of the niqab for women and polygamy.

One can only marvel at the fact that a work written in 2015 by one of the most prominent intellectuals on the right and entitled *Situation de la France* has, as its main or even sole subject, the presence of Islam in this country. Long limited to specialized studies, this question emerged in public debate only through political manipulation or media excess. It is now established at the heart of an existential reflection on the present and future of the nation, and it has been elevated to the rank of the society's central question. Nonetheless, as presented by Pierre Manent, Islam is understood not as a social object situated in a field—France—that is traversed by conflicts between actors competing for hegemony over its expression. Instead, it is posited as a religious entity pre-existing any social construction—a transcendent community characterized by a table of specific "customs" attributed to its faithful.

The approach that has guided the present book does not allow for an a priori essentialization of a social group by its mores—even in the Latin sense of the term, in which it refers to the whole set of a human group's habitual ways of life. Nevertheless, it is undeniable that Islamization is now more widespread in the banlieues of France than it was when I surveyed these same territories thirty years ago while writing *Les Banlieues de l'islam: naissance d'une religion en France* (*The Banlieues of Islam: Birth of a Religion in France*), published 1987. And yet the fact of this growing Islamization does not sum up the diversity of French population groups of Muslim culture or descent. Islamization is taking place in the context of a battle for hegemony over these groups being waged by movements and sects ranging from the Muslim Brothers to the jihadists by way of the Tabligh and the Salafists. The rise of these movements is undeniable. However, to concede victory to these zealots and to entrust their claim to represent the Muslim citizens or inhabitants of France as they have imagined it would be to underestimate the diversity of French people of Muslim provenance.

By analyzing the processes of sway over the expression of Islam—in particular, the political and social phenomena that cross Abu Musab al-Suri's *Global Islamic Resistance Call* with the emergence of Generation Y—we have tried to show that it is within the groups concerned that the most bitter battles are being fought. The elimination of "apostates" by jihadists who want to terrorize their co-religionists and force them to adopt their views constitutes the extreme form of this struggle.

Although the killers of 2015 have not yet won the battle, we have to admit with Pierre Manent that the incantation of the secular principles of the Republic by politicians who lack both inspiration and vision is far from being able to meet the challenge posed by a French jihad whose rise we have traced over the past decade and beyond. We can agree with Manent that beyond the monstrosity of the crimes committed against France by some of those who, in spite of themselves, are among its children, even if they have gone astray, terrorism in France is also the symptom of a malaise in our civilization.

Does that mean that we must also agree with Manent that "a certain communalism" (*communautarisation*) "is desirable" given the "ideological lie of the new secularism that seeks to force us to pretend to be only individual citizens" in a "nation marked by Christianity"? On the contrary, all through this book we have shown that the social actors who claim to follow "total" Islam in its diverse forms, from overexcited identity politics to the descent into violence, are resorting to religion to transform their social fury into a political strategy. In such a context, the places of religion or obedience to which the secularism of the Republic grants a legitimate place within human society—the church, the mosque, the synagogue, and the temple (whether Protestant or Masonic)—cannot be erected into the primordial relays of state intervention. If at the end of this development an institution seems to us to have to be re-founded and reconstructed in order to cope with this immense challenge over the long term, it is public education, from the nursery school to the university, that has now fallen into poverty as the result of a blameworthy incompetence on the part of the whole political class.

From my visit to Lunel, the ephemeral "capital of French jihad," in 2014, I have retained the image of a single place where all the city's components live together in a "friendship," to use Pierre Manent's term, that allows them, through work and shared values, to move beyond atavism and communalism: the *lycée*—the French high school. I hope this book has helped to show that the national debate and the implementation of public policies called for by terror in France cannot succeed without being based on the knowledge that can still be produced—but for how much longer?—by our universities.

ACKNOWLEDGMENTS

The research that enabled me to write this book was made possible by the support of the Institut Montaigne, which had already provided assistance for the investigations preparatory to *Banlieue de la République* (2012) and *Passion française* (2014). Here I would like to express my special gratitude to Claude Bébéar, who served as president until autumn 2015, and Henri de Castries, his successor, for their confidence, without which the trilogy that these three books form would not have appeared. Its director, Laurent Bigorgne, followed its stages with a fidelity that has never slacked and that has always been an element of intellectual stimulation.

Since *Passion française*, Hugo Micheron has been an indispensable and very valuable research assistant. Now that he is undertaking his own projects, it is a pleasure to wish him the full success that his merits deserve. It was with him that Antoine Jardin and I worked out the plan and the subject matter of this book. The association of a young doctor of political science, a research engineer at the CNRS specializing in electoral behaviors in working-class neighborhoods, and an Arabist in the autumn of his career was conceived as a dialogue between disciplines and generations. This is now, more than ever, necessary to meet the challenges of analyzing a phenomenon as exceptional as the killings of 2015 and beyond, putting it into perspective and context. Antoine Jardin wrote chapter 2 and part of chapter 5. I wrote the rest.

By conducting with me a seminar on violence and dogma at the École Normale Supérieure on the rue d'Ulm, my colleagues Mohamed-Ali Amir Moezzi and Bernard Rougier, along with Alexandre Kazeroumi, a brilliant postdoctoral fellow, restored my hopes for the university system after the termination of studies on the Arab world at Sciences Po in 2010.

Finally, I would like to thank all those who have agreed to talk with me, during my travels around France, about events that they have witnessed, sometimes in terrible ways. I think first of all of the families of the victims of terrorism and those whose children have gone to Syria, where some of them have died. They have shared their emotion with me and answered my questions about it. If this book helps them in their struggle, it will not have been in vain.

CHRONOLOGY OF EVENTS

December 3, 1983: more than 100,000 people converge on Paris to take part in the "March for Equality and against Racism," more popularly known in France as "la Marche des Beurs," to underline the heavy participation of French citizens and other residents of North African provenance. This demonstration led to the creation the following year of the organization SOS Racisme by those close to President Francois Mitterrand.

August 26, 1995: Paris Metro bombings perpetrated by Khaled Kelkal and his associates from the Algerian GIA. First wave of jihadist terror on French soil—followed by seventeen years of quiet until the Merah killings of March 2012.

March 2004: a law is passed in the French National Assembly prohibiting the wearing of "ostentatious" religious signs in French public schools.

October–November 2005: riots in disenfranchised banlieues throughout the whole of France after the accidental deaths of two Muslim boys hiding from police in a power station and the landing of a tear-gas grenade near a crowded mosque in Clichy-Montfermeil on the outskirts of Paris.

May 6, 2007: Nicolas Sarkozy is elected president of France.

November 2010–February 2011: the onset of the Arab Spring, a series of antigovernment demonstrations and a popular uprising against autocratic governments in the Arab countries of Tunisia, Egypt, Libya, Yemen, Bahrain, and Syria.

March 11–19, 2012: a series of shootings over nine days in the southern French cities of Montauban and Toulouse targeting French soldiers and Jewish civilians and leading to the death of seven people, including three soldiers (two of Muslim descent) and three Jewish children. The perpetrator, a twenty-three-year-old French citizen of Algerian descent named Mohammed Merah, had been a petty criminal and embraced extreme Salafist views several years before this attack. He claimed ties to al-Qaeda, although this is disputed by French authorities. Merah is killed in his apartment on March 22 by French police after attempts to negotiate failed.

April 22, 2012: François Hollande is elected president of France.

June 10–17, 2012: French parliamentary elections. Both votes witness a massive vote for the Socialists by electors who identified themselves as Muslims.

May 24, 2014: Ex-con and French jihadi Mehdi Nemmouche attacks visitors to the Jewish Museum of Belgium upon his return from the ISIS caliphate in Syria.

January 7, 2015: the Kouachi brothers massacre the staff of *Charlie Hebdo*.

January 9, 2015: Amedy Coulibaly attacks the Hyper Cacher supermarket in Porte de Vincennes.

January 11, 2015: a huge demonstration takes place in Paris protesting the January 7–9 attacks; this is the largest demonstration in French history.

April 19, 2015: Sid Ahmed Ghlam is arrested for planning an attack on a church in Villejuif.

August 28, 2015: Ayoub el-Khazzani tried to use a submachine gun on passengers on the Thalys train from Amsterdam to Paris.

November 13, 2015: Attacks on the Stade de France, several restaurants, and the Bataclan music hall in Paris leave 130 dead.

June 13, 2016: A police officer and his wife, a police secretary, are stabbed to death in their home in the town of Magnanville, France, thirty-four miles west of Paris, by Larossi Abballa, a twenty-five-year-old French citizen of Morocco living in their neighborhood. Abballa had been convicted in 2013 of associating with a group planning terrorist acts. During his attack, Abballa starts a Facebook Live broadcast on his mobile phone, pledges allegiance to ISIS, and gives out a list of people to be killed by jihadis. He is killed by French police in a gun battle at the scene after attempts to negotiate his surrender fail.

July 14, 2016: Mohamed Lahouaiej-Bouhlel, a thirty-one-year-old Tunisian man residing in Nice, drives a cargo truck into a crowd of Bastille Day celebrants on the Promenade des Anglais. Eighty-six people are killed—thirty of them Muslims, including ten children—and 434 are injured. The attack ends following an exchange of gunfire during which Lahouaiej-Bouhiel is killed by police. ISIS claims responsibility for the attack. Although the attacker's relationship with ISIS is unclear, French investigators discover that Lahouaiej-Bouhlel had become a sympathizer of ISIS shortly before his planned attacks.

July 26, 2016: two young men armed with knives storm a Catholic Church in the town of Saint-Etienne-Du-Rouvray in Normandy, taking several hostages and killing an eighty-five-year-old priest, Jacques Hamel. French police shoot and kill the nineteen-year-old attackers—ex-con Adel Kermiche and Abdel Malik Petitjean—shortly thereafter. French investigators reveal that both young men attempted to enter Syria to fight on the side of ISIS the previous year.

KEY PEOPLE AND ORGANIZATIONS

Abu Mussab Al-Suri—author of the *Global Islamic Resistance Call* (2005)

Abdelhamid Abaaoud—main jihadi involved in the November 2015 attacks in Paris

Abdulillah/Olivier Corel—leader of the Salafist settlement in Artigat

Mohamed Achamlane (aka. Abu Hamza)—founder of Forsane Alizza

Artigat Network—an Islamist network based in the town of Artigat in southwestern France

Djamel Beghal—convicted of terrorism in 2005. Mentored Chérif Kouachi in prison.

Salim Benghalem—French jihadi in Syria; involved in the November 2015 attacks in Paris

Farid Benyettou—Salafist "guru" to the Kouachi brothers in 2005

Buttes-Chaumont Network—an Islamist network based in the nineteenth arrondissement of Paris

Charlie Hebdo—a satirical French weekly newspaper

Fabien and Jean-Michel Clain—converts to Islam involved in the November 2015 attacks in Paris and former members of the Artigat network

Amedy Coulibaly—perpetrator of the January 9, 2015, attack on Hyper Cacher supermarket

Forsane Alizza—an Islamist group formed in 2010 and shut down in 2012

Sid Ahmed Ghlam—suspected to have planned an attack on a church in Villejuif in 2015

GIA—Groupe Islamique Armé (Armed Islamic Group), one of the main Islamist groups during the Algerian Civil War, 1992–1997

François Hollande—Socialist Party politician. Elected president of France in 2012.

Khaled Kelkal—terrorist affiliated with the GIA. He was involved in the 1995 Paris metro bombings, as well as other incidents. Killed September 1995.

Ayoub el-Khazzani—attacked passengers on the Thalys train from Amsterdam to Paris in 2015

Saïd and Chérif Kouachi—brothers who attacked the staff of *Charlie Hebdo,* January 7, 2015

Jean-Marie Le Pen—the founder of the National Front, the main far-right party in France

Marine Le Pen—a French politician who is the leader of the National Front and daughter of the party's founder

Dieudonné M'bala M'bala—French comedian, actor, and political activist who is strongly anti-Zionist.

Mohamed Merah—attacked several French soldiers and a Jewish school in March 2012 in Toulouse

Mehdi Nemmouche—suspected perpetrator of the attack on the Jewish Museum of Belgium, May 2014

Omar Omsen—Jihadi from Nice who joined the Islamic State in Syria. Creator of compelling recruitment videos.

Ségolène Royal—Socialist Party politician who ran for president in 2007

Nicolas Sarkozy—President of France 2007–2012

Alain Soral—far-right journalist and filmmaker. Founder of the website and political movement *Egalité et Réconciliation.*

INDEX

PRINCETON STUDIES IN MUSLIM POLITICS